St. Louis Community College

Library

5801 Wilson Avenue
St. Louis, Missouri 63110

GHANA

PROFILES · NATIONS OF CONTEMPORARY AFRICA
Larry W. Bowman, Series Editor

ABOUT THE BOOK AND AUTHORS

Despite its relatively small size, the West African state of Ghana has earned a special place in the political history of the African continent. From the days of the precolonial Asante federation, through the organized resistance to colonial conquest, rapid proliferation of Western-style education, adaptation to a cash economy, and initiation of the anticolonial struggle, Ghana has served as a model for other areas of Africa. In 1957, it became the first African state to achieve independence. Then it was the first to commit itself to the Pan-African dream and among the first to develop a one-party state and to undergo a military coup d'etat. Since independence, Ghana's government has changed eight times, its once viable economy has regressed at an alarming rate, and social unrest and civilian disorder have become widespread.

In this introduction to Ghana, the authors examine the historical roots of current patterns; trace the intricate features of the politics of independence; examine the bases, nature, and direction of social change; explore the causes of and reactions to the decline in the political economy; and assess the changes in Ghanaian international standing. In conclusion, they explore the implications of Ghana's inconsistent record for the future of the country, its people, and other African states.

Deborah Pellow is assistant professor of anthropology at Syracuse University. **Naomi Chazan** is senior lecturer in political science and African studies and head of the African Studies Department at the Hebrew University of Jerusalem, where she coordinates the African Research Unit at the Harry S. Truman Research Institute for the Advancement of Peace.

GHANA

Coping with Uncertainty

Deborah Pellow
and
Naomi Chazan

Westview Press • Boulder, Colorado

Gower • London, England

Profiles/Nations of Contemporary Africa

Unless otherwise attributed, photos are by Deborah Pellow.
Cover photo by Deborah Pellow.

Tables 3.1, 3.2, 4.1, 4.3, 4.4, 4.5, 4.6, and 4.8 are used by permission of Europa Publications. Table 4.9 is used by permission of Robert Price and *Canadian Journal of African Studies.* Table 4.10 is used by permission of *West Africa.*

Published in 1986 in the United States of America by Westview Press, Inc.; Frederick A. Praeger, Publisher; 5500 Central Avenue, Boulder, Colorado 80301

Published in 1986 in Great Britain by Gower Publishing Company Limited, Gower House, Croft Road, Aldershot, Hampshire GU11   3HR

ISBN (U.S.) 0-86531-369-5
ISBN (U.K.) 0-566-00776-2

Printed and bound in the United States of America

The paper used in this publication meets the minimum requirements of the American National Standard for Permanence of Paper for Printed Library Materials Z39.48–1984.

10   9   8   7   6   5   4   3   2   1

Contents

Tables

Illustrations

Preface

Ghana is a country that brings together people from all over the world and creates special bonds between them. We first met at the University of Ghana, Legon, in 1970, while each of us was engaged in separate doctoral research. Since then we have returned several times to Ghana: Deborah Pellow in 1979 and 1982, and Naomi Chazan in 1977 and 1980. We have maintained close ties with each other and with many friends in Ghana. To these colleagues and companions—too numerous to enumerate here—we owe our understanding of Ghana and our love for the country.

The opportunity to write a book on Ghana was appealing not only because of our continuing fascination with Ghanaian affairs, but also because of the chance it gave us to mesh anthropological and political science perspectives on recent Ghanaian history. We owe special thanks to Larry Bowman, the series editor, who gave us unstinting support throughout this project, and to Lynne Rienner and Deborah Lynes, who not only continually backed our efforts and exhibited much understanding of the difficulties of international collaboration but also became steadfast friends.

The Harry S. Truman Research Institute of the Hebrew University of Jerusalem offered a haven for both of us in the summer of 1982, when we first started work on this book. It has since furnished invaluable research facilities and administrative support. The Department of Anthropology at Syracuse

University also supplied research and secretarial assistance. Both institutions deserve our utmost gratitude.

A final thanks is owed by Deborah Pellow to Irving Thalberg and by Naomi Chazan to Barry Chazan, who both know too well how much this book depended on their warmth, support, and companionship.

Naomi Chazan,
Jerusalem, Israel

Deborah Pellow,
Syracuse, New York

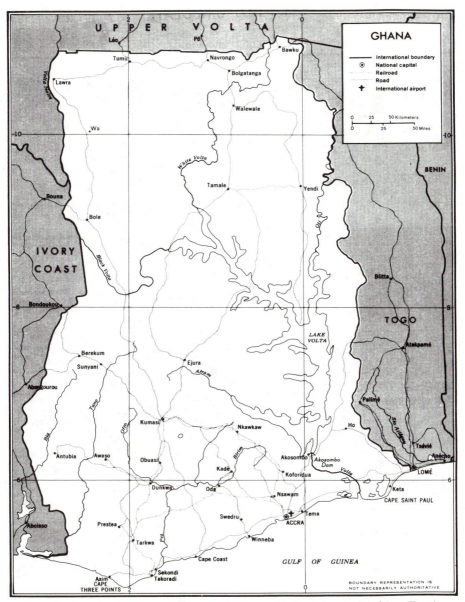

Physical map of Ghana (note that Upper Volta is now Burkina Faso).
Source: *Facts on File*, U.S. Department of State.

Poster sold by street vendors commemorating Ghana's heads of state since the country was granted independence

Summary of Ghana's Regimes, 1957–1986

Regime	Dates in Power	Leader (party affiliation)
Convention People's party government (First Republic, 1960–1966)	1957–1966	Kwame Nkrumah (CPP)
National Liberation Council	1966–1969	Lt. Gen. J. A. Ankrah
Second Republic	1969–1972	Dr. K. A. Busia (PP)
Supreme Military Council I (National Redemption Council)	1972–1978	Col. I. K. Acheampong
Supreme Military Council II	1978–1979	Lt. Gen. Fred Akuffo
Armed Forces Revolutionary Council	1979	Flight Lt. Jerry Rawlings
Third Republic	1979–1981	Dr. Hilla Limann (PNP)
Provisional National Defence Council	1981–	Flight Lt. Jerry Rawlings

CPP: Convention People's party; PP: Progress party; PNP: People's National party

Introduction

The West African state of Ghana, despite its relatively small size, has earned a special place in the history of the continent over the years. From the days of the Asante federation, Ghana has served as a model for other areas of Africa not only because of its precolonial legacy but also because of its organized resistance to colonial conquest, the rapid proliferation of Christianity and of Western education within the country, and its adoption of a cash economy. In 1957, Ghana became the first sub-Saharan African state to achieve independence from colonial rule. It was then the first to commit itself to the Pan-African dream, one of the first to set up a one-party state and to undergo a military coup d'etat, and the first to attempt a return to civilian rule. Even as Ghana's fortunes have declined in recent years, its governments have experimented with new political forms and its citizens have devised ingenious coping mechanisms. Anyone who comes into contact with Ghana can only be touched by the warmth of the people, fascinated by the richness of the culture and history, intrigued by the complexities of its contemporary experience, and troubled about the prospects for its future.

Ghana covers an area of 238,537 square kilometers stretching from a coastal plain along the fifth latitude in the south through a dense forest area to a small strip of savannah in the far north. It abuts on the Guinea Gulf and has common borders with the Ivory Coast, Burkina Faso (Upper Volta), and Togo (see Map 1.1). Like most countries bordering on the West African

1

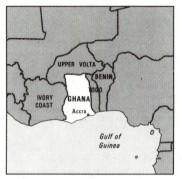

MAP 1.1 Ghana in relation to neigh-
boring countries (Upper Volta is now
Burkina Faso). Source: *Facts on File*, U.S.
Department of State.

coast, Ghana has three major zones. Along the Atlantic are the
Accra plains: a flat strip of land that gives way to a series of
ridges some forty miles inland. The climate along the coast is
humid and warm; in the mountains (especially along the Akwapim ridge) it is somewhat drier and cooler, making this area
a desirable spot during the particularly hot seasons. Most of
Ghana—in the middle strip—consists of tropical rainforest: here
the topography is hilly, and the area is covered by dense
vegetation. The humidity in this area is especially high; the
rainfall abundant. The forest gives way in the north to the drier
flatlands of the savannah, in which vegetation is sparse and
the humidity lower. Several rivers traverse the country from
north to south; the most prominent are the White and Black
Volta that lead into the Volta Lake in the east. The Afram, Ofin,
and Tano rivers flow farther to the south alongside the Pra and
Birim.

Accra, Ghana's capital, is located on the coast. The metropolitan Accra area has almost 1 million inhabitants—about
8 percent of the country's population. The second largest city
is Kumase (also spelled Kumasi), the capital of the forest zone,
with nearly 400,000 inhabitants. Tamale contains the major
urban concentration in the north, with a population of 100,000.
Other Ghanaian cities include Takoradi, Cape Coast, Sunyani,
and Bolgatanga. Ghana's present configuration, like that of most
African states, is a result of the colonial conquest and the
boundary adjustments made following the demise of Germany's
African empire after World War I.

An ethnic mosaic, Ghana's population is composed of a variety of sociocultural groups. The most important ethnic constellation, the Akan peoples (subdivided into the Asante, Fante, Akwapim, Brong, Akim, Nzima, and other smaller units), make up 44.1 percent of the population. The Mole-Dagbani constitute 15.9 percent, the Ewe 13.0 percent, the Ga-Adangme 8.3 percent, the Guan 3.7 percent, the Gurma 3.5 percent, and other groups 11.4 percent. Ethnic divisions in Ghana are accompanied by those of kinship and geography. In addition, status differentials based on income, education, and occupation have been superimposed upon those tied to sociocultural background. Special importance is attributed in the society to group affiliation and to group action, so that the social origins and bases of key actors have helped to define the nature of events in Ghana at any given juncture. Within this context, ethnic rivalry has been pronounced, as has been the conflict between populist and elitist strains active in Ghana's society and its polity. The continuous tug of war between these two broadly delineated social forces has exerted a major influence on Ghana since independence, a process that is the first ongoing theme in the contemporary Ghanaian experience.

Most of Ghana's 12,244,000 people (its population according to official 1982 midyear estimates) reside in rural areas. Although 73.4 percent of Ghanaians live in the countryside, rural-urban migration has increased in recent years. The population of Accra, the capital city, is estimated at 750,000. Other urban configurations—Kumase, Sekondi-Takoradi, Tamale, Tema, Cape Coast, Ho, Bolgatanga, Sunyani, Koforidua—have grown steadily in the past few decades. These urban concentrations have developed as centers for the country's nine administrative regions: Greater Accra, Eastern, Central, Western, Volta, Ashanti, Brong-Ahafo, Northern, and Upper. These regional divisions, which frequently coincide with ethnic groupings, have become important funnels for the distribution of services and have also become loci of development efforts.

The demographic composition and administrative structure of the country underline a second major theme that permeates the Ghanaian scene: the diffuse location of social, political, and economic activity. Events in and around the capital provide only one focus of public life. Another historically vibrant setting may be found in the intricate network of local institutions developed over the years. The complex interaction between the national level and the community endows culture, politics, and economics with a variety of meanings in different contexts. Local factors are as important in determining overall trends as the more readily observable forces operating at the state core.

Ghana's economy, like that of many other states in the tropical zone, is based primarily on agriculture. Cocoa is the export staple of the country and the main source of external revenues. Agriculture, forestry, and fishing constitute close to 50 percent of the gross domestic product (GDP), with manufacturing and mining (mostly gold and diamonds) contributing close to 20 percent. Wholesale and retail trade add 12 percent, services (including the government sector) some 14 percent, and transport and communication another 4 percent.

Despite the natural and skilled human resources at its disposal, the Ghanaian economy has not been able to sustain any measure of growth in recent years. Budget deficits have been endemic, the foreign debt has increased, inflation has averaged over 100 percent each year since the beginning of the 1980s, and food production has dropped at an alarming pace. The downward spin of the economy has been symptomatic of the political turmoil and social unease that have pervaded the country in the past few decades.

These circumstances highlight a third major theme of recent Ghanaian history: the centrality of economic considerations to the determination of postcolonial developments. Successive leaders have experimented with many different kinds of constitutional arrangements; however, the viability of regimes and of state structures has been as much a function of a government's ability to solve economic problems as of the validity of its organization.

Ghana's social, administrative, and economic structures have been influenced by foreign as well as domestic factors. For more than a millennium the country has maintained relations with other parts of the continent and with Europe along the trans-Saharan route. For almost 500 years the inhabitants of Ghana have been in direct sea contact with Europe.

These interchanges accentuate a fourth theme central to the Ghanaian experience: the importance of external forces in molding internal processes. Like many other African states, Ghana's ability to maneuver has been constrained by its growing dependence on the world outside its boundaries. The effects of foreign influences on Ghana and on Ghanaians have varied: Social, political, and economic matters within Ghana have developed in response to the global economic environment of which it is a part.

Contemporary Ghana encompasses a complex matrix of social forces, ecological conditions, economic resources, and foreign contacts. Its normative fabric manifests this diversity: Traditional values have retained much of their appeal at the same time as new codes have been incorporated. Deference and pride, fatalism and patience, participation and opportunism, tolerance and vindictiveness, humor and sullenness, rationality and a persistence of magical beliefs—all are apparent in everyday behavior.

Overall, present day Ghana is characterized by a sophistication, vibrancy, and awareness, which are a fifth key theme of this study. Few countries in Africa can boast of a population as politically informed, involved, and active as that of Ghana. Interest in communal affairs, whether at the local or the national level, is constantly in evidence. Actions of those in authority are scrutinized, evaluated, criticized, and frequently decried by a public that has ensured, however belatedly, that a modicum of accountability is always present in the Ghanaian arena. The curiosity and imagination of Ghanaians have thus guaranteed an atmosphere of debate and discussion that makes affairs in Ghana carry a special flavor of excitement and movement.

Since the heady years of early independence, Ghanaians have witnessed eight changes in government. Ghana's once viable and promising economy at first stagnated and then, in the late 1970s, regressed rapidly. Political instability and economic decline have been accompanied by social unrest and widespread civilian disorder, culminating in the populist coups led by Flight Lieutenant Jerry Rawlings in 1979 and on the last day of 1981. Drastic swings of the political pendulum, coupled with the persistence of common norms, economic disintegration and political volatility, and group adherence, together with individual mobility, localism, and national pride, have made Ghana into a paradigm of the complex processes of continuity and change in Africa. This cycle of elaboration and fragmentation constitutes the sixth theme of the contemporary Ghanaian experience.

An inconsistent record of continuity in a framework of political instability and economic uncertainty is the hallmark of the country since independence. Our interpretive introduction to Ghana first examines the historical roots of current patterns, then traces the intricate features of Ghanaian politics since independence. We devote a separate chapter to the bases, nature, and directions of social life and change. Our analysis then turns to the economic sphere: to an investigation of development strategies, economic performance, the causes for economic decline, and the reactions of Ghanaians to the constraints of growing impoverishment. We then assess changes in the country's international standing in an effort to come to terms with the anomalies of present-day Ghana. In the conclusion we evaluate the implications of this inheritance for Ghana, Ghanaians, and other African states and explore possible directions for future change.

1

Historical Background

The unique place that Ghana holds among contemporary African nations is due largely to the country's historical legacy of antithetical elements: struggles and capitulations, in-migrations and exoduses, personalities and events, Africans and expatriates. These various factors have molded the character of the country and given Ghana its special stamp. Together, they have undermined the country's stability and solvency while underlining its survival. The early migrations and the establishment of the northern trade routes brought the settled north into indirect contact with Europe and the Middle East. First Islam and later Christianity introduced new value systems, types of education, and economic networks. Local internecine wars created a nation of peoples whose historical enmities have periodically erupted in displays of tribalism. The maritime revolution and the country's cache of gold brought in one European power after another, each vying for control of the wealth for the good of the homeland. Ultimately, the European intrusion set the stage both for the amalgamation of the various peoples in a fight for independence and for the state of dependency and decline in which Ghana finds itself today.

STATES, TRADE, AND ISLAM

The modern state of Ghana, though remote from the great empires of the western Sudan that flourished between the tenth and the fourteenth centuries, nevertheless has several points of connection with them, both putative and direct. Ghana derives its name from the Sudanic trading state, described by Arabic

7

writers as "the land of gold," that evolved into a kingdom and reached the height of its power in the eleventh century.

Migrations

As Mediterranean peoples and trade routes spread farther out, the Sudanic centers operated as mediators in the commercial exchanges between black Africa and the Mediterranean. The two areas were linked with what is now northern Ghana through two major trade routes, both of which terminated in Asante. The northwest route from the area of the Sudanic empires, upstream of Timbuktu, began being used during the fourteenth century; carrying trade in gold, ivory, and slaves, it was controlled by Dyula (Mande) traders. Along the northeast route, gold, cowrie shells, salt, and kola nut from Gonja were exchanged for cotton cloth, leather goods, and slaves from Kano (the northern Nigerian Hausa state); established during the fifteenth century, the route was controlled by Hausa.

A less definite, although fundamentally significant, link was forged with the western Sudan, the place of origin of the settlers who begat the second-stage process of state formation that characterized the sociopolitical enterprise in the area for several hundred years. Prior to the eleventh century, kin-based societies inhabited what is now Ghana—Gur peoples in the northern savannah and Kwa in or near the forest in the south. Immigrants established their settlements along the two major trade routes. Whether or not the people of the ancient Ghana were ancestors of the contemporary Akan, traditions hold that the founders of this group were emigrants from the western Sudan. They moved into the lands of present-day Ghana in three waves between the thirteenth and fourteenth and the seventeenth centuries.[1]

The first group, the Guan, settled in the north and in the coastal areas of Accra and Winneba a bit to the west. Members of the second movement, composed of the ancestors of the Fante, established themselves in the central coastal area. And the third group, the ancestors of the Asante, moved down to settle between the two preceding peoples. A branch of the last group, the Akwamu, came into contact with the Ga in the seventeenth century. Many of these tribes developed democratic, decentralized forms of government, headed by a chief and his council. The Asante federation, the most famous of these, became a dominant power during the eighteenth and nineteenth centuries, until it was subdued by the British. The Fante became known for their trading abilities: They served as middlemen for Europeans and helped develop Ghana's renowned cocoa industry in the twentieth century.

The communities of the early Gur and Kwa speakers also hosted passing Hausa and Dyula traders. The role of Islam in state building among these autochthonous peoples is not absolutely clear, although it was significant to the growth of commercial activity. Arabic was the medium of trade contacts and accounting, and the prominent trade groups, such as the Hausa and the Dyula, proselytized Islam. The religion is said to have reached Dagomba, northeast of Asante, by the seventeenth century. In nineteenth-century Kumase, Muslims monopolized the distribution trades and worked as clerks in the royal court; those with learning wielded considerable influence.

The Ga-Adangme and Ewe of the south both migrated from the east in several waves, probably no earlier than the fifteenth century. Their center of culture had been among the Yoruba and Edo of southern Nigeria. The Ga moved in along the coast in extended family groups, founding villages among the Akan Kpesi. They were concentrated around Ayawaso, 8 miles northwest of modern-day Accra. Soon after, the (Ga) Accras moved their capital to Small Accra; their supremacy was acknowledged by other Ga tribes, who moved as well. By 1660, Accra was on the way to becoming capital of a Ga Federation, which extended from the plains to the Volta River.

Savannah Kingdoms

The founding ancestors of the savannah kingdoms of Dagomba and Mamprussi moved in from Hausaland and Lake Chad to the northeast as small groups of invaders. They arrived about the fifteenth century and attempted to impose new traditions with variable success. In western Dagomba, they totally eclipsed the original inhabitants, whereas to the east among the Konkomba (whose masses created the basis for the Dagomba state), traditional social forms survived. By the end of the sixteenth century, both Dagomba and Bono were established kingdoms that derived their power from the trade of salt, gold, and kola. The Mande forced the Dagomba people, their competitors in trade, to move their capital to Yendi; they also defeated the Akan state of Bono. Moreover, the Mande immigrants interfered with the Akan people already resident between Dagomba and the forest. These people lived in unproductive terrain, which in the fifteenth century was the focus of the northeast kola trade with Kano. In the seventeenth century, the Mande invaders took over these Akan and forged the state of Gonja.

Akan States

While the Accras were enjoying the prosperity during the seventeenth century, three major states monopolized inland-coastal trade—the Akwamu, the Akim, and the Denkyera. In the 1640s, the Akwamu began to expand their territory and to monopolize the trade routes. They occupied the state of Accra (at Great Accra) from 1677 until 1682. They burned towns, laid waste to land, and destroyed plantations. They reduced the Accra state to the position of a tributary province of Akwamu. From 1680 until 1730, Akwamu authority went unchallenged.

To the west, the Akwamu state was in competition with the considerably less powerful kingdom of Akim. In 1733, two Akim groups and other neighboring peoples took on the Akwamu. "The truth is that, as the Akwamu themselves relate with a sort of gloomy pride, they had been thoroughly bad neighbors to all around them, and every neighboring state jumped at the chance of expelling them."[2] The war lasted fifteen months and ended with Accra having recovered its independence.

In opposing Akwamu, Akim had allied itself with Denkyera to the west, which by the 1690s held sway over chiefs and peoples from the River Tano to the River Pra in the center of the country. Denkyera's merchants dominated trade on the western coast. The kingdom's rise was tied to the upsurge in the economic fortunes of the Gold Coast's interior. But the people of Denkyera were bad administrators and ruthless exploiters; ultimately they were defeated by the Asante.

The Akwamu, Denkyera, and Akim never consolidated their holdings on the coast, because the Fante, in 1720, founded a military confederation, and they could not centralize sufficiently to hold together their conquests.

Asante Expansion

The Asante nation emerged in the late seventeenth century.[3] Although its origins are obscure, Asante ancestors seem to have been Akan living in the southern part of the country. They migrated north in small kin groupings and settled at Tafo, the junction of the two northern trade routes.

Osei Tutu, chief of Kumase (an Asante state), was the architect of the Asante nation. The bond that cemented the Asante states had several facets. All belonged to the same Akan clan, and they all hated their former Denkyera overlords and after moving north wanted to prevent further exploitation by them. They desired land, which would have to be wrested from an already resident population. Their new location provided a means to wealth in commercial activity, and indeed gold became central to their polity. But they also gained mystical support: Okomfo Anokye, Osei Tutu's chief priest, created a bond of allegiance that would surpass that owed by members of each Asante state to their own chief or ancestors, by causing the Golden Stool to descend from the heavens onto Osei Tutu's knees; the Golden Stool was then perceived as the symbol of Asante unity and the Kumase chief regarded as its custodian (the Asantehene). The Odwira Festival, celebrated by all Asante peoples, symbolized solidarity. The Asante "constitution" and laws conferring citizenship substantiated unification, and Kumase was established as the nation's capital. It is not insignificant that Osei Tutu had spent his early years at the courts of both the Denkyera and the Akwamu. His drafting of the plan for Asante political and military organization presumably benefited from his mastery of the politics of these two powerful states as well as his understanding of the importance of firearms to their advancement.

During the eighteenth century the Asante empire was consolidated, and, it was expanded considerably under Opoku

Ware (1720–1750). Early on, the empire subjugated neighboring peoples and then incorporated them as citizens. In 1701, aided by the Akwamu, the Asante conquered the Denkyera state, absorbing its subjects and allies, and emerged as the dominant political power in the western Gold Coast hinterland, while also controlling the trade in gold, ivory, and slaves in the region. Conflicts continued in the south, including that in which the Akwamu betrayed the Asante, who were fighting the Akim in 1717. The Asante overcame such difficulties and in 1724 conquered Bono, the subject state of Tekyiman, which provided the nation with wealth and reknown and thereby facilitated the Asante push westward.

The Akim defeated the Akwamu in 1730, but they were an internally divided people that feared an Asante invasion—which finally occurred in early 1742 and made the victorious Asante the dominant political and economic power in the interior. The Akim, Akwapim (Akan), Accra, and Adangme peoples were also tributaries to the Asante nation. The only coastal area not controlled by the Asante was that held by the Fante Confederacy. The Asante, however, devoted their energies to subjugating the northern peoples—the Gonja and Dagomba—in 1745.

The Asante state was beset with internal and external problems of its own. By the 1740s, Kumase had become too powerful, causing Opoku Ware to set up an Asante royal bureaucracy as an attempt at government reform. However, his efforts were obstructed by the chiefs of other subdivisions, and civil wars broke out. Moreover, outlying vassal states were not governed by Asante administrators, and they continually rebelled. But the nation endured: By 1820, Asante had established its dominance over most of the territory of present-day Ghana. The Asante central government controlled foreign affairs, a large empire through an intricate communication network, and a state trading organization. The last aspect clarifies why the government was prepared to go to war to open closed trade routes, such as the roads leading to Accra.[4]

A Fante-Asante rapprochement in the mid-eighteenth century gave way to suspicion and strife over control of the coastal-inland trade in such goods as guns and gun powder, knives, and cotton cloths, and this discord smoldered during the better part of the last half of the 1700s. Relations between the Asante government and the coastal states worsened in the early 1800s. In 1806, when the Fante provided refuge to Asante rebels, the Asante declared war on them. Asante coastal victory, however, was only complete after ten more years and many more battles. As a result of Asante hegemony, the coastal states suffered economically until the 1870s.

The Asante push to the sea also entailed supportive expansion to the east and the west. This tied in with their access to the slave trade and the diversion of inland commercial activity from coastal traders to operators on the neighboring slave coast and Ivory Coast. This shift in turn provided the Asante with access to arms for campaigns against other states. Their imperialism was a means to control the economic system of which they were a part,[5] and it brought them face to face with European power.

EUROPEAN CONTACT

The colonial name for Ghana was the Gold Coast, a name that reflects the country's economic history. The Portuguese were the first Europeans to make the Gold Coast directly known to Europe. The development of European sea trade, which their arrival foretold, created new political and economic focuses in the south, which eclipsed northern trade routes. And in the nineteenth and twentieth centuries, the technology and ideology introduced from Europe overshadowed those from the Muslim world.

Initial Contact and Commercial Entrenchment

West African gold and particularly that mined in the Gold Coast where supplies were capacious and regular attracted the Portuguese in 1471. In 1494, papal award gave them a monopoly on African trade. This award, however, was disregarded by the English (arrival in 1553), Dutch (1595), Swedes (1640), Danes (1640), and Brandenburgers (1683). In 1482, the Portuguese built a castle at Elmina because they were threatened by competition—competition in commerce, not in colonization. Subsequently, many such battlements were erected by the various European powers drawn into the Gold Coast trade. Even though the Portuguese became known for brutality and native antipathy developed toward their forts, the trade they set up was sufficiently important to attract inland and coastal people to migrate to the new towns growing up around Elmina—foreshadowing the post–World War II western-based urbanizing boom.

The Portuguese, who had already built small fortified trading lodges and forts to the east and established their headquarters at Elmina, were driven out in 1642. The establishment of regular British trade with the Gold Coast dates from 1618, and through the mid-seventeenth century, Britain and Holland fought for hegemony. The latter years of the seventeenth and early years of the eighteenth century saw the construction of British forts alongside those built by the Portuguese and Dutch, which changed hands between the European powers. The forts became centers of economic and political power, often stronger than that in the traditional capitals. For example, the Ga chief agreed to the conversion of Dutch storehouses into a fort to protect his people against their neighbors, the Akwamu. This fort, called Crevecoeur (renamed Ussher Fort by the British), was finished in 1650. Two other forts were built in Accra: James Fort, 500 yards from Crevecoeur, was built by the British in 1673; Christiansborg Castle, 3 miles east of Crevecoeur in Osu, was built by the Swedes in 1657. By the mid-eighteenth century, and for about 100 years thereafter, ownership stabilized; along 300 miles of coast were scattered thirty well-fortified bastions: Those to the west of Accra were Dutch or British, those to the east Danish.

Slave and Legitimate Trade

European countries had long been dependent upon West African gold, and they relied upon Arab traders who traveled the northern routes for access to it. Thus, direct European trade with West Africa by sea, initiated by the Portuguese, was a breakthrough. As early as the beginning of the sixteenth century, the Portuguese were exporting about one-tenth of the world's gold supply, estimated between £100,000 and £350,000 per year.[6]

However, the slave trade really drew the Europeans into West Africa and led them to build forts to protect the occupants from both rival European countries and potentially hostile Africans. During the seventeenth century, slaves were not in demand in Europe; neither the English nor the Dutch engaged in slaving at that time. However, the discovery of the New World and the creation of the plantation system for growing sugar, cotton, and tobacco, with its insatiable demand for labor, produced the market for human beings. The Gold Coast was drawn into what became known as the triangular trade: Cheap manufactured goods were shipped from Europe to Africa, where slaves were bought or seized and shipped to the West Indies and Americas, and there exchanged for minerals and foodstuffs to be sold in Europe. Thus, 200 years before independence, the land that was to become Ghana was already an important source of raw material and a market for European goods.

From the mid-1600s until the late 1700s, the Gold Coast contributed no more than about 10,000 slaves each year, which at first constituted a large percentage of the total slave trade, but as the volume of the trade skyrocketed, the Gold Coast's contribution proportionately declined. The majority of Africans were shipped from further east.

Britain's economic and ultimately political primacy in the Gold Coast was a consequence of slaving contests with other European nations, especially with the Dutch. In 1807, Britain officially abolished the slave trade. Although humanitarianism played a part, the economic element really facilitated the official act of prohibition. For one thing, overproduction of sugar in the West Indies slowed down the pace of work and thus the need for workers (slaves). For another, the British economy was being industrialized and needed raw materials; hence a "legitimate" trade in raw agricultural products—palm oil and nuts, peanuts, cotton—was launched with the Gold Coast.

Nineteenth-Century Incursions

British influence along the coast grew as a result of a combination of economic policy and missionary, merchant, and administrative activities.[7] Following the abolition of slavery,

British missionaries (as well as others from Switzerland and Germany) arrived to preach a message of spiritual renewal to peoples suffering from the moral and material decay fostered by the slave trade. Their teachings had unexpected and far-reaching effects.

Altruism did not play a part in the arrival of the British merchants, whose activities in the Gold Coast date to the late seventeenth century and the formation of the Royal African Company. This association was succeeded by the African Company of Merchants, whose relations with local peoples living in the vicinity of British-held forts were formalized. In 1821, the imperial government assumed control over Britain's coastal possessions and forts when it became clear that the African Company could not deal with the Asante or secure the slave trade abolition.

In fact, British involvement in Gold Coast trade had an impact on native internal affairs and created new alignments. The Crown dropped its neutral position when the Asante-Fante wars disrupted trade and the Asante ignored the prohibition against slave trading, continuing to deal with other Europeans along the coast. As the British then backed the Fante, the Dutch backed the Asante, thereby creating another arena for the European contest.

Sir Charles MacCarthy, who in 1821 became governor of all the British West African possessions including the Gold Coast forts, led an unsuccessful battle against the Asante that resulted in his death. On the basis of this campaign, the British decided to avoid future alliances with native peoples that would involve them in local wars and to forego imperial expansion. In fact, the British government wanted to withdraw entirely, but the British merchants and the Fante protested because they were worried about their safety and continuing economic prosperity. Administration of the forts was then handed back to the company merchants under the presidency of George Maclean. During his tenure, the volume of British trade with the Gold Coast tripled, and Asante-Fante relations were quiet. The local public opinion supported Maclean fully, and the gradual development of British colonial authority began during his tenure. In 1843, the British government reclaimed the job of administering the Gold Coast settlements and forts and was also accorded judicial powers.

The British Conquest

Determined to maintain peace, the British in 1844 enacted the first of a series of bonds—special treaties with Gold Coast states—under which certain chiefs acknowledged the right of the Crown to intervene in the administration of justice but not to govern. From 1844 when the Fante Bond was signed until 1874, the states that entered into bonds were referred to loosely as the British protectorate, whereas the forts constituted the colony.

Although the Fante had conceded limited bond powers to the British, the latter subsequently usurped the judicial role of the kings and chiefs. Thus, although the Fante were under the protection of the British, they were also considerably cramped by the potential colonizer. Fante antagonism to the British led to the establishment of the Fante Confederacy and a widespread movement by this ethnic group in the 1860s to oust British authority. Although short lived, the confederacy was a forerunner of Ghanaian nationalism, which threatened the British economically and politically and led the latter to take a more active and expansionist role—indeed, to become a colonizer.

Unlike the Fante, the Asante had always resisted British intervention. Asante expansionism was the force that had driven the Fante and other peoples to commit themselves to British protection. The Asante were "officially regarded by successive merchant and colonial governments, as wealthy but disturbing neighbours, whose power continually offered a potential threat to British trade and influence."[8] The British-Dutch exchange of forts in 1872 gave the British possession of Elmina. The Asante war of 1873-1874, marked by the state's invasion of the Cape Coast–Elmina area, was inspired by its determination to drive out the British. The British, in turn, initiated an imperial war by invading Kumase with the Gold Coast Hausa Constabulary (a defense force of foreign recruits) and destroying the town. The Asante signed a treaty with the British in 1874, renouncing all claim to the latter's coastal possessions.

Between 1875 and 1890, the Asante union was troubled by secessionists (who were encouraged by the British, in hopes of breaking up the nation). By using negotiation and military force the Asantehene succeeded in subverting British influence—discouraging their interference in domestic politics and their claims to trade routes under Asante domain. Fearing that Asante political organization and alliances would result in their being barred from the interior trade, the British again invaded Kumase in 1895, arrested Prempeh the Asantehene, and exiled him to the Seychelles Islands. The final Asante attempt to drive out the British, the 1900 Yaa Asantewa War, failed.

The British Colonial Presence

In 1850, under pressure from the merchants the Gold Coast was separated from Sierra Leone and designated a distinct colony. The British purchased the remaining Danish forts, and the influence that the Danes had enjoyed passed on to them. The governor and his administrators resided at Cape Coast Castle. In 1877, they transferred their headquarters to Christiansborg Castle in Accra.

By proclamation, Britain's powers extended to preservation of public peace, protection of individuals, life, and property; civil and commercial jurisdiction; extinction of human sacrifices; abolition of slave dealing; measures regarding domestic slavery and pawning; and establishment of police force, administration of health and education, and the raising of revenue.[9]

In 1885, the colony of the Gold Coast represented the largest area controlled by Britain on the west coast of Africa and included the forts and chiefdoms to the immediate interior that had been annexed in 1874. Not until 1901 were the Asante lands annexed as part of the colony and the Northern Territories made a protectorate. In 1902, the Gold Coast was a British Crown colony made up of three separate but related territories, which fifty-five years later gained independence as Ghana. After World War I when British and French troops occupied the Gold Coast's eastern neighbor—the formerly German-held Togoland—under a mandate from the League of Nations, the western part was placed under British care to be administered as part of the

Black Star Square, Accra

Gold Coast. This area became an integral part of the Gold Coast, and later, of Ghana.

The Structure of Indirect Rule

In administering its West African colonies, Britain enjoined indirect rule, which entailed governing the native peoples through their already developed indigenous political institutions.[10] In the Gold Coast, the British pursued one type of indirect rule until the 1930s and another type following that date. Initially, their rule can be characterized as laissez-faire, which was intended to back up the native authority in the colony states and no more. Thus, from 1874 until 1927 the colony chiefs maintained their internal autonomy, and the colonial government merely buttressed their power. After 1904, the governor was empowered to confirm the election and installation of new chiefs. Any reduction of chiefly powers translated as the limitation of judicial competence. In those Northern Territories that had no tradition of chieftaincy, the British simply accorded executive powers to the clan elders and ruled through them.

British colonial policy of indirect rule after the 1930s was more interventionist and was similar to British policy regarding the Asante—the only chiefdom not left to govern itself. The British had been bent on destroying the Asante union since 1874, and the conquest of Kumase in 1896 allowed them to implement that intent. After the arrest and exile of the Asantehene, the Asante nation had the status of a protectorate with no real administrative system. In 1896, a resident was appointed by the British and given civil and criminal jurisdiction over the territory. Each Asante state was administered separately, isolating Kumase and diminishing its authority. But in 1919, when Sir Gordon Guggisberg became the new governor, the Asante federation was reconstituted so that the British could simplify their governance of the state by using indirect rule.

The British system of administering the Gold Coast by indirect rule suffered from two contradictory trends: (1) showing respect for the traditional institution of the chief and (2) equivocating on the ultimate source of his power—the stool or the Europeans. As a consequence, it also created an ambivalence in the populace, who were torn between serving two structurally very different masters. The confusion was exacerbated by the variance between laissez-faire and active rule.[11]

In any case, the governor was appointed as the representative of the Crown in the colony. He was assisted by the district officer or district commissioner, who represented the Crown in the field. A system of native authorities enabled some decisions to be screened through traditional means. This device, which is integrated into the Western bureaucratic structure was distinctive in the Gold Coast because it was instituted considerably after—not before—the central government. The district commissioner supervised the native authority, which was responsible to the state council. Above the latter, at the pinnacle of the native authority structure, were the provincial councils, established to create a link, along with the chiefs, between the local administration and the central government. The councils strengthened the chiefs by providing them with an additional source of legitimacy and giving them national prominence.

Executive and Legislative Councils, which were advisory bodies, served as additional instruments of governance. The

Sir J. P. Rodger, governor of the Gold Coast, Nii Obi (the Ga chief) and his elders to the governor's right, and Malam Bako (Hausa headman), Ibrahima Braimah (Yoruba chief of Accra's Muslims), and Kadri English (Hausa headman) and their elders to the governor's left, c. 1909. Source: copy of original lent to Deborah Pellow by Alhaji Ali Kadri English, chief of Accra Central Hausa community.

Legislative Council, established in 1850 to give taxpayers representation in decisionmaking, had the power to make the laws for the colony. In fact, its setup implicitly acknowledged the autonomy of the colony in creating legislation, as separate from the British Parliament or the Colonial Office in London. A few Africans, representatives from the elite class, were appointed— perhaps as early as 1850. The Executive Council was composed of government officials who presented matters like financial estimates to the Legislative Council. Appointed by the governor to advise and assist him, the Executive Council had few internal or external checks. Only the colony came under the Legislative Council's jurisdiction. Asante states and the Northern Territories were both ruled by proclamation. Not until 1946 was Asante territory incorporated under council jurisdiction, and even then British colonial rule did not extend to the north.

Christianity, Education, and Westernization

Preceding and accompanying the colonial administrators into Ghana were missionaries, who established schools and preached sermons that carried the lessons of the West, lessons often antithetical to those taught by the traditional sages. New codes of conduct, based upon the Bible, were introduced. British missionaries touted the nuclear family, monogamy, and domestic roles for women, at the expense of Ghanaian social institutions, such as extended family ties, the polygynous farming household, and the economically autonomous woman. People came to be respected for the status that they achieved through education rather than that accorded for age and lineage. Access to mobility through new roles threatened traditional authority.

Governor Guggisberg regarded Western education as the mechanism for development; by acquiring it young men could move into the civil service. The British criteria of privilege, very much a function of social and economic position, were absorbed by those desirous of making their way in the comparatively open Ghanaian society. Indeed, whereas the British colonizers created disunity by introducing a new social system with a role structure supported by foreign norms and values, African "converts" took over where the British left off. The educated became a new elite, which mediated between the British and the African masses. In their desire to reform traditional society, they began to compete with the traditional elite for power. The early elite of the Gold Coast began to emerge along the coast during the second half of the nineteenth century. Its members monopolized the commercial and political posts created by British colonial policy. They adopted English names and the Victorian life-style, and they nominally accepted Christian teachings. Bourgeoisification became their hallmark. Members of this incipient class were influential in the Fante Confederacy.

The Cash Economy: Gold and Cocoa

Gold was the initial commercial attraction that the Gold Coast held for Europe, and it remained an important export throughout the colonial period.[12] An indigenous industry, which employed such comparatively unsophisticated techniques as panning or mining by shafts, gold mining became an exclusively foreign-run enterprise by the 1890s. The development of the modern gold mining industry in the Gold Coast brought enormous revenues into villages just at the time when the range of desirable European imports was expanding. Tribal authorities profited greatly from mining concessions, as did African lawyers and speculators involved in land deals. Early on, educated Africans tried to prevent the wholesale expatriate takeover by setting up modern mines, but they were obstructed by lack of capital and technology.

The mining industry developed slowly, and production did not exceed 18,000 fine ounces until the turn of the century. The early concessionaires mined in areas already known to Africans. The Obuasi mine, which the Denkyera had worked two centuries earlier, was opened to the Europeans in 1897. The colonial British government constructed a railway from the coastal city of Sekondi northward, which passed through Tarkwa, site of a gold field. The prospects of enormous profits produced a boom, and by the beginning of the twentieth century, 400 gold mining companies had been formed. Between 1912 and 1931, the Ashanti Goldfields Company was producing an annual average of 105,263 fine ounces. The African territories' dependence on European technology to profitably exploit their mineral deposits facilitated the European takeover.

Unlike the mineral industry, export agriculture was never taken out of African hands. And the cocoa industry remained under the control of the small-scale farmer. Despite a small market, cocoa bean cultivation was begun in earnest in the 1870s by a man in Mampong-Asante. In 1895, 13 tons were exported; by 1905, the figure had risen dramatically to 5,000 tons and by 1911, to 40,000 tons—a result of the Cadbury Company's decision to buy cocoa from the Gold Coast rather than Saõ Tomé and Fernando Po. Unlike other forms of food production, which followed a pattern of shifting fields, cocoa farms were permanent, encouraging individuals to hold land. The cocoa farms were established first in the Eastern Province, and then in the Asante, Western, and Central Provinces. After 1915, cocoa was the colony's primary crop export; in the 1920s, it constituted 78 percent of the Gold Coast's total exports.

The colony thus developed a monocultural dependence on cocoa. Attempts at diversification failed, either because farmers were uninterested in cultivating different crops when cocoa revenues were high or because diversification schemes could not be funded when cocoa revenues were low. In any case, the boom in cocoa production and export was perhaps the major factor in the development of the Gold Coast's money economy.

In return for minerals and agricultural products, Gold Coast residents spent a lot of money on a variety of imported manufactured consumer items—indicating their incorporation into the world economic system. Many of the imports were products that they could not produce for themselves. Unfortunately, however, some imported products replaced those indigenously made—for example, enamelware replaced pottery. Further fueling the country's dependency, foodstuffs and provisions that could have been produced locally were imported. Cash-croppers preferred not to be bothered with subsistence farming, for example, eschewing the producing of rice or sugar. As early as 1889, a government report remarked on the irrationality of the food dependence, but the colonial government never attempted to rectify the situation because its interest centered on the production of palm oil and cocoa. Thus, by the 1930s, the structure of the economy was transformed; the political implications of this shift were also clearly evident.

POLITICAL RESPONSES TO BRITISH COLONIALISM

Ghana is the first African country to successfully become decolonized. The three phases it underwent on the road to independence—national awakening, direct confrontation with the colonial authorities, and consolidation of domestic power—foreshadowed the development of similar processes elsewhere on the continent. As this dynamic evolved, larger numbers of individuals and groups were drawn into the new political orbit. The manner and sequence of their inclusion in the nationalist effort were to affect profoundly the direction of political change in Ghana after independence. The anticolonial struggle thus provides the essential foundation for an understanding of trends in contemporary Ghana.

The Anticolonial Awakening

The imposition of colonial rule in the Gold Coast and its permeation into the hinterland sowed the seeds of anti-British sentiment. The first indications of dissatisfaction with the colonial presence in the Gold Coast emanated from the group that had been most consistently exposed to its influences and had most directly benefited from this proximity: the intelligentsia.[13] As early as 1897 a small group of educated Africans established the Aborigines' Rights Protection Society (ARPS), which successfully thwarted the British administration's attempt to transform all uncultivated tracts into Crown lands. This early political party went on to dominate coastal politics during the first two decades of the twentieth century. It demanded and received greater unofficial representation in the Legislative Council and controlled municipal politics in Accra.

The ARPS was superseded in the 1920s by the National Congress of British West Africa (NCBWA), whose leadership was drawn from all territories under British rule in West Africa. During the interwar period, the NCBWA pressed for a greater African role in the colonial administration, for the expansion of Western education, and for more indigenous participation in decisionmaking bodies. The moderation evident in these demands reflected the narrow social base upon which the first political aggregations stood. Only a handful of well-educated and well-connected individuals were involved in these activities. Little effort was made to represent the interests of a broader public or to appeal to it.

Although the ARPS and the NCBWA were more concerned with finding ways of integrating their members into the colonial network than with devising means of uprooting it, they did point out some of the more glaring inequities inherent in the colonial system. In this way, they contributed to the creation of the more encompassing political movements of later years.

The breeding ground for anticolonial feelings at this juncture was not the formal political parties but rather a vast array of voluntary associations, ranging from ethnic groupings to labor organizations and from religious bodies to self-help societies and literary clubs.[14] These organizations provided much needed

personal security in a situation of social flux and rapid urbanization. They assisted new migrants by cushioning the difficulties
encountered in adjusting to the new conditions and unfamiliar
mores of the city. Precisely because voluntary associations constituted frameworks in which Africans could control their own
destiny (albeit in limited spheres), they rapidly became the
arenas for political debate and leadership training, and inevitably,
for the accumulation of political experience so necessary for
participation in full-fledged liberation movements.

The potential inherent in this wide range of voluntary
organizations was felt initially in 1937 and 1938, when an
alliance of cocoa planters and Akan chiefs organized a cocoa
boycott that effectively immobilized the economy of the Gold
Coast for four months.[15] By the late 1930s, as more students
from the Gold Coast were exposed to European currents and
became increasingly sensitive to the dynamics of the colonial
situation, the voluntary structures began to assume more stri-
dently political overtones. The radicalization process was spearheaded by educated young people who came together to form
the Gold Coast Youth Council in 1937. Joseph Boakye Danquah,
who headed the movement at that time, was among the first
to demand a drastic change in the colonial status of the Gold
Coast. He and his cohorts organized meetings, published pam-
phlets, and set up branches to disseminate their nationalist
principles. Their assertiveness was indispensable to the promulgation of the anticolonial message prior to the outbreak of
World War II. More significant, this group of Ghanaian intellectuals consolidated an ideology of political liberation that was
to become the cornerstone of the mass struggle that later
developed against the British colonial administration.

The first signs of Ghanaian nationalism assumed a variety
of cultural, economic, religious, social, and political forms. These
diverse activities built up interest in the colonial problem,
nurtured a renewed pride in local history and institutions, and
established the groundwork for more concerted efforts at colonial
disengagement.

The Confrontation with Colonialism

In the aftermath of World War II, the heterogenous strands
at work in the Ghanaian arena were brought together as a

cohesive national liberation movement. The enfeeblement of Britain during the war, the participation of Africans in combat side by side with Europeans, the emergence of the superpowers, and an international environment more favorable to national self-determination—all combined to create an atmosphere conducive to the alteration of the colonial system.

In the Gold Coast, as elsewhere in Africa, the mantle of direct anticolonial activity was taken up at the outset by the educated elites who had been involved in prewar voluntary activities. In 1947 Danquah and other intellectuals and chiefs established the United Gold Coast Convention (UGCC), whose declared goal was to achieve self-government within the shortest possible time.

Although the UGCC viewed itself as the political embodiment of the entire population, its leaders and members were drawn primarily from the select group of wealthy planters, traditional rulers, prosperous business people, and professionals who flourished in and around the colonial center. Aware of the fragile basis of their popular appeal, the UGCC leadership decided to invite Kwame Nkrumah, then a political activist in the Pan-African movement and the West African Student Union in London, to become the secretary-general of the organization. In November 1947 Nkrumah returned to the Gold Coast and began to create an effective political organ not only to promote Ghanaian independence, but also to serve as a model for other such movements throughout the continent.

Nkrumah's vision, style, and ambition clashed with those of the more conservative leadership of the UGCC, but his policies were probably more attuned to the popular mood of discontent rapidly spreading throughout the country. In early 1948, a boycott on foreign firms set in motion a series of strikes, demonstrations, and protests that culminated in the deaths of two exservicemen in a rally in Accra. These actions gave vent to wide-spread feelings of political frustration, economic dissatisfaction, social malaise, and general impatience with British rule. "Should we not fight for liberty? . . . Why should we be bound under unheard of restrictions and oppressions? Shall we not be free?"[16]

The 1948 outbursts were a critical turning point in the decolonization process. They brought the youngmen—the

Ghanaian term for the commoners, the elementary school drop outs—to the forefront of the political scene. This group struck out not only against colonial authority as such, but also against the intelligentsia that upheld many of its precepts. The populist component of Ghanaian politics that first surfaced at this juncture had been underestimated both by the colonial administration and by the UGCC leadership. Although the UGCC had not organized the strikes, it did support their instigators and tried to capitalize politically on the growing waves of discontent. Although its leaders were jailed by the British, the split between Nkrumah and the UGCC old guard intensified. After the release of the politicians, Nkrumah began to act on his own: In September 1948, he established the *Accra Evening News* as the mouthpiece of the nationalist movement and set up the Committee on Youth Organization (CYO), which was directly subject to him, not to the convention as a whole.[17]

By the end of 1948, it was apparent that the uneasy alliance between Danquah and Nkrumah could not be sustained. On June 12, 1949, Nkrumah and the CYO seceded from the UGCC and established the Convention People's party (CPP). The division in the anticolonial movement was significant for two reasons: (1) It represented a symbolic rupture between the colonially nurtured intellectual class and the common people represented by the CPP; and (2) it brought to a close a period of united activity against colonial rule in the Gold Coast.

A phase of mass politics, from 1949 to 1954, was about to commence; the most salient characteristic of this period was its overt militancy. The qualitative change in the political atmosphere was underlined by the diversification of tactics and the reorganization of structures. On the organizational level, Nkrumah set out to mold the CPP into a political vehicle capable of achieving its goals quickly and efficiently. First, he made a concerted effort to expand the leadership of the anticolonial movement. Although the executive was still drawn mainly from the exceedingly narrow group of the Western educated and colonially sponsored elite, the CPP actively sought and incorporated heads of voluntary associations, traders, farmers, students, urban unemployed, and chiefs into its leadership nexus. Each of these newcomers had direct access to distinct groups in Ghanaian society and could therefore help the party establish deep roots in the countryside. On the second leadership rung, the CPP nurtured a group of professional politicians, drawn mostly from the ranks of young men (commonly dubbed the Verandah Boys), who devoted themselves exclusively to party activity.

Second, Nkrumah stressed the importance of structural cohesion in the nationalist effort. The CPP itself was composed of numerous local cells linked first to district and then to regional committees; these in turn were represented in the party's national institutions. Despite a clear emphasis on the functional diversification of tasks at each level, the various wings of the party were placed under the immediate control of the top executive. This complex yet highly centralized party structure was justified on the grounds that it facilitated decisionmaking without sacrificing social depth.

The third principle of organization advocated by Nkrumah resulted from his quest for broad mass support. Nkrumah believed that the success of the CPP depended on its ability to transcend urban areas and to reach the largely rural inhabitants of the country. He achieved this aim through an all-out mobilization drive that utilized symbols, party colors, a unique dress code, hymns, and even prayers to attract active support. It employed both formal modes of information dispersal—the press, radio—and traditional means of political communication such as the well-known bush telegraph and talking drums, rallies, mass gatherings, and well-publicized assemblies were used to mobilize public support. The CPP judiciously dispersed goods and services to members and sympathizers. With his concurrence, Nkrumah was elevated to the position of a national hero, endowed with semimythical charismatic powers. Within less than two years, the CPP had constructed the prototype of an African anticolonial movement.

Once the initial organizational phase was completed, the CPP focused its attention on confrontation with the British. Nkrumah voiced his demand for immediate independence in the party's main slogan of the late 1940s: "Seek ye first the political kingdom and all things will be added unto it."[18] In 1950, he launched a Positive Action campaign that advocated noncompliance, resistance, and sanctions as means to pressure the British to withdraw from the country. These activities, although strident in tone and unsettling, were not accompanied by extreme manifestations of outright violence.

At the height of the Positive Action campaign, the CPP presses were shut down, and its activists, including Nkrumah, were jailed. The British, in what now appears as an overreaction, helped to create a group of political martyrs who made a prison sentence into a prerequisite for respect and status in the anticolonial movement. At the same time, however, the Colonial Office created the Watson Commission to investigate the 1948 disturbances, and it recommended a transition toward self-government in the Gold Coast. The Colonial Office also set up the Coussey Commission to study constitutional change; in 1950, the commission called for an African majority in the Executive and Legislative Councils and for the extension of voting rights to most segments of the population.

In 1951, elections were held in the Gold Coast. Although Nkrumah was still in detention and the CPP had announced its opposition to the Coussey constitution, the party leaders decided to contest the election. The CPP won thirty-four of the thirty-eight seats in the Legislative Council. The day after the elections, Kwame Nkrumah was released from prison and was appointed leader of government business. The second, confrontational phase of decolonization in the Gold Coast had come to an end.

The focus of political agitation between 1946 and 1951 was the attempt to eliminate the colonial presence in the Gold Coast: The conflict therefore pitted the Africans against the British administration. In the Gold Coast, this contest was initially conducted by elite classes and then developed mass support under Nkrumah's guidance. By 1951, with the British agreement in principle to grant independence to the colony, this stage of decolonization gave way to a period of domestic struggles for power on the eve of independence. At this juncture the internal tensions that had been kept somewhat in check erupted into an open clash over control of the colonial (and postcolonial) state.

Political Struggle Before Independence

Nkrumah's victory in 1951 heralded the commencement of a period of dyarchy that lasted until the Gold Coast attained independence in 1957. Once in power, Nkrumah (whose title was changed to prime minister in 1952) sought to use his position to consolidate his hold on the government apparatus and to expand the foundation of his popular support: He placed CPP activists in key government positions, gained control of the pivotal Cocoa Marketing Board, and dispensed benefits to his backers. Nkrumah also elaborated a vision for a new Ghana. Because of his ethnic background (Nzima) and nonestablishment roots, he advocated a unitary system of government that would not only facilitate the immediate goal of political independence but also help to fulfill the second objective of the anticolonial struggle—development and social justice. As the promulgator of the aspirations of the common people, Nkrumah called for the complete transformation of society, the elimination of the privileged position of traditional authority, and the equitable reallocation of resources.[19]

The promise of a munificent future had a special allure for a population that had systematically been held back by colonial and sometimes traditional constraints. This appeal was further enhanced by the cult of personality that evolved around Nkrumah himself. Osagyefo (the victor) Nkrumah was crowned with titles ranging from Showboy to Messiah. His movements were followed with a mixture of pride and awe; his words were consumed with a fervor that transformed politics into a new form of religion. Minority ethnic groups, young people, and urban constellations, seeking ways to improve their lot in the colonially determined hierarchy, were particularly drawn to the Nkrumah message. This diverse group became the solid backbone of the CPP structure.

Nkrumah's administrative acumen and his popular support appeared to favor an early transition to full independence for Ghana.[20] In 1954, elections were called to determine the precise complexion of the government prior to the final transfer of power. Organized opposition to the CPP was weak, coming almost entirely from the veteran leaders of the UGCC, then

united under the banner of the Ghana Congress party, which
had been established in 1952. Despite the seemingly invincible
position of the CPP, the party succeeded in drawing only 55.4
percent of the votes (the remainder went to a disparate group
of independents who opposed CPP candidates in various locales).[21]

The poor showing of the CPP in the 1954 elections raised
demands from intellectuals as well as from ethnic, regional, and
religious groups to delay independence until the political picture
could be clarified. Another landmark in the decolonization
process had come into evidence: one that superimposed special
interests on the mass-elite divisions that had characterized
anticolonial politics in the postwar era. A myriad of political
parties, all representing specific groups or interests, came into
being. The most important new political constellation to appear
at this time was the National Liberation movement (NLM),
whose center was in Kumase. The NLM grew out of a coalition
of wealthy cocoa farmers (concerned with the low prices offered
by the CPP to producers), traditional chiefs, and the largely
Asante and Brong remnants of the UGCC. These groups were
joined by the Asante Youth Association, which rebeled against
the CPP and joined the NLM in demanding greater regional
autonomy. The NLM "met the nationalist appeal of the CPP
with a rival nationalism of its own, through an impassionate
demand for recognition of the traditional unity of the 'Ashanti
Nation.'"[22]

The appeal to traditional revered objects and values—the
Asantehene, the Golden Stool, Asante history, and Asante
rights—masked other, more specifically political concerns. J. B.
Danquah and Kofi Busia, the leaders of the NLM, were as
committed to protecting the interests of the social groups they
represented as they were to forwarding specifically local concerns.
Their fear of the CPP and of their own possible exclusion from
the sources of state power, coupled with their genuine reservations about Nkrumah's deviations from liberal principles,
fueled their opposition to the governing party.

Other political constellations advocating similar goals began
to spring up throughout the country. The Northern People's
party came out against the systematic neglect of the Northern

Territories and the disinterest evinced toward its special problems. The Togoland Congress persisted in the demand for the reunification of Togo. The Muslim Association party championed the needs of adherents to Islam, who lived mostly in the cities of the coast and the forest. The Ga Shifimo Kpee came out in favor of greater Ga representation in the political process.

The emergence of particularistic politics reflected both the extent of the politicization that had taken place during decolonization and a growing realization of the political stakes involved. Although each new agglomeration derived its strength from different parts of the country, the new parties were united in their demand for a federal constitution that would take into account the heterogeneous needs of the different groups and the divergent cultures that made up the Ghanaian social mosaic.

The introduction of the ethnic component compelled the British administration to reconsider the format and the timetable for independence. At a conference held in Achimota (boycotted by the opposition parties), it was decided to maintain the unitary structure expounded in previous constitutions. The Bourne report of 1955 did, however, take local demands into account by suggesting that regional assemblies be created in which local disputes could be resolved and specific concerns aired. The absence of agreement among the various parties led the British to decide to hold another set of elections that would bring these issues before the electorate.

The 1956 elections pitted the mass anticolonial party, the CPP, against a coalition of particularistic parties. The CPP openly championed a unitary government, a relaxation of the restraints of traditional authorities, a concern for the lot of commoners, a distaste for ethnicity as a basis for political organization, and a reformist outlook. Its opponents rallied around federalism, tradition, localism, and deference, and showed a marked preference for preserving existing social arrangements.

The CPP cast the issues facing the voters in terms of two fundamental questions: Do the citizens of Ghana want to revert to the days of imperialism and colonialism? Do they want to delay independence? Party militants suggested that if the answers to these queries were negative, it was vital to support the CPP and its leader. The NLM and its allies based their appeal not only on a call for the revitalization of traditional norms, but also on an outright attack against the CPP, its questionable methods, and its authoritarian tendencies. The volatility, tension, and periodic violence that accompanied the campaign indicated the enormity of the political issues involved.

The CPP emerged from the 1956 elections triumphant. It garnered 54 percent of the popular vote and 71 of the 104 seats in the national parliament. The victory of the CPP may be explained by several factors. First, in a period of decolonization, the party enjoyed a special position by virtue of its leadership in the anticolonial struggle. Second, acceptance of its constitutional formula meant the immediate achievement of independence. Third, the CPP was already in office and could therefore take advantage of its position to foster further support. Fourth, Nkrumah's personal standing was unrivaled by that of any of his opponents. Fifth, the CPP maneuvered local disputes, specific conflicts, and particularistic interests astutely to manipulate the opposition for its own purposes; the particularistic coalition, on the other hand, could not compete effectively on a nationwide basis with the CPP machine.[23]

The timing and the circumstances of the 1956 elections enabled the CPP and Kwame Nkrumah to consolidate their power on the eve of independence. The small margin of the CPP victory highlighted the fragile basis upon which this power rested. The 1956 elections therefore exposed the rifts within Ghanaian society at the same time as they accentuated the vibrancy and common pride that are essential parts of Ghanaian political life.

Framework for Ghanaian Independence

The British granted Ghana independence on March 6, 1957. Ghana's emergence as the first postcolonial African state was a watershed in the history of the continent. For Africa, Ghana spearheaded the quest for African liberation and demonstrated how this goal could be achieved. Its experience also highlighted the limitations of political sovereignty and the obstacles facing those responsible for realizing the potential ingrained in the people and the resources of the continent.

For Ghanaians, the manner of decolonization determined the framework of public life in the immediate postcolonial era. The excitement of political participation and the promise of a new and better future were tempered by a growing awareness of the social, cultural, historical, economic, and external constraints unearthed during the years of anticolonial activity. Contradictions between populist and elitist interests, between the local and the national levels, between reformist and conservative impulses, and between parochial and universal outlooks came to the fore at this juncture. These factors have guided events in contemporary Ghana since the successful achievement of independence almost three decades ago.

2

The Pendulum of Ghanaian Politics

Ghana's political history since independence has been marked by sharp fluctuations and growing uncertainty. By the time Ghanaians celebrated their country's silver jubilee in 1982, they had lived under eight different regimes (see Table 2.1). The swing of the political pendulum began with the self-proclaimed socialist regime of Kwame Nkrumah. It then shifted in 1966, when a group of moderate army officers established the National Liberation Council, which consequently relinquished power to Kofi Busia's Western-oriented Progress party in 1969. The vacillation continued in 1972, with the return of the military under the initially reformist administration of I. K. Acheampong. Acheampong himself was ousted by Lieutenant General Fred Akuffo in 1978. The political gyrations of 1979 were exceptionally severe: First Flight Lieutenant Jerry Rawlings effected a coup of the lower ranks, and then political control was handed over to a middle-of-the-road civilian government led by Dr. Hilla Limann. The latest chapter commenced on December 31, 1981, when Rawlings returned as head of the Provisional National Defense Council.

Even though each regime has possessed its own distinctive outlook and attempted to establish its own institutions and promote certain activities, and even though social, political, or economic circumstances seem to go from bad to worse as regimes rise and fall, so far the evidence does not indicate that one administration was either better or worse than any other. What we see in Ghana's modern history is a decline consequent upon

36

a cumulative pattern of internal mismanagement coupled with exogenous misfortunes.

Succeeding regimes had to reorder political priorities and were constrained from selecting options already tried by their predecessors. Over time this dynamic reduced the ability of Ghanaian state structures to control events in the country. The vulnerability of the state apparatus has been accompanied, however, by a capacity to survive and to endure. Politics in Ghana after 1957 has evinced a complex admixture of weakness and vitality, and no regime seems to maintain a monopoly on either.

The purpose of this chapter is twofold: to delineate the features that have characterized Ghana's rise, decline, and uncertain rehabilitation and to isolate the common threads of postcolonial political history, with a view of uncovering the design that underlies the unpredictable framework of politics in the country since independence.

NKRUMAH'S VISION AND FAILURE, 1957–1966

The cycle of deterioration and persistence that has come to characterize Ghanaian politics was set in motion during the tumultous tenure of Kwame Nkrumah and the CPP. Ushered into office on the wave of euphoria accompanying independence, the first government of Ghana gradually whittled away its public credit and eventually became isolated from the support base that it had so carefully nurtured during decolonization. The rise, elaboration, and decline of the Nkrumah regime serve in retrospect as a prototype of the dynamics that have characterized all succeeding regimes in Ghana.

Leadership and Instruments of Power

The government of the new state of Ghana was confronted, as were those of other recently independent countries, with a myriad of problems that had to be dealt with simultaneously. These included not only the almost insurmountable challenge of meeting expectations with meager resources, but also the need to grapple with continued dependence on the metropole,

TABLE 2.1
GHANA'S REGIMES, 1957-1986

Regime	Dates in Power	Leader (ethnic background)
Convention People's party government (First Republic, 1960-1966)	1957-1966	Kwame Nkrumah (Nzima/Akan)
National Liberation Council	1966-1969	Lt. Gen. J. A. Ankrah (Ga)
Second Republic	1969-1972	Dr. K. A. Busia (Asante/Akan)
Supreme Military Council I (National Redemption Council)	1972-1978	Col. I. K. Acheampong (Asante-Akan)
Supreme Military Council II	1978-1979	Lt. Gen. Fred Akuffo (Akwapim/Akan)
Armed Forces Revolutionary Council	1979	F.Lt. Jerry Rawlings (Ewe/Scots)
Third Republic	1979-1981	Dr. Hilla Limann (Sisalla)
Provisional National Defence Council	1981-	F.Lt. Jerry Rawlings (Ewe/Scots)

to incorporate a diverse population into a workable whole, and to establish the guidelines for a distinctive Ghanaian path of constructive change.

As a precondition for coming to terms with these issues, the government had to create a viable administration capable of handling a multiplicity of often conflicting pressures. Thus, between 1957 and 1960, the Convention People's party (CPP) was made into the instrument for exercising power and the main channel for the implementation of policy—a reasonable tactic in light of the leadership's ambivalence toward traditional and colonial structures.

The entrenchment of the CPP network rested on two strategies. By the first strategy, opposing parties were systematically enfeebled. Initially, they were coerced into a merger; however, when opposition leaders later refused to be wooed they were harassed, some were placed in preventive detention (most notably J. B. Danquah), and the support of their followers was undermined. By the second strategy, which aimed more directly at expanding the CPP's organizational capacity,[1] re-

Type of government	Means of Gaining Power	Political Party in Power
Civilian: president, elected parliament	Election	Convention People's party (CPP)
Military: eight-member council	Coup d'etat	--
Civilian: ceremonial president, elected parliament	Election	Progress party (PP)
Military: advisers to head of state, government commissioners	Coup d'etat	--
Military: military advisory council, government commissioners	Internal putsch	--
Military: ten-member council	Coup d'etat	--
Civilian: executive president, council of state, unicameral parliament	Election	People's National party (PNP)
Military: seven-member council, special adviser	Coup d'etat	--

sources were channeled from the state to the party, whose headquarters in Accra became the pivot of political activity during the early years of Nkrumah's tenure. The central committee of the CPP, its key coordinating branch, was made responsible for the selection of members of parliament and lower functionaries.[2]

The CPP extended its control over the population at large through vertical and horizontal institutions. The CPP penetrated from highest to lowest levels through party appointment of regional commissioners, district commissioners, and town (or local) development committees (see Map 2.1). The horizontal broadening of the CPP depended on the creation of functional groups under party control, the most notable of which were the Ghana Trade Union Congress (TUC), the United Ghana Farmers Council (UGFC), the Young Pioneers, the Workers Brigade, and a variety of party-run women's associations and self-help organizations.

Although the CPP effectively neutralized the opposition and curtailed avenues of dissent, it was not always able to

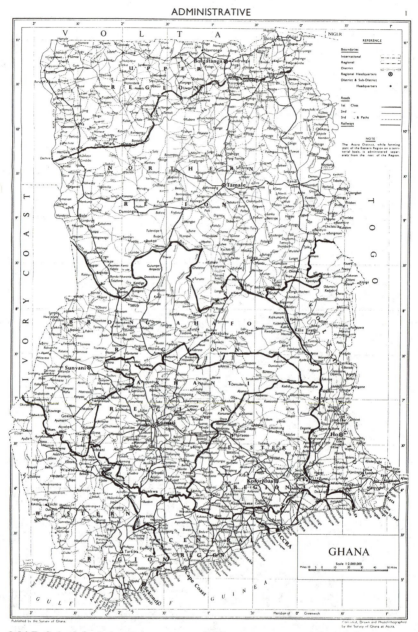

MAP 2.1 Administrative map of Ghana, prepared by the government of Ghana and included in Walter Birmingham, J. Neustadt, and E. N. Omaboe, eds., *A Study of Contemporary Ghana*, vol. 1 (Evanston, IL: Northwestern University Press, 1967)

permeate the social fabric or to garner the support it desired. Party allegiance was often accomplished through coercive means—vigilante groups, such as the Asafo Companies and the Party Vanguard Activists, were butressed by the security branch and the president's Own Guard Regiment, a private military auxilliary.

Despite its consolidation, accomplished by 1960, the CPP never became a totalitarian party because its authority was never unequivocally acknowledged. Fraught with bickering and structural impediments to communication, the CPP came to represent an increasingly narrow group of devotees who benefited from its patronage. Nkrumah became a cult figure, a deity, and the sole decisionmaker in Ghana. His charismatic aura, which substituted for a critical institutionalization of power during the earlier period of transition, came to dominate the political arena as the party became unwieldy. The CPP state became synonymous with Nkrumah, and Nkrumah became the embodiment of the party and its aspirations.[3]

The 1960 constitutional referendum, overwhelmingly approved in a special ballot, augmented the powers of the executive and redefined Ghana's position in the British Commonwealth. Kwame Nkrumah was elected president of the First Republic, and thus, for all intents and purposes, by 1960 Ghana had become a one-party state with Nkrumah as its leader. The authoritarian tendencies apparent during decolonization were officially entrenched in the centralized and personalized pattern of government that emerged at this juncture.

Ideology

Once the regime had been consolidated, the Ghanaian government, in late 1960, could move on to elaborating policy. The force behind the government's political policy was Nkrumaism—Ghana's brand of African socialism.[4] Designed to serve as a comprehensive philosophy and a blueprint for action, Nkrumaism rejected the rigidity of existing traditional institutions and opposed all manifestations of colonialism, neocolonialism, and external interference. As a socialist development strategy, Nkrumaism rested on several pillars: an outright attack on underdevelopment, the rapid expansion of state intervention in the economy, industrialization as the key to economic growth, and diversification of foreign contacts. The party was seen as the main vehicle for social reconstruction. Pan-Africanism—the creation of a unified, all-African superpower—was to be the culmination of the unique African contribution to socialism.

Nkrumaism offered a coherent, if not always cohesive, framework for thought and behavior. Its psychological appeal was enormous: It attributed existing problems to the machinations of alien intruders; it presented a way toward self-fulfillment and real growth; and it gave a vision of the future as enticing as it proved to be elusive.

But as an ideology, Nkrumaism was inconsistent: It drew haphazardly from Marxism and Leninism, from Fabian socialism and British libertarianism, from a mystification of the African past, and from a variety of Christian sources. Far removed from Ghanaian realities, it became an abstract vision, which could not provide the concrete guidelines needed to help Ghana overcome the economic and political difficulties it confronted at the outset of independence.

Administration and Policy Implementation

The foundation of the CPP's bureaucracy was the administration inherited from the colonial era. Bureaucratic growth, necessitated by the emphasis on state control over society and economy, involved expansion of offices, absorption of graduates into the civil service, creation of new ministries, and state monopoly on technical expertise.

Two sets of bureaucratic networks, frequently with overlapping responsibilities, were gradually created. Nkrumah, afraid to leave political matters in the hands of the civil servants, developed a parallel political administration that received instructions from his operational center and was directly responsible to the party. Predictably, conflicts between CPP functionaries and ministry personnel broke out repeatedly, impeding policy implementation.

Not surprising in these circumstances, the performance of the Nkrumah regime was unimpressive. During the early period,

Nkrumah was committed to infrastructural development: The primary focus of the first of Ghana's string of development plans, inaugurated just before the CPP came into power in 1951, was communications and education.[5] The Second Five-Year Plan, launched in March 1959, played down infrastructure and stressed agriculture and industry. In fact, fewer than 150 of the 600 proposed establishments were put into production, and of these only 37 were government owned; after two years the plan was abandoned. Nkrumah's goal was to set up not only a socialist economy but one free of foreign control. The government's policy from 1957 to 1961 was one of gradualism and restraint: It allowed the coexistence of private enterprise, cooperative units, state-private enterprises, and state corporations and made no direct efforts to eliminate foreign interests. In fact, the government brought on internal policy contradictions by attempting to achieve economic independence while remaining dependent upon the same foreign capitalist interests to which Ghana was tied during the colonial period. In his Dawn Broadcast of April 8, 1961, Nkrumah officially launched the socialist phase of the First Republic by nationalizing the cocoa trade. Two documents amplified the details of Ghana's socialist development: the Program of the Convention People's party for Work and Happiness (1962) and the First Seven-Year Development Plan (1963–1970). The economic provisions included heavy emphasis on centralized planning, shift from infrastructure to industrial production, nationalization of foreign enterprises, establishment of state-owned companies, and creation of a mixed enterprise system as the first step toward state socialism.[6]

Indeed, the creation of a wide network of state corporations further enhanced the pattern of bureaucratic growth. These bodies, autonomous from the administrative institutions but integrally linked to the state, were the means to the rapid industrialization and thus economic progress Nkrumah envisioned. The state corporations ranged from industrial firms to infrastructural concerns, from agricultural units (state farms) to external trade organizations (the Black Star Line), from distributive networks (the Ghana National Trading Corporation) to marketing monopolies (the Cocoa Marketing Board).

Political components of these policy instruments stressed the centrality of the party and its role in ideological indoctrination. The Kwame Nkrumah Ideological Institute at Winneba was transformed into the major center for the promulgation of Nkrumaism. The CPP journal, *The Spark,* became a further vehicle for political education, supplemented by the CPP's newspaper, *The Evening News.* Nkrumaism was to become a subject of instruction in the schools.

In 1961 Ghana's economic problems began: Imports and government expenditure (especially investment in productive facilities) rose whereas export proceeds (from cocoa and mining) began to level off. Consequently, the government introduced an austerity budget and borrowed extensively from the Central Bank of Ghana and abroad. It also set up the Compulsory Savings Act. When on September 4 workers received their first pay packets from which 5 percent savings had been exacted, a general strike broke out, led by the railroad workers in Takoradi.

Some of the early expenditures nevertheless did pay off. By the 1960s, in education and health mortality Ghana's record was impressive. Tema Harbor, which would be too expensive today to build, carries the bulk of the country's shipping, and the Akosombo Dam has eased the oil price squeeze. However, production in government plants during the 1961–1966 period declined, the foreign debt burden grew at an alarming pace, real urban wages were cut by half, sectoral imbalances were magnified, and in the name of socialism, gold mines, plantations, and even Accra's laundries were nationalized, draining resources and generating no return. Agricultural production stagnated and in some cases dropped.

Kwame Nkrumah set out to free Ghana from external dependency. The Ghanaization of personnel accelerated after 1960, especially in the public sector; however, the country remained tied not only to the export sector but especially to cocoa. A large proportion of the lower classes developed standards of consumption based on the high cocoa prices of the early years. But the country's productive capacity never grew at a rate commensurate with that of consumption; the import dependency was greater than ever and without external financing, the country could not fund any major investment.[7]

Thus Nkrumah and the CPP not only failed to bring prosperity to Ghana, they created economic havoc, introduced new social cleavages, and by 1964, reduced the role of the state to that of a dispenser of patronage. By advocating the construction of a ramified bureaucracy, Nkrumah established a new social stratum directly dependent upon the state. By curtailing the freedom of movement of these state functionaries through the diversion of administrative tasks to political ends, the regime contributed directly to undermining their effective performance.

Political Conflicts: Challenge and Response

During the First Republic, the political significance of an already existing and intricate network of corporate groups, social formations, and community structures crystallized. Political conflict during the CPP years proceeded in several well-defined stages. First, the party set out to weaken the power of the established intellectuals, professionals, chiefs, and large cocoa farmers—the same groups that had opposed Nkrumah in the 1950s and that were concentrated in the Asante region. For example, the large cocoa farmers were subordinated to the UGFC, and their independent action curtailed. And in 1961, after appropriating Stool lands and restricting chiefly authority, the government passed the Chieftaincy Act, which granted the government the right to confirm chiefs elected in specific areas and to dismiss them at will. Although the regime had enfeebled the opposition, it was not able to squelch its discontent.

Second, in 1961 a series of workers' strikes erupted, spearheaded by the Takoradi railway workers, a group that had helped bring Nkrumah to power and defined its objective in populist terms as a struggle of "the common people versus the big men in government."[8] The government's attempts to allay discontent were ineffective, and vociferous trade unions were joined by religious groups that opposed the attribution to Nkrumah of godly qualities. Simultaneously, policy conflicts intensified within the party; after an attempt on his life at Kulungugu in the Upper Region, Nkrumah came to rely on the CPP's radical elements. As a result, the breach between the president and his supporters widened.

Third, a generalized wave of protest arose as students, women's associations, professional organizations, and disenfranchised ethnic groups joined in dissent. In response, the Nkrumah administration resorted to force to obtain compliance with regime dictates.

In 1964, through a manipulated referendum the regime transformed Ghana into a one-party state. Support eroded and discontent soared; in its last two years in office the CPP conducted a holding operation, complicated by a cut in the world market price of cocoa, reduced foreign credits, and growing regional isolation.[9]

The 1966 Coup and the End of Nkrumah's Tenure

On February 24, 1966, a group of army officers, led by Colonel E. K. Kotoka, Police Inspector General J.W.K. Harlley, and A. A. Afrifa, carried out a coup d'etat against the Nkrumah regime while he was on a state visit to China.[10] Support for the coup came from all social sectors, and the CPP virtually disintegrated overnight. There has been continuing debate over the causes for the demise of the First Republic—that socialism was unsuitable, that the brand of socialism was inadequate, that the president was too authoritarian, too weak, too inconsistent. The First Republic, much like its leader, has been characterized by polarizations—egalitarian versus elitist, exciting and disillusioning, innovative and inefficient—thereby conveying an image of achievement and promise constantly tempered by problems inherent to dealing with the concrete present.

The legacy of the CPP is ambivalent and paradoxical: Although not an outright failure, it did highlight the problems intrinsic in accomplishing a complex agenda of political construction, economic elaboration, and social betterment. But the legacy is important. In the political realm, the Nkrumah government set up the boundaries for politics in independent Ghana. The problems it confronted—constraints on policy implementation, balancing of social forces, authoritarian and personalistic inclinations of the leader—have plagued successor regimes. And in the economic policy sphere, Nkrumah set the pattern for the country's downward spiral and was unable to lead Ghana out of the dependence and underdevelopment bequeathed by its colonial rulers. Above all, however, Nkrumaism furnished a lesson in the problems of governance in Ghana, an issue at the forefront of all subsequent politics in the country.

AN ERA OF DECLINE, 1966–1981

During the fifteen years following the overthrow of Nkrumah, Ghana was governed by six regimes: two elected civilian governments and four military ones. These regimes differed— sometimes radically—in terms of their social bases of support, internal structure, composition of leadership, policy approaches, and conduct in office. At the same time, however, they all exhibited problems of performance: tendency toward authoritarian rule, ethnic favoritism, intolerance of criticism, and above all, inability to overcome economic deterioration. Although one is hard-pressed to judge which regime was better or worse, the cumulative effect was one of social, political, and economic decline.

Leadership and Instruments of Power

Every post-Nkrumah administration encountered internal difficulties in governing the country. The eight-person ruling council of the first military regime was headed by Lieutenant General J. A. Ankrah.[11] Although army and police interests were balanced, the council's ethnic composition was skewed toward Ga and Ewe and away from Akan representation.

The support of the National Liberation Council (NLC) was broad based. The backbone of the NLC was the civil service, and its tripartite military-bureaucratic-chiefly alliance was applauded by university lecturers, members of the legal profession, and members of Nkrumah's opposition. These groups were prominently represented on the Political Committee, which became the National Advisory Council (headed by Busia), on the Board of the Centre for Civic Education, and later on the Electoral Commission and the Constitutional Commission. Concerned with administration rather than reform and with regulation rather than innovation, the NLC coalition was bonded by an antipolitics, anti-Nkrumaist bent; it set out to rectify distortions of the preceding period and to lay the foundations for a return to civilian rule.

Kofi Busia followed in the steps of the NLC. A member of the NLM opposition during the 1950s, he was, like members of the NLC, anti-Nkrumah and went into exile during the first president's tenure. Lacking Nkrumah's charisma, Busia's style was paternal. Influenced by his background as an anthropologist and as a member of the royal house of Wenchi, Busia (and his allies) found in Ghanaian history and culture a reservoir of the crucial values of democracy, humanism, and individualism,[12] in contrast to Nkrumah, who looked outward in search of inspiration. Busia's worldview highlighted gradual change, pluralism, and decentralization—a very different approach from the Nkrumaist perspective.

Although Busia's Progress party was itself amorphous, its ruling backbone was composed of the middle-class establishment that had been excluded from the CPP. The young newcomer activists, however, did not always share the elitist outlook of the older generation and their conflict with the latter compounded the party's ethnic cleavages. The issue of ethnicity and social background in leadership problematic during the tenure of the NLC came up during the Second Republic as well, when not a single Ewe sat on the first cabinet. Busia's government was both ethnically slanted and elitist, and the key party figures were all professionals from the Akan regions. Party structure remained undeveloped, and with the lack of internal cohesion, neither the parliament nor the party could become the regime's power instruments.

In stark contrast, the coup of the National Redemption Council (NRC), led by Acheampong, initiated a phase of military reformism. This second military regime, composed of six middle-echelon officers and one civilian, had a narrow support base; it rested on the creation of a pact between the army, the civil service, and the chiefs, as did the NLC base. However, its leaders insisted upon a rigid army-based hierarchical structure. Civilians were subordinated to their counterparts in the army, and appointments and decisionmaking were controlled by the head of state. Thus, like the regimes of Nkrumah and Busia,

Acheampong's rule took on an authoritarian flavor. Like Busia's administration, I. K. Acheampong nurtured a concern for traditional authorities; unlike Busia, he decried ethnicity and constructed the most ethnically balanced cabinet in independent Ghana. He also sought to depoliticize life; yet, as under Nkrumah, strict limitations were placed on freedom of speech. In his reordering of state-society relations, Acheampong established a new form of incorporation based on solidifying institutional links.

After a few years, Acheampong became aware of the many difficulties confronting his regime; he chose not to reassess policy but to reorganize his administrative apparatus. In November 1975, Acheampong formed a Supreme Military Council (SMC), composed exclusively of the commanders of the various branches of the armed forces. The NRC took on advisory functions, and its original members resigned or were forcibly retired. The original coalition of soldiers and bureaucrats was broken. All state organs were placed under military control. The structure of the SMC reflected Acheampong's aversion to criticism. As under Nkrumah, the center of power was highly personalized, revolving around the whims of the head of state.

Acheampong's six-and-a-half years of arbitrary rule ended on July 5, 1978, when a group of senior officers demanded his resignation. He was replaced by his chief of defense staff, Lieutenant General Fred W.K. Akuffo. Not unlike the NLC, Akuffo's SMC II was explicitly transitional in conception and design; its object was to guide Ghana back to civilian rule.

But before that happened, in the midst of the first political campaign in ten years, Flight Lieutenant Jerry Rawlings intervened for a brief, four-month stint. Unlike the previous military administrations, the ten-member Armed Forces Revolutionary Council (AFRC) was noteworthy for the youth of its leadership—especially in a society that so honors age and its ascribed attributes of sagacity and ability to guide. The AFRC succeeded in doing what no other government in Ghana had done before: molding the have-nots of Ghanaian society into a potent political force. Rawlings spoke to and for the common Ghanaian; his views on politics were those of the nonpolitician, and though genuine, his moralistic reformism was naively conceived and amateurishly implemented. Inevitably, he provoked fear and insecurity among the middle classes, and class antagonism, defined in populist versus elitist terms, intensified. Ethnicity also became an issue: The Akan and particularly the Asante perceived the AFRC to be a largely Ga and Ewe construct. But at this point in his political career, Rawlings was not concerned with undertaking a major structural transformation.

This mission fell to Hilla Limann, who in 1979 was elected the president of the Third Republic. Limann, the heir apparent to Nkrumah, appointed an impressive array of academics and technocrats to the cabinet. The elitist composition of his cabinet, like that of Busia, was also ethnically slanted—in this case toward Ga and (for the first time) toward northern groups. But also for the first time, antiestablishment sentiments had been unleashed (by Rawlings) and Limann's choice of advisors did not take this into account.

Unlike any of his predecessors, Limann relied heavily on formal institutions to maintain contact with the population. He viewed seriously the National Assembly (the main representative forum) and the Council of State, which encompassed such important groups as chiefs, academics, and professionals. A major weakness of the ruling coalition was its inability to mobilize the civil service and the army, the mainstays of the state apparatus. Barely two months after he assumed office, Limann dismissed the chief of defense staff, Brigadier Nunoo-Mensah; other armed forces personnel were fired and some resigned. Rawlings was forcibly retired. Northerners were given command posts, and the AFRC-created vigilante groups were employed. However, the People's National party (PNP) never succeeded in managing the military. Thus its hold over state institutions was never firmly established.

The trend toward personal authority began with Nkrumah and continued through Busia: The centrality of each man served as the pivot of power. Both surrounded themselves with like-minded advisors who were granted undue access to state resources and through such patronage became the major intermediaries between various groups and the government. Acheampong used the same tactic but with far less subtlety; he bought houses for friends and family, indiscriminately handed out import licenses, and gave favors to weeping women. Rawlings attempted to clean up such abuses and hand over power to the people, but his first foray into politics was too brief and the job too grand. Limann, a novice, inherited a dubious legacy: a bureaucracy whose capacity to function was minimal, a population wary of the machinations of political leaders, local communities that maintained a conscious distance from a state whose autonomy had been drastically reduced, and an economy in complete disrepair. None of the leaders of Ghana during this era, despite his various efforts, was able to devise a formula that would regulate or institutionalize state-society relations.

Policy and Implementation

Every administration during this era of decline constructed its own approach to dealing with Ghana's social, political, and economic problems, often reacting against the policy of its immediate predecessor. Each of these regimes, nevertheless, was unable to carry out its program. By the end of this phase, these attempts and failures resulted only in greater hardship for Ghana's citizens.

Stabilization and Anti-Nkrumaism. The policy outlook of the NLC was based upon a pragmatic worldview that reflected its administrative makeup. Its approach was to blame Ghana's problems on the personal mismanagement of Nkrumah and his cronies and the ideology they preached. It sought to promote individual responsibility and reduce state functions to supervising the population without intrusion. At the time of the NLC coup, corruption was rife, percolating down from the highest echelons of government to the individual on the street. Politics and party membership were used to justify the worst abuses, such as the siphoning of public funds. NLC policy measures included a campaign to eradicate Nkrumaism, which meant the banning of all political activity, the prohibition on the spreading of rumors of any sort, and the establishment of a bewildering array of commissions of enquiry charged with investigating virtually every facet of CPP rule. One aspect was the push to reeducate the population; the Centre for Civic Education gave courses and materials debunking Nkrumaism were distributed.

The NLC launched a program of divestment of state corporations and state farms. In overseeing Ghana's economic recovery, the NLC was concerned with restoring order and efficiency and (unlike Nkrumah) with doing so nonideologically.[13] The First Republic had been ineffective in controlling prices because it persisted in heavy public expenditure and allowed the money supply to grow. The NLC sought to complete potentially productive unfinished projects and otherwise retrenched labor in the public sector. The state relinquished the weighty control it had exercised under Nkrumah and pursued pragmatic participation—for example, lifting import restrictions on spare parts for public and private industry. Western powers proffered support in part to ensure the repayment of loans extended to the First Republic. The NLC strategy gave high priority to rescheduling loans and grants. To secure foreign finance, the NLC also subjected its policy to the scrutiny and approval of the International Monetary Fund (IMF) and the United States.

This approach led the government's economic advisors to adopt an IMF-backed stabilization program that commenced with the announcement of a 30 percent devaluation in July 1967. This program was aimed at creating an atmosphere of confidence conducive to attracting private investment, strengthening economic planning in the public sector, and encouraging local enterprise.

The statistics for 1967 showed stability: The government ended the worst errors of commission in the agricultural sector. Even though the receipts of cocoa farmers fell 40 percent in 1966, they recovered slightly the following year. By mid-1967, commodity prices were believed to have declined to a bearable level. The stabilization program also paved the way for a new development effort. In mid-1968, the NLC inaugurated the *Two-Year Development Plan: From Stabilization to Development.* The plan signaled the end of stabilization and new interest in planned economic growth; it was regarded by the government as the forerunner to a more comprehensive plan to be carried out by a civilian administration.

To implement this program, the NLC contracted with foreign firms and as a result was charged with preferring outsiders to

Procession for opening of Ghanaian parliament, 1971

local entrepreneurs. To repair its image, the government passed the Ghanaian Enterprises Decree in December 1968. The decree not only curbed immigration in response to demands from local businessmen for protection against foreign competition but also stipulated that retail trade would be handed over to Ghanaians within five years.

In retrospect, the NLC allowed Ghana a breathing space. Although it was spurred initially by revenge and was forced to rely on technocrats in the state bureaucracy, it freed the system for international economic bargaining and more private enterprise. It moved cautiously to indigenize the economy while leaving long-term politicoeconomic rethinking to the civilian regime to follow.

Private Enterprise and Political Favoritism. The Second Republic was launched on the optimistic promise of a new beginning. But the postelection euphoria overlooked some of the very real constraints operating on the Progress party leadership: the ongoing need to deal with the political and economic legacy of Nkrumah; the difficulties resulting from three years of military rule; and, ironically, the problems of coping with the inflated expectations that accompanied the return to civilian government.[14]

Busia's policies, unlike those of the NLC, aimed at gradual reform and rehabilitation. The role of the state was purposefully limited to acting as a framework within which individuals could fulfill their aspirations. Therefore, unlike Nkrumah, who viewed the state as a vehicle for social transformation, Busia saw it as a regulatory body. Because of his intellectual roots, he conceptualized the ideal society—a perplexing mixture of moderation and self-righteousness. Like Nkrumaism, Busia's philosophy of government was internally inconsistent: It simultaneously emphasized compromise and supervision, civil rights and reduced state tasks, and government regulation and individual liberty.

The Second Republic had little economic policy, and its development strategy followed the path laid down by the NLC—fortification of the private sector and renewed stress on agriculture and rural development, as set forth in the Two-Year Plan—but in a capitalist mode.[15]

To pursue this objective, the Progress party undertook a variety of measures. In 1969, it enacted the Aliens Compliance Order, whereby all foreigners were expelled, in order to combat rising unemployment and the growing resentment against foreign intrusion in commerce. The Ghanaian Business Bill, reminiscent of the NLC's Ghanaian Enterprise Decree, called for Ghanaian ownership of small retail companies; in actual fact, like the Aliens Compliance Order, it did little to protect the economy from foreign involvement.

In the interests of private enterprise, the government courted Western investment, including a short-lived flirtation with South Africa. It also offset any gains from this policy by the wholesale liberalization of imports and a massive increase in government spending in 1970 (caused by the government's belief that the regime of controls and centralization guiding the economy for a decade was to blame for Ghana's economic woes).

This liberalization, occasioned by exceptionally high revenues from cocoa sales, created a severe balance-of-payments problem. There was a 44 percent rise in food imports—19 percent of the total import bill of £30 million ($45 million)—much of which (tobacco, rice, fish) could have been produced at home under the right conditions. Import bills ate into the foreign exchange reserves. As a result, the government enacted an austerity budget in 1971, a year that also saw a terrific drop in world cocoa prices.

The government directed its energy toward assisting private entrepreneurs and developing the rural sector. As a result of biases built into earlier development plans, the agricultural sector was disadvantaged. To realign the relationship between rural and urban sectors, the Rural Development Fund was established in 1970. The agricultural program promulgated by the PP administration provided incentives to producers, upgraded rural services, and sought to improve infrastructure in the countryside. These measures were supplemented by a campaign to eliminate bribery and corruption and, by efforts, spearheaded by the Centre for Civic Education, to instruct Ghanaians of their rights and obligations as citizens.

To carry out its program the Busia government first sought to delineate its relationship with the civil service. It accomplished this by conducting a politically motivated purge: Over 500 employees, not one of Akan extraction, were summarily dismissed. When the Ghanaian Supreme Court ordered their reinstatement, Busia refused. The bureaucracy clearly lost its independence, and standards for access to officials gave way to favoritism on the basis of kinship, ethnicity, and friendship.

The PP established two state institutions that provided further ways of bypassing existing structures. The National House of Chiefs brought together rulers from all over Ghana and authorized them to adjudicate according to customary law. And the National Service Corps, conceived as a volunteer, self-help rural organization, was situated in the prime minister's office. The middle class was strengthened and its Akan backers rewarded.

After dealing with the civil service, the government decentralized administrative tasks and diffused the functions of ministries. Consequently, lines of communication were confused, inefficiency prevailed, and corruption blossomed.

In an effort to regulate state-society relations, the PP gave preference to its own supporters and allowed them a free hand to implement policy. Not surprisingly, performance was frequently weak and inept. Administrative malfeasance was rampant. Charges of corruption and elitism, which this government had leveled at Nkrumah, were leveled against Busia's entourage as well. Many citizens felt that the government maintained one set of rules for the common people and one for government personnel. At the same time that Ghanaians were asked to exhibit restraint in consumption, government ministers were driving late-model Mercedes-Benz. The state emerged as a tool of narrow class interests. Although, on one hand, Busia seemed unable to control his cohorts, on the other, he exhibited a kind of authoritarianism.[16]

The ineffectiveness and capriciousness with which the PP pursued its efforts toward social consolidation not only fostered ethnic and class cleavages, but also capitalized on the predatory facets of Nkrumah's legacy rather than on his managerial and innovative achievements. The PP administration took only two years to accumulate debts equal to those compiled by Nkrumah in nine years. The economic situation reached crisis proportions as the deficit rose to ₵202.4 million.

According to the *Ghana Economic Review* for 1971-1972, Ghana's economy suffered from three structural weaknesses: the dominance of cocoa, which accounted for 65 percent of the country's foreign exchange; the burden of the foreign debt; and a population growing in tandem with a stagnating economy. The workers needed more money, especially with the upward spiraling of prices. Yet at the same time, the trade unions had to be controlled.

The final straw in the political-economic conundrum was the fall in cocoa prices. This development removed the last firm support from the promising but fragile economy and led Busia, like the NLC before him and Akuffo and Rawlings after him, in December 1971 to devalue the cedi[17]—in this case by 43.8 percent. This desperate measure was aimed at boosting exports and cutting down imports. Cocoa farmers were given a raise in wages to stimulate production while workers received a minimum pay increase from 75 pesewas to 1 cedi per day (₵1 = 100 pesewas). Six weeks later, the military took over the government.

Self-Reliance and Economic Catastrophe. The National Redemption Council (NRC) came to power in an atmosphere of dwindling expectations and widespread disillusionment. Impatient with the patronizing elitism of Busia and the ideological verbiage of Nkrumah, Acheampong publicly declared his intention to pragmatically tackle Ghana's economic, social, and political ills. The main policy principles of the new regime, presented in the National Redemption Charter, aimed toward "a complete and systematic transformation of our peoples into a self-reliant nation, unique in its economic, social, cultural, political, technological and all-round development, a united nation with a spirit of its own."[18] Self-reliance, the linchpin of the NRC's early policy, was viewed as a means to extricate Ghana from cumbersome external entanglements, to capitalize on domestic resources, and to pave the way for tangible improvement in standards of living. It meant, in contrast to Busia's policy, a reduction of foreign intrusions into the economy.

A concerted effort was made to engage the local population in productive activities. The backbone of the government's program was Operation Feed Yourself (OFY), a plan for the development of food self-sufficiency in Ghana. When the NRC took over, Ghana was importing more than 50 percent of its food and raw materials even though it had the natural and human resources necessary for local crop production. By raising local food supplies through OFY, the government hoped that Ghana would achieve greater autonomy from the fluctuations of the world market in other spheres as well. Three years later, Operation Feed Your Industries (OFYI) was launched to produce raw materials required for agrobased industries, such as palm oil for soap and margarine.

These programs were policy instruments undertaken within the framework of the Five-Year Development Plan, 1975–1980, the operational companion to the charter. Like the NLC plan, this one identified and addressed three long-standing constraints on Ghana's economic growth and development: the openness of the economy and balance-of-payments problem, inflation, and unemployment. The plan made self-reliance the central goal of its economic effort.

The execution of the NRC's reformist policies depended to a large extent on the bureaucracy. Besides allowing the civil service leeway in formulating and implementing specific measures, the NRC also paid particular attention to institutional restructuring outside of Accra. It decentralized decisionmaking in rural development by creating Regional Development Corporations (RDCs), which supervised the day-to-day activities of OFY.

Self-reliance came to imply an emphasis on more equitable reallocation of resources.[19] Acutely aware of the regional and class discrimination practiced by Busia, Acheampong sought to overhaul the system of resource dispersal. He saw the state as primarily a manager of public affairs, a position midway between Nkrumah's activism and Busia's paternalism. Its task was to point out needs, define directions for action, and assist individual and group activities.

The promotion of Ghana's self-reliance also necessitated changes in foreign policy. The NRC repudiated debts totaling $94.4 million incurred by previous regimes, established the outlines of a plan to expropriate foreign holdings, and prepared to indigenize most enterprises. By abrogating some debts, the NRC displayed a different demeanor from that of the earlier military government: It conveyed less concern for the opinion of Western leaders. As a consequence, Ghana could no longer expect to receive credit for imports, which in turn underlined the policy of self-sufficiency.

For a while the NRC's initiatives appeared to produce a formula that would meet Ghanaian needs and cause a resurgence in its political economy. The year 1975, however, proved to be a critical turning point, and by 1977, the economic disorder was unprecedented. The credit extended to the state by banks had skyrocketed from ₵17 million in 1973 to ₵781 million in 1977. The impetus of the RDCs and OFY had not been sustained, production had dropped, shortages were recorded in essential commodities, inflation soared, and smuggling was rampant. Hoarding and profiteering, as means of survival, had reached such heights that the term *kalabule* ("to keep the lid shut"; used to refer to economic malfeasance) was coined to denote economic malpractices. Corruption was everywhere. From March to April 1977, the Consumer Price Index jumped from 964.5 to 1128.7 because of the skyrocketing cost of locally produced food. Working people were unable to afford their staple foods made from corn and cassava. Those with enough money bought yellow corn even though they expressed shame at eating what was normally used for animal feed. The crisis was by no means abstract: The estimated cost for a meal for five was ₵15—at a time when the minimum wage was ₵4 a day.

Although the economic catastrophe of the late 1970s can be laid at his door, Acheampong also inherited a host of problems. His early proclamations—especially appealing after the patronizing attitude of the Busia regime—were narrow in time, space, and substance. The reformist promise of the second military government was systematically squandered by an incompetent and self-serving leader. His government was characterized by mismanagement and riddled by corruption. The Border Guard was at the center of the nation's smuggling, and state distribution agencies were responsible for shortages. During this era, private fortunes were amassed at the same time as the country was becoming impoverished.

Economic Stabilization Again. When Fred Akuffo took over as head of SMC II, he declared his intention of relinquishing power to civilians in summer 1979. Party politics went into full swing, and the Constituent Assembly was called into session. Akuffo's task was to subject the country once again to a program of economic stabilization—and to stick to it. This approach involved stringent economic measures (the austerity budget of 1978) demanded by the International Monetary Fund. Akuffo's aim was to alter the pattern of budget and balance-of-payment deficits, inflation, and declining productivity in agriculture and industry.[20] In fact, while Acheampong remained in military custody, the disintegrative trends he had unleashed continued to affect nearly every facet of life in Ghana.

Akuffo employed orthodox devices to implement his economic policy. To curtail inflation, he reduced the monetary supply by holding back increases in government expenditures to 11 percent in 1978–1979 (in contrast to 59 percent the previous fiscal year), which in turn necessitated clamping down on government borrowing from the central bank. Acheampong had refused to devalue, despite a black market rate ten times the official exchange rate. In August 1978 under Akuffo's administration, the cedi was devalued 58.2 percent against the U.S. dollar, from ₵1.15 to ₵2.75. To reestablish Ghana's international economic credibility, which was damaged by Acheampong's debt repudiation, Akuffo appointed a fifteen-member National Economic Advisory Committee to advise his government on measures that would move the country into a period of sustained growth. Interest rates were increased to encourage savings, and commercial lending rates were raised.

These stringent provisions resulted in an *increase* in inflation to 300 percent—the prices of consumer goods doubling and quadrupling by October 1978—accompanied once again by terrific shortages in consumer goods, especially local foodstuffs, and a consequent decline in real wages. Although by spring 1979 inflation had dropped to 150 percent, SMC II failed to control prices. Commodities were in short supply. Hoarding persisted as the order of the day; it included anything that could be resold—soap, canned foods, flour, toilet paper, spare parts, and cars themselves. Kalabule brought in extra money, but even money was not the answer if there was no milk to buy.

Anticorruption and Public Accountability. Like the three previous military interventions, the June 4 coup took place when economic conditions were in a state of crisis. Rawlings's arrival highlighted the fact that the political measures introduced by the enfeebled Akuffo government and acceded to by aspiring politicians were largely irrelevant to the conditions prevailing in the country. The revolt also served notice that the ills of the Acheampong regime could not be redressed merely by replacing the current political leadership: A basic realignment of the foundations of the power structure was required.

The Armed Forces Revolutionary Council (AFRC) under Rawlings's direction, set three goals for itself: the eradication of all vestiges of corruption, malfeasance, ineptness, and exploitation left by Ghana's leaders; the restoration of probity into the political arena to revive notions of public accountability and to awaken the mass of Ghanaians to their rights and duties; and the implementation of the return to civilian rule.

The first events in the "housecleaning" of the armed forces and upper echelons of civilian society concerned the arrest and trial of top NLC and SMC personnel before a hastily assembled revolutionary court. Before the end of June 1979, Acheampong, Akuffo, Afrifa, and five other men were executed. Indeed, by mid-1979 only J. A. Ankrah, the erstwhile head of the NLC, was still alive. Kwame Nkrumah died in exile in Conakry in 1972. Kofi Busia passed away in exile in Britain in 1978, and Afrifa of the NLC, Acheampong of the NRC/SMC, and Akuffo of SMC II were eliminated by the AFRC. These events demonstrated the extent of the anger that had built up against the SMC; they also indicted the AFRC's determination to overhaul the power structure. Next, middle levels of the officer corps were scrutinized, with lists of wanted persons published daily. People's tribunals heard the cases, and severe sentences were meted out to those found guilty of betraying the public trust. The junior ranks, the have-nots of the military, were the ones who forced a major upheaval in the armed forces.

The AFRC then turned its attention to the civil service: Senior position holders, principal secretaries, and supervising senior secretaries (regarded as the source of administrative corruption) were dismissed, and lower-level personnel were investigated. Only the Special Branch was left virtually untouched because its intelligence services were critical for the AFRC to implement its designs. Thus the bureaucrats, civil servants, and senior officers, who had operated without any constraints during the SMC years, were served notice that they would henceforth be held accountable for their actions.

In its goal of moral reform, the AFRC hit the worst instances of black-marketeering, hoarding, and other corrupt practices. It instigated probes, property confiscations, and tax collection drives. The "empty" house of a former government commissioner contained ₵45 million in goods, including 100 cases of margarine, 20 cases of sardines, and 50 cylinders of gas for cooking. The loot was distributed to the urban masses and village people. Hoarders and profiteers, along with common thieves, were publicly flogged.

Moreover, the AFRC re-instituted control pricing, but, unlike SMC II, it vigorously enforced it.[21] Sometimes its surveillance of traders bordered on an illegal practice—the occasional soldier insisting on a low purchase price for an item and obtaining it by making threats with his gun. Market women were regarded as among the most flagrant abusers, and Makola Market in Accra, in the minds of many, was the hub of the underground economy. Generally, however, the resistance of the market traders was tied to the government's insistence on standard pricing, which was invariably much below that formerly asked and tied to the black-market price the trader had paid. The licit supervisory and illicit extortionist activities of the military in the marketplace proved disruptive—merchants closed down to protest controls or because they were frightened—resulting in more shortages and in the razing of Makola.

By focusing on local distributors rather than foreign investors and multinationals, the AFRC collected millions of dollars in back taxes, which it handed over to the civilian government that succeeded it. These actions, however, caused a loss of confidence among overseas investors: The IMF and other sources of investment and aid dried up. Moreover, in protest against the political executions, foreign suppliers engaged in an informal economic embargo, inducing further food and crude oil shortages. A Japanese shipment of canned fish mysteriously never arrived. An oil tanker from Nigeria entered the Tema Harbor, turned around, and steamed back to Nigeria as news of Akuffo's execution was announced; Ghana's credit period for Nigerian oil was cut back from ninety to thirty days.

The message of the AFRC's actions was unambiguous: Moral rectitude was required of the servants of the state and popular vigilance was necessary to ensure good government. Unfortunately, Rawlings was not successful in attaining his goals. The perhaps long-overdue social upheaval initiated by the AFRC was not accompanied at this time by the development of a suitable replacement. Under the circumstances, as has been said of the programs of preceding regimes, the Rawlings policy lacked substance and direction.

Pragmatism Without Policy. Rawlings's third goal of return to civilian rule was taken up by Limann. In stark contrast to his model Nkrumah, Limann approached policy formulation in a piecemeal fashion. In his outline for PNP concern and action, he made agriculture the cornerstone of policy.[22] The government introduced a two-year agricultural plan in May 1980, intended to encourage food production and enhance the profitability of agricultural exports. As a corollary, the government advocated improvement in the infrastructure of rural sector and alleviation of income discrimination against rural workers. A second component was mining and mineral exploitation. The third target was industrial rehabilitation to overcome the neglect of previous years. And finally, the Limann administration set out to obtain the capital necessary to underwrite its program: Taxes were raised, restrictions on foreign investments were lifted, an appeal was issued for greater aid allocations and a campaign was mounted to secure IMF funding.

Like early NRC leaders, Limann has been described as pragmatic rather than ideological. His budgets reflected his pragmatism: The austerity budget of December 1979, aimed at reducing inflation and debt service, presented a bleak outlook. Yet, instead of underlining the necessary sacrifices, Limann promised to flood the market with consumer goods (which Ghana could ill afford). The 1980-1981 budget, although pragmatic, revealed the many shortcomings of adopting an incremental approach to an all-encompassing economic crisis. In 1980 the government increased its spending as a result of the tripling of the minimum wage; however, the hike was offset by indirect taxes on oil and consumer goods. The government's answer to shortages in essentials was to allow any business possessing foreign exchange to import under a special license. The 1981-1982 budget gave further testimony to the desperate state of the state. Yet it was defeated because it was regarded as inadequate to the task. The inflation rate registered 70 percent and the estimated deficit $1.5 billion, or 30 percent of the gross national product (GNP).

The policy measures of the Third Republic's administration included the liberalization of foreign investment, and it made special efforts to locate outside support to revive industry. Another policy instrument was the 10 percent reduction in government spending ordered in late 1981. But the enormous budget deficits persisted: By December 1981, halfway through the fiscal year, the government had overspent the budget by ₵5000 million (although the planned deficit for the *entire* year was ₵4500 million).

The value of the cedi had fallen precipitously, but instead of increasing the domestic product or reducing the supply of currency, the government printed 55 percent *more* money to finance deficit spending. Although the official exchange rate stayed at $1 = ₵2.75, the actual market rate rose to ₵42. Smuggling as an avenue to gaining higher prices flourished, and profiteering was rampant: These devices did not so much indicate rapaciousness as serve as mechanisms of survival. Many house-wives reported that during the Limann years they could afford to cook only one family meal per week because the prices of foodstuffs had risen so high; inflation had shot up to 116 percent.

The Third Republic's listless approach to policy formation was compounded by inadequate implementation procedures. Cumbersome bureaucratic regulations impeded efficient action. The reluctance of producers to cooperate with the government hampered its efforts to generate changes in the rural areas. The government's inability to supervise the civil service invited mismanagement and massive bureaucratic corruption—undoing the AFRC's good deeds.

The results of these half-hearted efforts were hardly en-couraging. Government services had eroded. Acute food short-ages were widespread. The Food Distribution Corporation could barely keep up with demands for the most essential commodities. Cocoa production recorded the lowest levels since decolonization. And, because world cocoa market prices fell, foreign debt increased and external dependency grew. The Limann admin-istration, like its predecessors, failed to make a dent in the economic morass or to set up a program to improve the country's economic future.

Political Conflicts

Internal Divisions in the NLC. The precarious structures and poor performance of all the regimes in the era of decline generated increasingly vocal and broad-based dissent. This trend com-menced with the ouster of Nkrumah. Students, workers, and displaced politicians quickly expressed their discontent with the NLC. Likewise Akan leaders felt that their political access was circumscribed by the coastal ethnic complexion of the NLC leadership. These dissatisfactions came to a head in April 1967 when Lieutenant S. Arthur led an abortive coup during which Colonel Kotoka and others were killed. Arthur and a Lieutenant Yeboah were executed following a brief trial. However, in a constructive response to the in-house threat, the NLC established an Executive Council that included civilians and upgraded the National Advisory Council headed by Busia.

These measures could not effectively restrain the discontent that grew out of the government's stringent economic measures, and those adversely affected coalesced into a bona fide opposition. They were led by the trade unions, which launched a series of debilitating strikes during 1968 and 1969. To prevent a resurgence of the strength of the old CPP leadership, the NLC excluded former CPP politicians from participation in any preparations for civilian rule.

At the same time, ethnic tensions within the NLC grew between A. A. Afrifa and A. K. Ocran, and J. A. Ankrah and his supporters; they peaked when Harlley accused Air Vice Marshal M. Otu and Navy Lieutenant Kwapong of subversion. In 1969 as a result of these internal divisions, the NLC leaders hastened the return to civilian rule in an effort to maintain the cohesion of the military as a corporate unit.

A Constitutional Assembly, dominated by educated young men, debated the draft proposals presented by the Constitutional Commission. The members voiced concern about careful division of powers, civil rights, and independence of the judiciary. In May 1969, the NLC lifted the ban on political parties, which it had instituted when it came to power in 1966, and prohibited CPP activists from participating in the campaign. The two main parties were the pan-Akan Progress party (PP) of K. A. Busia and the National Alliance of Liberals (NAL), headed by K. A. Gbedemah, the former CPP stalwart who broke with Nkrumah in the early 1960s. Gbedemah, an Ewe, faced two drawbacks: the anti-Ewe sentiments of the populace and the anti-CPP bias of the NLC.

Elections were held on August 29, 1969.[23] The PP polled 59 percent of the votes, won 105 of the 140 seats in parliament, swept Akan regions, and gained strong majorities elsewhere. The PP victory resulted from the support it received from the NLC and A. A. Afrifa, its new head, as well as the excitement generated by the young PP activists. The support base of the PP thus differed from that of both the first civilian government and the NLC.

PP Versus Students and Trade Unions. Ethnic conflict also characterized the Busia years. From the start, non-Akan groups felt excluded from mainstream politics. They claimed that national interests were subordinated to those of the Asante and that Accra was subordinated to Kumase.

The Progress party alienated other groups whose support was critical to smooth government. The dominant professional alliance neglected workers and farmers. At the local level, reinstatement of chiefs upset the local balance of power and provoked communal strife. Government policy measures that adversely affected target groups caused enmity: The Alien Expulsion Ordinance undermined Muslim support; meddling in the bureaucracy placed many civil servants on guard; reduction of military budgets sparked rumblings in the ranks of the armed forces.

A coalition of students and Trade Union Congress (TUC) activists organized an opposition to Busia:[24] The former group was unhappy with Busia's rejection of some essential tenets of modern nationalism, the latter with the PP's blatant entrepreneurial favoritism. Together with other groups, they pleaded for more even-handed policies, equitable distribution of goods and services, consideration of the needs of common laborers, and the affirmation of Ghanaian national pride.

As the opposition grew, Busia lashed back by suppressing rural agitation, berating student leaders, quashing strikes, censoring critics, and detaining opponents. These measures brought on a series of student demonstrations and worker strikes in spring and summer 1971. Fearful that these actions heralded a resurgence of Nkrumaism, the government banned the display of Nkrumah's picture. The national workers agitated for more pay, spearheaded by an attack on the government by TUC leaders for creating the National Development Levy (which imposed a 5 percent tax on income for development projects and was rife with nepotism/tribalism in the specific projects chosen). The government in turn accused the TUC of "economic subversion" and enacted the Industrial Relations (Amendment) Act, which dissolved the TUC, made trade union membership optional, and led observers to dub 1971 along with 1961 (when strikes broke out after the Compulsory Savings Act) as the twin "Nightmare Years" of trade unionism in Ghana.[25] Busia also disbanded the National Union of Ghanaian Students (NUGS) and replaced key army personnel with regime sympathizers.

Political poster advertising Prime Minister Busia's anticorruption campaign, 1971

Busia's overreaction to his opponents served as a timely reminder of the intolerance of Ghanaian leaders to criticism of any sort—regardless of their political orientation. The PP's mishandling of the opposition displayed an authoritarianism fundamentally at odds with the democratic precepts it espoused.

Within two years after its inauguration, the government of the Second Republic was floundering. However, the military intervention on January 13, 1972, was directed at forwarding the interests of a small group of disgruntled officers. Although the citizenry was displeased with Busia's government, it was not happy to see the military back in power. Thus, the popular legitimacy that the Progress party initially enjoyed and subsequently forfeited was never Acheampong's from the start.

Acheampong and Growing Turmoil. Politicization and protest accelerated in four distinct and increasingly violent phases. The first phase spanned the NRC period and was relatively controlled. Most ethnic groups cooperated with the NRC, whose communal policies they viewed as even handed. The sole source of ethnic protest was mounted by the Ewe; some felt excluded from the centers of power,[26] whereas others were displeased with Acheampong's antipathy toward Togo's Ewe president Etienne Eyadema and began to revive Ewe claims for autonomy that dated back to decolonization. The Movement for the Liberation of Western Togoland actively agitated for the separation of the Volta Region from Ghana. These separatist tendencies were dealt with firmly.

The concept of self-reliance rallied workers, students, women, and civil servants. However, expoliticians and a handful of professionals and academics—in other words, those favored by the former administration—were now openly disgruntled, and they instigated a series of coup attempts. The ringleaders of each of these failed plots were tried publicly for subversion and sentenced to lengthy jail terms, serving notice that armed efforts to bring down Acheampong's government would not work.

The second phase of protests, triggered by the reorganization of the government (as the SMC) in 1975, was characterized by broad-based dissent. Urban elites, mostly professionals organized in the Association of Recognized Professional Bodies (ARPB), spearheaded agitation and were joined by students, by traders stifled by arbitrary controls, and by some Muslim factions. Bureaucrats began to voice their discontent about their much reduced power and prestige, and, significantly, Akan ethnic and regional protest increased.

Acheampong's intolerance of dissent was reflected in his response to the growing tide of civilian unrest. He harassed his opponents, issued decrees prohibiting criticism of the regime, and stifled the press. Coercion became less effective in controlling public outcries, and in October 1976 Acheampong announced his intention of constructing a union government (Unigov) that would include representatives from the population at large— the army, police, and major social groups. The concept of Unigov was presented as the linchpin of the SMC's transition plan for a return to civilian rule, and a committee was appointed to clarify the main ideas in this notion of no-party government and a program for the return to civilian rule.

The Unigov proposal set in motion a third wave of protest. Between early 1977 and spring 1978, students and lecturers, professionals and business people, clerics and traders, farmers and workers, and women and young people joined forces to oppose Unigov because it would perpetuate the military's term in power under a different guise and because Acheampong suggested it. Antigovernment activity spread throughout the country, and the combined opposition launched a civilian revolt against the SMC. In May 1977, students demanded the immediate resignation of Acheampong. In June the ARPB joined them, and on July 1, the professionals instigated a general strike that effectively immobilized the country.

Rather than abdicate, Acheampong announced a two-year timetable for return to civilian rule, which was agreed to by his opponents. First there was to be the referendum on Unigov in March 1978. In anticipation, civilian agitation intensified, and anti-Unigov forces united around the People's Movement for Freedom and Justice and the Front for the Prevention of Dictatorship—both led by ex-Progress party leaders who enjoyed widespread support in Akan areas and among the middle class. In return, the SMC sponsored the pro-Unigov Ghana Peace and Solidarity Council (backed by ex-CPP activists and non-Akan leaders) and mobilized the National Charter Committees to lobby for its plan.[27]

The campaign was intense and ugly, and despite a crude attempt to manipulate the results, Acheampong barely mustered 55 percent of the vote: His support came from the Upper, Northern, Central, and Western Regions whereas Greater Accra registered only 51 percent in favor. The referendum's results highlighted the extent of civilian discontent with the SMC, and it resolved none of the issues that induced the challenge. Moreover, after the vote Acheampong lashed out against the most minor expressions of discontent.

In spring 1978, Ghana was plunged into a state of almost complete turmoil.[28] Mass rejection of the government took on several distinct forms: Some people chose to continue their struggle, triggering a series of strike actions in spring 1978 that ground the country to a halt; some populist urban groups demanded a redefinition of the rules of the political game, including the elimination of patronage structures; entire rural communities withdrew from all contact with the state, reasserting their own indigenous modes of self-reliance; and the disgruntled people who were unable to manage economically simply left the country. Indeed, between 1974 and 1978, Ghana suffered a significant loss in human resources, as uneducated and educated men and women emigrated in search of better conditions. The events of these months in 1978 doomed the first Supreme Military Council.

Popular Unrest and the Multiparty System. Despite the desire of SMC II (the successor to Acheampong's regime, which was ousted by Akuffo in July 1978) to institute some order in the country, the government's efforts at containing popular unrest were largely unsuccessful: Acheampong remained in military custody (public demands for his trial notwithstanding) and the economy continued to deteriorate. The long-suffering people, particularly the urban working and middle classes, were hit by the double insult of rising prices and devaluation. They expressed their fury in a series of strike actions: Over eighty occurred between August and November 1978, at which point the civil service—backbone of the state—stopped work. Akuffo declared a state of emergency that remained in effect for two months.

Labor unrest continued throughout the Akuffo interlude, culminating in simultaneous strikes by teachers, nurses, lecturers, sanitation workers, miners, and students in spring 1979. Government measures to stabilize the economy, including an austerity budget, a devaluation, and a cedi exchange program (during March the borders were closed for ten days) did little to alleviate social tensions. The discontent peaked in May when a student demonstration degenerated into a bloodbath, leaving one student dead and two others seriously injured.[29]

With no apparent warning, on May 15, 1979, Flight Lieutenant Jerry Rawlings led an abortive coup. Upon his capture, Rawlings declared that Ghana needed "an Ethiopian solution . . . a bloodbath to purge the army." Rawlings was described by friends as an idealistic but bitter young man (thirty-one years old) who, like Akuffo, wanted to repair the military's tarnished image. Reminiscent of Nkrumah's early success at unleashing popular support, Rawlings's subsequently successful June Fourth (1979) Revolution was a populist uprising aimed at redefining the political structures and norms in Ghana.[30]

It was a credit to Rawlings himself and his commitment to the ideas of popular participation and public accountability that scarcely two weeks after the June Fourth Revolution, on June 18, 1979, elections were held to return Ghana to civilian rule. The Constitution of the Third Republic, drafted in 1978 and revised by the Constituent Assembly in early 1979, provided for an executive (rather than ceremonial) president to be elected directly by a majority of the voters. The parliamentary structure of the Second Republic was retained. The new constitution emphasized the establishment of safeguards against the recurrence of official abuses.

Two dozen parties surfaced when the ban on politics was removed in December 1978; six survived to contest the elections. The People's National party (PNP), the successor to Nkrumah's CPP in philosophy and personnel, was reinforced by a new guard of young men. Dr. Hilla Limann, a Sisalla from the Upper Region and the party's presidential candidate, held a Ph.D. in political science. Although a political unknown, Limann did not become a candidate by accident: He was the nephew of Imoru Egala, the moving force behind the PNP. The main opposition to the PNP was the Popular Front party (PFP), successor to the Progress party; its candidate was one of Busia's former cabinet ministers, Victor Owusu. Many PFP leaders were from the central Akan zone. The United National Convention (UNC) was led by A. A. Afrifa, who directed the coup that overturned Nkrumah, and Paa Willie Ofori-Atta, a sentimental favorite who had spent years in detention during Nkrumah's reign. The support base of the UNC relied strongly on Ga and Ewe groups, although its ideology was essentially the same as those of the PFP and PP. The other three parties did not gain nationwide appeal.

The parties exhibited continuity with previous political constellations, the leaders dated back to the First and Second Republics, and the platforms reiterated the rhetoric of Nkrumah's socialism or Busia's free enterprise. On key issues, all referred to the same list of grievances and jointly issued a plea for national unity, protection of human rights, and economic reconstruction. The factor that most affected the outcome of the elections was the social sources of support. The PNP won 71 of the 140 parliamentary seats, securing seats in every region of the country. The PFP did well in the central Akan regions of Asante and Brong-Ahafo, whereas the UNC gathered votes in the Accra, Eastern, and Volta Regions.

The PNP victory was rooted in several interrelated factors. First, because of the PFP/UNC split, the parties vied with each other for the same voters and thus helped the cause of the PNP. Second, the PNP brought in new young politicians, a strategy that appealed to Ghanaians anxious for real change. And yet, third, the PNP inherited the mantle and the organizational skill of the CPP; many voters, discontented with the immediate past, remembered the CPP era with joy. And fourth, the PNP attracted votes outside its northern foothold; many people voted less for PNP and Limann than against the PFP as the heir to PP.

Unity and Disintegration of the PNP. PNP's convincing victory may have been as much a reflection of general political trends in the country as of the political skills of its leadership. The trying years of military rule had disrupted the networks linking individual citizens to the state center. The previously powerful patrons of the south lost their position whereas those in the north remained strong because they maintained good relations with the military. The northern politicians had a distinct advantage in that they attracted voters whose patrons had lost their access to state resources. The election results were quite revealing: (1) For the first time, minority northern ethnic groups dominated state politics; (2) despite Rawlings populism, the middle class was entrenched; and (3) the number of politically active citizens had shrunk.[31]

The Third Republic fell victim to criticism from the start. Rawlings had gained support for his campaign from the groups of have-nots. These highly politicized groups injected their antiestablishment views. They were backed by the June Fourth movement (a Rawlings creation) and the New Democratic movement—both of which were concerned with upholding the AFRC's moral revolution. Ethnic discontent surfaced among the Ewe, who would not cooperate, and many Akan leaders withheld allegiance to the central government.

The labor unrest that broke out during the first year of Limann's tenure included rampaging by university workers and strikes by lecturers angered by the high inflation. The actions were dealt with by a government directive to fire administrators. At a time when the minimum daily wage was $1.50, members of the Ghanaian parliament were awarded salary increases resulting in monthly incomes of $1,500. The minimum wage made workers' incomes fall below starvation level—a loaf of bread cost more than a day's wages—and the cost of living rose to such an excessive degree that the TUC, which broke with the government on the dismissal of strikers, threatened a nationwide strike.

Limann attempted to absorb new groups into the administration and when that failed, like his predecessors, he resorted to coercion: censoring the press, suppressing student demonstrations, and closing down campuses; stifling ethnic dissent; and coming down particularly hard on the military, focusing his concern on the charismatic Rawlings. Retired from active military service, Rawlings had assumed the role of resident critic. The government set out to curb his activities, but by linking coup attempts with his name, they bolstered his visibility and gave him a special status in the public eye.

Moreover, since its formation the PNP had suffered from internal conflict revolving around the rivalry of the old guard of CPP activists and the new guard of younger politicians. President Limann stood between the two factions, and when Imoru Egala, the PNP strongman, died, a vicious struggle for party leadership erupted. By fall 1981, the PNP was fragmented and disunited.

In 1981, two years after the return to civilian rule, the situation in Ghana bordered on chaos. The government of the Third Republic was unsuccessful in dealing with the growing impoverishment of Ghana's people and with their highly politicized and agitated condition. Operating under severe constraints, Hilla Limann could not rise to the task of providing leadership. When Jerry Rawlings handed over power to Hilla Limann in 1979, he warned him that he would be watching and waiting, ready to return if the changes promised eluded the Third Republic. The second coming of Rawlings, on New Year's Eve 1982, abruptly ended Ghana's third experiment in civilian government and began the fifth successful occurrence of military intervention.

Summary. Ghana's era of decline bred leaders who failed in their leadership, who were criticized by their constituencies for this fundamental deficiency, and who were insensitive and reacted ungenerously to popular distress. From the time of the arrival of the NLC, the opposition grew as economic conditions worsened and the leadership unsuccessfully tried to control the situation. No matter what regime held power, social tensions brought out workers, former politicians, students, and professionals (although in each regime the dominant group varied). Ethnic tensions were also characteristic of each of the governments, and the economic austerity brought about strikes led by the trade unions, professionals, and students.

The most significant inheritance willed by the NLC was the introduction of the military dimension into Ghanaian political life. During the NLC phase the army became a potent institution in the political arena and an obvious mechanism for political change. The failure of Ghana's second attempt at civilian government exposed basic political difficulties that went far beyond the limitations of a single regime: the inability to come to grips with the diverse social interests and economic complexities in the country. The civilians had not yet devised a workable formula to enable popular participation. The departure of Busia heralded the entrenchment of instability as the single most salient feature of contemporary Ghanaian politics.

The destruction left by Acheampong was immeasurable. During his years in office, he institutionalized a kleptocracy that ravaged the economy, trampled civil rights, and undermined the commitment of many Ghanaians to their state. Although Acheampong inherited from his predecessors a failing economy and a set of severe structural problems, under his inept guidance these difficulties intensified and became almost insurmountable. By 1982, with the ouster of Limann the center of Ghana had virtually collapsed. The number of people still involved in the formal state arena had dwindled. A large segment of the population was disillusioned, hungry, and alienated. These people thrived on the rejection of the power structure and the promise of a real social upheaval. Still others had simply given up on the state, withdrawing into local self-enclosed communities.

No matter whether the government was military or civilian, the economy state controlled or free enterprise, the policy one of stabilization or liberalization, each regime was remarkable in its inability to deal with immediate problems of state and economy and unsuccessful in containing dissent and unrest, and each was unable to master the task of governing Ghana.

THE RAWLINGS REVOLUTION, 1981–

Today we initiated a holy war. . . . There is no justice in this society and so long as there is no justice, I would say there shall be no peace.

—Jerry Rawlings, *West Africa,*
January 11, 1982

The 1981 policy of Jerry Rawlings, the first military leader in Africa to successfully carry out a second coup, differed in design and intent from that of his first intervention. The Provisional National Defence Council's (PNDC) action was directed against a duly elected civilian government, not a military regime. It was far less violent than its AFRC precursor. And the PNDC, unlike the AFRC, seemed determined to stay in power for as long as necessary to effect a sweeping transformation of Ghanaian society and its political economy. The nonestablishment groups that Jerry Rawlings had molded into a political force in 1979 had now taken over.

Leadership and Instruments of Power

The return to power of the young, handsome, populist, and charismatic Rawlings was greeted with enthusiasm. People said that the coup was inevitable, given the extraordinary degree of corruption and black-marketeering. The housecleaning that Rawlings initiated in 1979 had not been completed. Corrupt business and politics had, if anything, increased during Limann's sojourn, as citizens used every trick, every personal or political connection, to stay afloat. A new Mercedes-Benz, the status car, cost ¢1,500,000, and some people had the money to buy it. Limann had been incapable of controlling prices; if a worker earned ¢12 per day and bought a small can of milk for ¢10, how much was left for himself and his family?

Rawlings's second coming carried with it the hope of national resurrection. The new/old leader created a Messianic atmosphere during the early months of 1982 that revolved around his person. As "savior of the nation" and "father of the revolution," Rawlings promised to return power to the people and to wage a "holy war" against corruption, privilege, and inequality.

In its initial populism, the new government relied for support on students and urban unemployed, on trade union members and farmers, on the military rank and file and radical intellectuals, and on petty traders and rural wage laborers. These diverse groups were united by the fact that they had been excluded for twenty-five years from Ghana's ruling establishment. In contrast, the urban elite—professionals, technocrats, businesspeople, wealthy farmers, expoliticians—was now purposely excluded from the PNDC coalition.

DON'T JUST STAND AND STARE

......GET INVOLVED.

Head of state Jerry Rawlings depicted in a political poster, 1982

PNDC membership, originally composed of six council members and the chairman, encompassed civilians, soldiers, liberals, and Marxists. Secretaries (ministers) were appointed to handle day-to-day affairs on the basis of their qualifications and their commitment to a complete national overhaul. Because Rawlings was seeking widespread support, he included people within his medley of advisors whom he neither knew well nor trusted entirely.

As in previous regimes, the decisionmaking power devolved upon the chairman, and in time, he came to rely increasingly for advice on the Ewe clique that surrounded him and especially on his army companion Kojo Tsikata. Even the populist Jerry Rawlings was not free of the bogey of ethnicity! Like Nkrumah before him, Rawlings became increasingly invisible, and members of the ruling circle acted as spokespersons and emissaries for him.

The consolidation of the PNDC therefore rested on two quite different foundations: the highly personal and at times authoritarian basis centered on Rawlings and the heterogenous, antiestablishment forces guided by revolutionary zeal. Under the PNDC, a new pattern of populist incorporation was devised as the balance of power shifted.

Ideology

Jerry Rawlings returned to power with a vision of and ideology for social revolution: He saw the transformation of the country into a participatory democracy as the driving force for change. People's power, in the PNDC worldview, translated into popular involvement in overseeing the affairs of state. Every citizen was charged with eradicating wasteful institutions, supervising public officials, judging offenders; through constant vigilance, inequality and exploitation could be eliminated.

External forces, in Rawlings's view, were as guilty as unscrupulous elites for the continuous subjugation of the country. And by placing Ghanaians as watchdogs against the excesses of foreigners, Rawlings hoped to protect Ghana's autonomy and highlight the indigenous quality of the new order.

At the start, the new government was characterized by radical rhetoric, which depicted the creation of a vibrant community based on egalitarian values. People's socialism was to be the vehicle for the establishment of a state that truly reflected the capabilities and aspirations of the average Ghanaian man and woman. Rawlings painted for Ghana's downtrodden citizenry an enticing picture of a just and better future in which they would take an active part.

The PNDC ideology took on a life of its own: naive, appealing, and remote from the harsh realities of present-day Ghana. But the regime's policy orientation was both realistic and practical.[32] Policy guidelines, published in May 1982, called for "the creation of a material basis for ensuring a democratic and popular education as well as health schemes, housing, food and transportation to ensure the physical, spiritual, moral and cultural quality of life of our people."[33] In time, the PNDC adopted a series of measures that would help increase agricultural and industrial production at a modest rate, lower inflation, expedite the distribution of goods and services, and eliminate expatriate and local malpractices. The PNDC's *Programme for Reconstruction and Development,* unveiled in late December 1982, gave special attention to improving infrastructures and repairing the rail, road, and communication networks.

The Rawlings regime first employed radical and later conventional approaches: The former was promoted by a strong group of neo-Marxist advisors who advocated a massive campaign against what they regarded as retrogressive social forces that had ruled Ghana since independence; the latter by liberal academics voicing social welfare concerns. By late 1984, the radical approach was replaced by the more cautious measures of liberal advisors; the PNDC's main priority in its return to democracy was to move away from political and ideological labels, which in effect meant a move away from Marxism. It sought instead to examine the society's African traditions and review the progress of Ghana's independence, looking for a better mix of its constituent elements, such as the legacy of anticolonialism, Nkrumaism, and the December 31 revolution.

Administration and Policy Implementation

PNDC activities focused on two major actions: imposing a new system of justice and setting in motion the program of economic recovery. In both spheres the government tried to introduce institutional changes and help popular groups assume power directly. In both fields, the Rawlings regime also supervised the detailed implementation of its proposals. According to the PNDC, the regime's first task was to establish the means not only to bring those guilty of corruption to trial but also to ensure the constant monitoring of public officials. The PNDC took over executive and legislative branches of government. The judiciary was transformed: Various investigating commissions as well as public tribunals were established to involve the public in the administration of justice and to reform institutions mishandled by private individuals.

Activities of individuals were scrutinized by a series of investigating commissions. Those traders, businesspeople, journalists, and professionals, who were suspected of flouting revolutionary doctrines, were questioned. A National Investigations

Commission was set up to oversee public behavior. Citizens' Vetting Committees (CVCs) were created to review the existing organization of government structures and to judge the suitability of its incumbents. The CVCs systematically examined the bureaucracy, retired troublesome civil servants, eliminated superfluous positions, and established themselves as the watchdogs of the state apparatus.

People found wanting by these investigating bodies were brought before public tribunals; unlike the conventional courts (which continued to operate), the tribunals had criminal jurisdiction. These people's courts meted out justice quickly and often harshly. Lengthy sentences (sometimes amounting to sixty years or more) and large fines (not infrequently amounting to millions of cedis) were handed down to PNP leaders, senior civil servants, and officials of public corporations. Army personnel were judged by military tribunals composed mainly of members of the lower ranks.

The new structures created by the PNDC did not replace existing institutions; they complemented them. As with the courts, they operated along parallel lines and dealt with similar issues. Together, these various institutions established an alternate and dualistic system of supervision and adjudication. This network did not engage in implementation per se, but by taking precedence over the courts and the civil service, it did constitute a significant check on continuing activities.

The entrenchment of popular guardians was a precondition for tackling the second and far more difficult challenge of reforming the economy. Here, too, the first steps of the PNDC centered on institutional changes. Although the bureaucracy was still responsible for carrying out many projects, the government sought means to incorporate Ghanaians into the planning and implementation process. In every community and neighborhood, People's Defence Committees (PDCs) were created to organize development programs; in factories, banks, industries, and universities, Workers' Defence Committees (WDCs) were similarly set up for policymaking and execution. At the village level, local management committees were charged with similar functions. Thus the structure of government was decentralized. Small groups of activists throughout the country initiated and carried out a variety of schemes according to regime guidelines but with very little supervision.

Through these mechanisms, the PNDC mobilized the population to begin the slow, trying process of socioeconomic transformation. In the early phase, the Rawlings administration's economic programs were devoted almost entirely to salvaging exports and to improving distribution networks. A campaign was launched to evacuate the cocoa crop, primarily utilizing student task forces, and to pool food production. Volunteer work groups repaired the roads. Through the PDCs and WDCs, the government took over the allocation of essential commodities. Persons in the PDC/WDC structure also monitored the people's behavior and oversaw the country's borders. In a drastic measure announced in September 1982, all land borders were closed to curb smuggling, black-marketeering, and currency trafficking. Only in January 1983, after the forced exodus of 1 million Ghanaians illegally living and working in Nigeria, were the borders reopened. The returnees, the bulk of whom were unskilled men in their twenties, were sent back to their hometown areas to farm. The "Green Revolution," like Acheampong's OFY, sought to make the country self-sufficient in food production.

During the first year of PNDC rule, the Castle (government headquarters) was peopled by economic advisors and consultants, but no systematic policy was announced. As in the political arena, Ghana's economic program had catchy rhetoric, most of which alluded to breaking out of dependency relationships with the "imperialist West." Ties with Libya, cut by Limann, were restored and economic agreements signed. Crude oil was shipped in at higher market prices but more favorable credit terms. Libya's Muammar Qaddafi flew in food to ease Ghana's plight, although the planes were rumored to contain arms and ammunition.

The PNDC revised the 1981-1982 budget so that the projected deficit would be contained at ₡4800 million. Interest rates were raised by almost one-half to encourage capital investment. The amount of money in circulation was sharply curtailed. About two-thirds of the country's money supply (₡6 billion) was circulating (or hoarded in ₡50 bills), so that the government had little money with which to work. In February 1982, the largest denomination, the ₡50 note, was withdrawn. Bank chits were given in return for the withdrawn bills, with no assurance of when the equivalence would be paid back. The "big-money" people, including expatriate businesspeople, were noticeably absent from the long bank lines, absorbing their losses rather than facing investigation by the CVC; in fact, everyone suffered (as the money was not returned in any case), but at the time it was the farmers, especially, who lost most of their capital..

Banking rules changed daily; accounts were frozen and unfrozen in the government's zealous search for profiteers, tax evaders, and illicit operators. As a consequence, the ordinary person feared having more money confiscated and chose to hide cash rather than to bank it. This practice exacerbated the country's capital flow problem.

The PNDC set stricter controls on government spending; one-quarter of Ghana's embassies were temporarily closed to save money. Price controls on goods and services were reinstituted with a vengeance. The initial delight of the citizenry turned sour as commodities and services disappeared. Market women were again maligned as the source of everyone's misery. Lining up for two cans of milk or one cake of soap became a way of life. Fights broke out in bread lines, until bread became unavailable because of the absence of flour. Control pricing of transportation (taxis and buses), coupled with the scarcity of spare parts (or their terrific cost) and the expense of gas, resulted in many transport owners and operators retiring their vehicles rather than taking a loss.

After Kwesi Botchway, the secretary for economic planning, introduced the objectives of government policy in December 1982, the regime acted swiftly to carry out a series of much needed fiscal measures. The four-year *Programme for Economic Reconstruction and Development* allotted one year for setting down a strong basis for changing social, economic, and political conditions and three years for building the foundations of a self-reliant and integrated national economy. Harking back to the days of Nkrumah, the plan mandated state control of the economy. To improve the distribution of goods and services, a national network of people's shops was set up. Cocoa continued to be the principal export staple.

During its first two years in power, the PNDC unquestionably took the lead in managing the economy. In 1983, the cedi was so overvalued that the black market rate for $1.00 fetched ₵50 to ₵60, about twenty times the ₵2.75 bank rate. Staple items had become unaffordable, whereas imported foods continued to be brought in at the unofficial rate; as a consequence, local agricultural productivity was unprofitable and farmers cut back—further increasing the price of the less plentiful locally grown foodstuffs. In March 1983, the government took the explosive but economically essential step of effectively devaluing the cedi. This step, as well as budget proposals that imposed a severe austerity regimen, was a precondition for the extension of a $300 million loan from the IMF.

In September 1982, Ghana had closed its borders to control smuggling and to deter mercenaries said to be determined to overthrow the Ghanaian government. Six months later the borders were re-opened to reabsorb the Ghanaians expelled from Nigeria. This influx added to the economic hardship that accompanied Ghana's acquiescence to IMF conditions as the level of consumer prices rose by 750 to 990 percent. Acute shortages were recorded in every single sphere: Manufacturing was virtually at a standstill; unemployment and inflation were rampant. As a result of the worst drought in years and several disastrous bush fires, the food shortage had reached such monumental proportions that even the Ghanaian magicians were unsure of where their next meals would come from. A second devaluation in 1983 revalued the dollar at ₵30, and the minimum wage rose from ₵12 to ₵25—its real value in fact was a mere 13 percent of the 1975 level.

In November 1983, the PNDC convened a donors' conference in Paris and received pledges of some $750 million to support its plan to revamp the country's shattered infrastructure and to pay for the importation of raw materials necessary to revitalize industry. In early 1984, new import restrictions were imposed. That same year, three further adjustments caused the cedi to be deflated to $1 = ₵50; the minimum wage was raised to ₵40 whereas a yam cost between ₵150 and 200!

In a courageous but nevertheless ruthless way, the PNDC adopted some drastic measures to extricate Ghana from its economic morass. The unconventional methods were aimed at carrying out an economic plan contained in most classical textbooks. There was, indeed, a gap between the radical rhetoric of the Rawlings government and its commitment to IMF policies. The forces unleashed by the PNDC were unpredictable and not easily subject to central control. Policy was therefore frequently confused and implementation uncoordinated. In 1984, the government undertook a recovery program that aimed at restoring real growth and maintaining public financial and monetary discipline. Foreigners expressed a new confidence in the viability of Ghana's political economy. Aid money, so necessary if the devaluation policy instituted in 1983 was to work, had been slow in coming, but now the IMF and the World Bank seemed committed to supplying it. Also foodstuffs were relatively abundant because of the combination of normal rainfall, the incentives of 1983 scarcity prices, and government encouragement of increased planting. But by late 1984, the recovery program had slowed down, as economists disagreed on policy and conditions worsened for consumers after the cedi was again devalued ($\cancel{C}70$ = \$1).

The effect of the structural innovations was not clear cut. On one hand, by deconcentrating authority, the PNDC expanded the scope of government and encouraged many people previously excluded from the public sphere to actively participate in the political economy. On the other hand, the PDCs and WDCs lacked the expertise and skills necessary for the implementation of the government's program. All too often they interfered with executive bodies, which still continued to implement government policy. An institutional dualism set in between PDCs/WDCs and the bureaucracy that sometimes confused lines of communication and complicated daily activities. At the end of 1984, the PDCs/WDCs were renamed Committees for the Defence of the Revolution (CDRs). The National Defence Committee (NDC), the revolutionary organ responsible for the defense committees, was dissolved and its functions taken over by the PNDC secretariat itself, perhaps eliminating some of the dualism. CDR executives were known as organising assistants, and coordinators at the regional and district levels as political heads of administration. The CDRs were viewed as instruments for social justice and social transformation. The change in name actually reflected the move away from ideological dissemination: The role of these units was redefined in Rawlings's words—"to mobilise people not to achieve certain political objectives of the revolution."[34]

Thus in both political and economic domains, there was a move away from the rampant populist rhetoric and policies espoused in 1982 to a realignment of institutional processes in 1984. Under the chairmanship of Justice D. F. Annan, a member of the PNDC, the National Commission for Democracy (NCD) was created to work out an appropriately Ghanaian democratic process of constitutional rule—to represent a compromise between the PDCs and the concept of an elected parliament.

The performance record of the PNDC was ambiguous: The course of action that the PNDC pursued held the prospect of an economic turnabout; at the same time, conditions in Ghana worsened during its first two years in office. It succeeded, albeit under threat, in creating some level of worker consciousness and unity of purpose in fulfilling necessary economic tasks; however, classism and tribalism became rampant. Although popular participation was achieved, it cost the country the expertise of Ghana's skilled technocrats. Specific groups were encouraged to launch their own communal initiatives; these frequently had a debilitating effect on official programs. The dualism apparent in the PNDC's structure was reflected in the results of its activities.

Political Conflict

Rawlings's return to power was not welcomed in certain circles, and within months, a solid opposition had been formed. The backbone of the dissident camp was the urban elite—the professionals and bureaucrats who had been deprived of their access to power. These groups, led by the ARPB, challenged the activities of the PDCs and WDCs, decried the regime's curtailment of civil rights, and berated the Rawlings revolution. In time, they were joined by other groups.

As in all previous administrations, ethnicity became an issue. Akan groups, uneasy because of the Ewe-based takeover, resisted the soldiers' authority and in consequence were unduly harassed. The clergy expressed doubts about PNDC tactics, and the Catholic Bishops' Conference questioned the legality of the defense committees. Students voted out the radical leaders of NUGS and joined the anti-Rawlings protest. Many Ghanaians substituted *warabeba* (literally, "you will bring yourself"; i.e., if you want black market goods, you must seek them undercover) for kalabule and tried to keep their distance from the new government.

Opposition to the regime peaked following the brutal murder of three justices of the High Court and a military aide in summer 1982. Although Rawlings hastily set up a special investigations board (SIB), headed by the respected Justice J.V.C.C. Azu-Crabbe, this move hardly placated a strong constituency appalled by the official sanction of organized terror. Six months after the PNDC takeover, the government was beleaguered. Rawlings lashed out against his critics—another leader intolerant of criticism: He imposed a dusk-to-dawn curfew, closed Ghana's borders, and muzzled the press.

Dissent arose both outside and inside the military. In an October 1982 coup attempt, A. Akate-Pore, one of Rawlings's trusted lieutenants, failed to dislodge the PNDC leadership; a similar effort in November was also unsuccessful. Measures instituted to avoid a recurrence of such attempts triggered unrest in the military and further threatened Rawlings's control. In late February 1983, another coup effort was uncovered, this one instigated by Brigadier Nunoo-Mensah, the PNDC's most senior military figure and a major moderating force in the ruling coalition.

Dissent grew throughout 1983. The budget proposals caused resentment within the TUC. Rumors about the possible SIB exoneration of Rawlings's aides in the murder of the High Court justices exacerbated tensions. On June 19, 1983, a group of rank-and-file soldiers in another attempted coup actually seized key government offices in Accra, but they were eventually subdued by pro-PNDC units.

By summer, Ghanaians in exile had formed an overseas movement to oust Rawlings. The Campaign for Democracy in Ghana, led by Major Boakye Djan, the former AFRC spokesman, mounted an international protest against the regime. At home, lawyers, church groups, and professionals called for Rawlings's immediate resignation; all three universities were closed after students' antigovernment demonstrations.

At this point, Rawlings decided on a course of moderation. In the SIB report published in June 1983, a former PNDC member (Amartey Kwei) and three soldiers were found guilty of the assassination of the justices, and the government ordered their immediate execution. To the dismay of leftist supporters of the revolution, Rawlings clamped down on abuse of power in the armed forces: Soldiers found guilty of abusing their position were given stiff sentences, whereas civilians were treated lightly.

The Ghana New Democratic movement was formed in London in 1984 by former politicians; led by J. H. Mensah, a member of Busia's cabinet, the group was interested in the restoration of democracy in Ghana. Exile groups also developed among exsoldiers in Togo and the Ivory Coast. Many other exiles were careful to keep their distance from such opposition politics to improve their chances for an easy return to Ghana.

Internal strife grew in Ghana, especially among the ranks of the military. In March 1984, an attempt by two groups of armed dissidents to infiltrate Ghana was put down; three of those executed were former soldiers who had participated in the June 1983 failed coup.

Hoping to achieve some kind of national reconciliation, Rawlings began to make plans to establish a people's parliament. In the 1982-1983 period, an ideological split took place within the Left; having been associated with the radicals since the 1979 coup, Rawlings adopted a more centrist position. The cleavage between the rightists, who favored the IMF solution to Ghana's woes, and the leftists, who did not, smoldered, and the latter group lost power.

By early 1985, the regime was engulfed in an ideological battle. The ideologues [through the political vehicle of the New Democratic movement and including a Dutch priest and former head of the Ghana Broadcasting Corporation (GBC)] wrote a letter criticizing the dissolution of the PDC/WDC structure and the return to the prerevolutionary elitist control of the instruments of governance. The resignation of Warrant Officer Adjei Buadi, the last original PNDC member, indicated how the regime's original purpose had been altered. Moreover, the GBC attacked the leadership of the TUC for having condemned the IMF-directed economic recovery program. It also accused it of undemocratic behavior because the TUC demanded a higher minimum wage ($\cancel{C}$70 per day being unrealistically low), which would upset the IMF's tables.

Despite the tension that accompanied the PNDC's rise to power, it worked increasingly toward creating a more institutionalized basis for regime legitimacy. Jerry Rawlings returned to power at a time when Ghana needed fundamental reform. The PNDC offered a program that was both innovative and problematic. The populist regime was a bundle of contradictions. A charismatic ruler supervised a process of real decentralization; a self-styled revolutionary adopted policies that provided incentives for private entrepreneurs. A forceful leader remained in office, although he could not impose even the most elementary order. Mass participation in development was nurtured when standards of living dropped to an all-time low. The PNDC period came to be characterized by a growing gap between Rawlings's convincing promise of political salvation and the stark realities of Ghanaian life. The record of Ghana's experiment with people's power was equivocal. Rawlings left unanswered the question of whether the gains made by his regime could have been achieved without the widespread disruption and social upheaval that accompanied his rule.

THE REGRESSIVE CYCLE OF GHANAIAN POLITICS

Politics in Ghana since 1957 has undergone manifold changes and multiple dislocations. Differences in the style and character of politics have unfolded in every phase of the country's recent history. Ghanaians have experienced a series of regimes, each of which possessed a distinctive flavor and left its own unique legacy.

Some features have nevertheless been common to all regimes. Every government in Ghana since independence has had to deal with the lack of organic cohesion of state institutions and with the fragility of inherited colonial structures; virtually every option of governance has been explored and every conceivable political combination tried. All governments have shared the common objective of establishing a system of rule that would ensure order and facilitate progress. Certain similarities therefore have characterized Ghanaian political processes. Authority, in very diverse ruling coalitions, has become personalized, and authoritarian tendencies have surfaced time and again. National politics has assumed the character of a zero-sum game. The inability to translate policy into practice has plagued every regime. No administration has evinced much tolerance for criticism or dissent, and successive regimes have employed force to curb discontent.

Several persistent problems account for the fragility of Ghanaian politics: the country's inability to establish adequate mechanisms for policy formulation and public accountability, and a modicum of governability. Ghana's political difficulties have been personal, social, and structural. Over the years, two large social constellations have vied with each other for power and influence: the haves and the have-nots. The challenge of finding a workable formula for linking diverse social groups together in a way that would relieve Ghana's dependence of other countries and permit it to equitably use its resources was not met during the first twenty-five years of independence.

Consequently, Ghanaian politics has developed a rhythm of incoherence and uncertainty. The overall pattern of decline and endurance remains the most constant single theme of the political history of the country. Ghana has experienced a steady and unremitting political enfeeblement. Misguided leadership and systematic mismanagement highlight personal explanations. But these factors are related to historical variables, external vulnerability, deep social inequities, dualistic economic structures, and the absence of a unifying value system. In recent years, Ghana's difficulties have been compounded by the effects of the global recession, natural disasters, and an unrelenting crisis of poverty. The swings in the political pendulum that have become part and parcel of the weakening of the state have both reflected and contributed to the process of decline.

Today Ghana is at a political crossroads. Experiences under past regimes have nurtured widespread disillusionment among its people and growing alienation toward its government. The prospects for the stabilization of political life in the near future are not promising. Although change is necessary to avert complete disintegration, Ghana has not collapsed and by the mid-1980s, showed some signs of stabilization. State institutions have retained an intrusive quality. At the local level, Ghanaians have devised their own means of coping with political uncertainty: In some instances, traditional authorities have been revived; in others, new political structures have been constructed. Alternate systems of justice have been created and new mechanisms for resolving conflict have been devised. A distinctive process of political implosion is taking place. Within the framework of political instability, Ghanaians are coping.

3

Society and Culture

The majority of Ghana's inhabitants are rural dwellers—farmers and craftspeople who observe customary modes of social, political, and economic behavior, as did their parents and grandparents before them. But they are no more untouched by the modernization of their country, concentrated in three or four major cities, than are their urban compatriots cut off from their rural roots. Modernization in Ghana, as in much of the Third World, has not effected a sharp distinction between the rural and urban sectors. Circular migration has introduced the farming population, either directly or through mobile kin, to the benefits and opportunities of urban living, whereas hometown festivals and family connections have prevented tradition from dying off.

Differences between urban and rural life-styles, however, do exist—in part as a function of an expected growing apart, a movement in different directions, and in part as a function of the different penetration and impact of the modern state and its institutions. Although the heterogeneity of the city has caused an erosion in traditional structures, the state has stepped in to replace them with more encompassing ones. Politics (not just the quest for and the use of power but the ideological vacillations underlying directions of control) and economics (which like politics has followed cycles in its policies and its fortunes) have deeply affected social patterns. Normative roles, social groups, and the basis for societal structures have been redefined. Ghanaians have been badly abused by outsiders, by their leaders, and by one another as political and economic security have become imperiled.

At the same time, their cultural heritage has given Ghanaians the strength and ability to survive (see Map 3.1 for cultural divisions). Although the populace showed an initial enthusiasm about state control and the various regimes established the basic infrastructure, a stable system of central institutions has not been developed. Ghanaians have, however, weathered the breakdowns, either fatalistically shrugging their shoulders and patiently waiting for a change or—increasingly—playing a larger role; participating more; resurrecting activities, behaviors, and strategies; and taking over in the wake of the state's disrepair.

SOCIOCULTURAL STRUCTURES

The Centrality of the Group

Traditional societal organization in Ghana is focused on kinship. The family—an economically productive unit and a socially and demographically reproductive unit—reinforces natal group solidarity and even operates as a microcosm of the larger society. Although not itself perpetual, the family feeds into the larger unilineal descent group, a corporate body that does live on in perpetuity and is reckoned according to one line of descent—generally the patrilineal in the north, the matrilineal in the south.

Kinship ties in with political, religious, economic, and juridical structures. The particular level that carries greatest salience varies from culture to culture. For instance, the matrilineal Asante family, if under a female head, consists of her, her sister, and her sister's children and perhaps her own and her sister's uterine grandchildren; if under a male head, it consists of him and his wife (wives) and children or of his sister and her children in addition to his nuclear family. The matrilineal Akwapim household is composed of a man and his wife and children or, more likely, a woman with her children and/or her children's children. In contrast, members of the patrilineal Ga lineage live in sexually segregated households—in one household the men, possibly three generations, joined at night by their wives; in another household several generations of the women and their young sons. The clan in the patrilineal Tallensi and

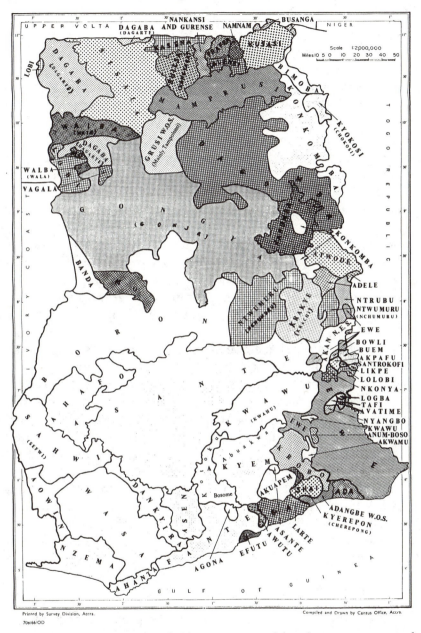

MAP 3.1 Cultural map of Ghana, prepared by the government of
Ghana and included in Walter Birmingham, J. Neustadt, and E.
N. Omaboe, eds. *A Study of Contemporary Ghana*, vol. 1 (Evanston,
IL: Northwestern University Press, 1967)

Konkomba societies is basic to their political systems, even though the members do not live together and do not know their exact relationship to one another. From kinship, the individual derives a sense of security, a right to citizenship, and access to resources. Reciprocally, the member owes certain obligations and duties to the kin group and its members. The kin group provides a point of reference.

In the countryside, the unilineal descent group is most operative, and social interaction is framed by membership in localized kin groups. In the south, land is held in common by family groups, among the Akan symbolized by the authority of the stool[1] and sanctioned by the ancestors and elders. In the north, as among the Konkomba, even though land is the property of the Earth God and thus separate from tribal authority, rights to it are associated with groups who are symbolized by a land shrine and overseen by elders. Because the group owns rights to the land, the individual group member is entitled to use that land.

An individual's membership in a group is ratified by connection with the ancestors; they are propitiated, and in reciprocation they look out over their descendants. The ancestors do not lose their membership in the kin group when they die; only their status has changed. Just as the individual's social niche is ascribed by birth into a family, so is his/her future predestined. According to the philosophy of the various ethnic groups, each person is endowed by the deity with a soul and through that essence a destiny or fate in all areas of endeavor.[2] This folk fatalism encourages acceptance of one's lot in life and more generally of life itself, which may not produce, but certainly does mesh with, the patience and tolerance so characteristic of Ghanaians.

Urban and Rural Settings

Rural areas are characterized by the predominance of one so-called tribal group. Stranger populations—nontribal immigrants residing in the tribal area—are tolerated at the pleasure of the chief, who grants them only custodial rights to land as the lands belong to the tribal ancestors. In the past, chiefs were

Housing in northern Ghana among the Dagomba

regarded as political leaders, lawmakers, spiritual heads, economic heads, and custodians of the people's land, who ensured fair allocation; as a consequence, a chief was the focus of the tribe's unity.

The primary focus of production in Ghana is agriculture. In southern Ghana the land is farmed by women; Ga, Akan, and Ewe women all grow crops. Cocoa farming in the forest area of Asante and Brong-Ahafo was established prior to the turn of the twentieth century and grew rapidly because men were free to devote their time to the crop. Women are seldom the outright owners of the food farms they cultivate, and they share the labor with their husbands; in the Akan areas, however, a significant percentage of women own cocoa farms.

Rural families live in one or more huts, arranged in a compound around a common yard where household activities such as cooking and eating take place. In the farming household, marriage can be polygynous, and variance in domestic residence technically affects spouse residence (e.g., Akan matrikin live together, whereas among Ewe the conjugal family is the basic unit). In fact, with the exception of some wives in matrilineal groups, most spouses in matrilineal, patrilineal, and bilateral farming households live together in households headed by men. Polygyny guarantees every younger woman the right of re-marriage; as such, it operates as a social security system for them. Moreover, divorce rates are high, since women know that remarriage is easy. Thus, in northern Ghana, at any one time 70 percent of the men have more than one wife, and 25 percent have two. With respect to domestic economy and social activities, marriage bears little resemblance to the European form. Ghanaian couples enjoy little conjugal companionship: Spouses rarely sit and talk; they eat separately, and they engage in separate ceremonial and recreational activities. In the rural sector, people behave according to patterns enshrined in the past—patterns that are legitimate because they are interpreted as pleasing to the gods or ancestors or because they work.

A growing number of people are leaving the countryside and moving to Ghana's cities (localities of 5,000 or more). The number of urban dwellers has increased from 29 percent in 1970 to 33 percent in 1975 to 36.6 percent in 1981, making Ghana the most urbanized country in West Africa (see Tables 3.1 and 3.2).

No part of Ghana is ethnically unmixed, a phenomenon well-rooted in history. Hausa, Fulani, Mossi, and Arab traders were certainly dealing with Ghanaians by the eighteenth century. And the growth of the urban areas is due partly to migration, which in turn is tied to economic fortunes. According to the 1970 census, one-third of both internal migrants and immigrants from other countries were enumerated in Ghana's urban centers. The immigrants from outside Ghana were more likely to settle in cities than were indigenous migrants, but between 1960 and 1970 many aliens moved to the rural sector or emigrated. More than one-half of the immigrants from Liberia, Nigeria, and Mali live in Ghana's cities. In 1970, 3.5 million interlocality lifetime adult migrants were located in Ghana; 17 percent of these had moved from village to town. The greatest increase during the 1960–1970 decade was in the number of urban-rural migrants; however, the number of urban localities also increased—from 93 to 135. In any case, most rural-urban migration was to the

TABLE 3.1

POPULATIONS BY REGION (Census enumerations)

Region	20 March 1960	1 March 1970	1970 Density (per sq mile)
Western	626,155	770,087	83
Central	751,392	890,135	235
Greater Accra	491,817	851,614	851
Eastern	1,094,196	1,261,661	164
Volta	777,285	947,268	119
Ashanti	1,109,133	1,481,698	157
Brong-Ahafo	587,920	766,509	50
Northern	531,573	727,618	27
Upper	747,344	862,723	82
Total	6,726,815	8,559,313	93

Chief Tribal Groups (1960 census, percentage of total population:
Akan 44.1, Mole-Dagbani 15.9, Ewe 13.0, Ga-Adangbe 8.3, Guan 3.7,
Gurma 3.5.

Source: "Ghana: Statistical Survey," Africa South of the Sahara,
1984-85. Fourteenth Edition (London: Europa Publications, Ltd.,
1985), p.424.

TABLE 3.2

POPULATION OF PRINCIPAL TOWNS (1970 Census)

	City Proper	Conurbation
Accra (capital)	636,067	738,498*
Kumase	260,286	345,177
Tamale	83,653	--
Tema	60,767	--
Takoradi	58,161	160,868**
Cape Coast	51,653	--
Sekondi	33,713	--

*Accra-Tema Metropolitan Area.
**Sekondi-Takoradi City Council.

Source: "Ghana: Statistical Survey," Africa South of the Sahara,
1984-85. Fourteenth Edition (London: Europa Publications, Ltd.,
1985), p.424.

Accra Central, facing the Ghana National Trading Corporation department store on the left and the main post office adjacent to it

Accra Region, although the Northern Region's cities gained 23 percent of the total.

Urbanization is a multidimensional process of transformation, which in Ghana has been heavily influenced by the West. The Ghanaian urban milieu is characterized by dense settlement, which offers a wide range of personal contacts; increased mobility in identities and loyalties available; heterogeneity of peoples and situations; and economic differentiation. The migration process has been very significant in molding and transforming the urban demographic structure, which is visible in the variance between Ghanaian towns. Occupational diversification, for example, can be seen among cities as a result of their different economic development and functional specialization: Accra is an administrative center, Kumase a trading center, and Sekondi-Takoradi an industrial center.

A breakdown and redefinition of traditional value systems has taken place in Ghana, resulting in both detribalization and retribalization. The city is the locus of social structural change.

The affective importance of the group has carried over; migrant Frafra, for instance, are generally unwilling to disregard kinship obligations. However, the centrality of the kin group has been modified: Individuals are no longer defined merely by their kin group affiliation; they can achieve new roles, especially through Western education. Kinship is less primary in terms of economic ties; materialism dominates the kinship mode. Moreover, contract replaces kinship—individuals now represent themselves. Kin groups no longer regulate behavior to the extent that they did in the countryside; that role has been taken over by voluntary associations. In the city in contradistinction to the village, compounds are heterogeneous with respect to both ethnicity and kinship. This diversity contributes to a broadening of cultural awareness and a breakdown in traditional behavior.

The urban household differs from the rural one. Polygynous marriages are less frequent in urban areas, especially for persons exposed to Western orientation, for women have unequivocally stated that a man should have only one wife. The functional equivalent of polygyny, the "friendship" between a woman and a married man, is, however, quite common. Life in the city is costly, and women generally earn less than men because their opportunities are more limited. With the lessening of the kin group's control and the postponement of marriage for girls in school or beginning an occupation, many young women have assumed this typically urban role of girlfriend. Meanwhile, the marital unit continues to operate much as it does in rural areas: Husband and wife pursue their lives quite separately. However, among the urban elite, movement has begun toward the Western conjugal family type and toward marriages performed according to the civil Marriage Ordinance (which, unlike native law, does not permit polygyny), both of which are approved in the modernizing milieu.

The physical aspects of city life in Ghana are very different from those in the rural sector. Modern amenities, such as electricity and piped water, are the rule. The streets are alive with modern vehicular traffic, which must contend with pedestrians, hawkers, and animals. There are traffic signals. The markets are open daily and carry food-stuffs, provisions, cloth, household items, and so on. In addition, there are supermarkets and department stores.

But in Ghana, as in much of Africa, the behaviors of rural and urban dwellers are not as distinct as in the industrialized West. Value orientations rather than geography are decidedly influential, and in Ghana, one is never far from the pull of the traditional group. Migration not only brings country folk to the city; it also sends new urban dwellers back to the hometown for visits. Thus people at both ends keep in touch. Hometown voluntary associations are a reinforcing mechanism for members of the same ethnic group in the city. Fostering children is especially salient in this regard. Among such different peoples as the Ga, Gonja, and Dagomba, children are shared among kin and their upbringing is a group responsibility. For those who have relocated to the city, sending children home to the extended family reaffirms bonds.

Ethnic Groups

In Ghana as elsewhere, social differentiation may be based upon either ascribed or achieved status. The former is commonly associated with traditional behavior as dictated by the specifics of ethnic group membership. In Ghana, there are about 100 ethnic groups. The government's position has always been that national unity is "good" and tribalism "bad," and it is possible to speak of a national whole, which is aided by the adoption of English as the language of the country. However, the ethnic groups are bound culturally (through ideology, language, marriage), structurally (through roles and relationships), and geographically (in a regional sense). Ethnic groups are self-defined as separate entities, and in times of political stress tribalism has emerged and been fanned by the party line.

Throughout Ghana, internal and external migrants, whose movements are economically motivated, have crossed the geographical boundaries of settled groups and established themselves temporarily (seasonally) or permanently. Geographic migration has not created new or extinguished old natal memberships; even when intermarriage has occurred, ethnic groups do not simply fuse by virtue of propinquity. But the salience of ethnicity may undergo change. This criss-crossing of traditional allegiance and assimilation is particularly marked in the urban milieu.

Cases of supertribalism, observed among the immigrant Hausa some years ago, have occurred when group members have rejected assimilation in favor of insular ways of life. But many people also have chosen to drop their tribal identity and become townspeople—perhaps to escape the not infrequent derisive ethnic labeling that categorizes Ewe as jujumen (practitioners of black magic) or Frafra as backward. More commonly, in accordance with what is called situational selection, the individual chooses the identity, including the ethnicity, and the behavior appropriate to the given situation.

Ethnic groups often inhabit economic niches—the Kwahu are businesspeople, Ga are fishermen, Hausa are kola nut traders—and by activating the ethnic network, individuals can benefit from the inherent reciprocity and trust and find their place in the niche.

Broadly speaking, Ghana's ethnic groups fall into two regional categories: the southern Akan, Ga-Adangme, and Ewe, who speak Kwa languages and make up 70 percent of the population, and the northern Gur speakers, who constitute 20 percent. The southerners, who are dominated in numbers and influence by the Akan, have had the longest and most far-reaching contact with Christianity and modern European life. The northerners, on the other hand, are distant from the coastal areas and the European presence, and although they have fallen under the influence of Islam, their traditional mode of life has remained remarkably constant. The northerners, who also include immigrants from Nigeria, northern Togo, Mali, and Burkina Faso (Upper Volta), are distinguished from the southerners by ethos, religion, and education.

The fluidity of ethnicity facilitates the redefinition into more encompassing regional units. Frafra, like other migrants to Accra, maintain their ethnic identity through mutual dependence and structures like the hometown associations. The latter help sustain a sense of belonging to the group. They reserve their primary social interaction for members of their ethnic group; celebrate festivals together; reinforce traditional norms and behaviors; and maintain contact with the community where they were born. The Frafra, like other northerners, however, have become absorbed into urban *zongos* (stranger quarters)—social/physical agglomerations that are distinctly Islamic in tone. In fact, as seen in residential isolation, migration status is more likely to differentiate urban dwellers in Ghana's cities, as it is in new cities throughout Africa, than is ethnic group or family status.

Class

Under British rule, the traditional Ghanaian conceptions of social status and self-respect were supplanted by new role definitions, based upon achievement rather than ascription, and by the beginnings of a stratification system based on economic class rather than ancestral prerogative. Individual mobility was franchised, most evidently in the emergent urban social system.

As migration enables movement across boundaries, mobility allows movement within boundaries. Mobility is evident in the city: Indeed, on one level, urban living carries cachet; on another level, the particular city neighborhood inhabited is what counts. Ethnic status—a criterion of social stratification—can be manipulated, telescoped, or diminished through situational selection, but it is crosscut by other axes. For example, economic position generally correlates with education. There are the traditional elites—chiefs and ritual specialists; there are wealthy traders and farmers; there are even workers who earn more in the informal sector than their compatriots in the formal one. But well-educated professionals, senior civil servants, and members of government, hold more prestigious positions. In Ghana, the distribution of occupation, education, and similar advantages is tied to the historical penetration of British colonialism inland from the coast.

Education was initially applauded among Ghanaians because it served as an avenue to European-type occupations—to the most highly regarded and highly paid occupations. Moreover, it gave esteem to the new African elite, whose affiliations and aspirations challenged traditional values. This new elite entered the comparatively open society of the Gold Coast as a new prestige group with new political and social roles.

The coincidence of ethnic-cultural and occupational lines of division clearly ties in with economic position and education. The first Ghanaian men to be educated came from trading families and were members of the Fante peoples (Akan) near the European forts. When the British moved their administrative headquarters to Accra, Ga males joined the ranks of the educated and well-employed. Among today's railroad employees, the unskilled and semiskilled road workers are from the Northern and Upper Regions and the skilled and semiskilled workshop employees are southern, primarily Fante workers. The so-called laboring poor—the skilled and semiskilled employed in the formal sector, the small-scale entrepreneurs, and informal sector workers—are primarily migrants. Migrant status, in turn, provides a criterion for determining social status.

An enormous gap exists between the masses of low-paid workers and the elite stratum of politicians and senior civil servants. From 1968 to 1971, the differential between the highest- and lowest-paid employees in government service was in the proportion of 39:1. And the relative distribution of income has deteriorated badly; in 1965, the upper 6 percent of earners accounted for 12.9 percent of Ghana's total national income, whereas by 1968, the upper 4.6 percent accounted for 24.7 percent of the total.[3] Although statistics on income are not available, World Bank estimates indicate that by 1978, poverty levels were high (Tables 3.3 and 3.4).

In Ghana, class is reflected in people's life-styles. The large cities like Accra are differentiated into two population groupings, a differentiation reflected both physically and socioeconomically. On the one hand, the inner city is occupied primarily by the masses and some long-established indigenous families. Inner-city dwellers live in crowded compounds and share rooms and public spaces. Their senses are continually bombarded by traffic noise and blaring music and by cooking smells produced by street-side food traders and odors of uncollected night soil. They are confronted by open rubbish dumps. Drivers navigate alongside open sewers; children often use the channels for playing and passersby for disposing of food wrappings and garbage. The urban workers are physically segregated from those who control them—expatriates and Ghanaian professionals, politi-

A commemorative statue at a central traffic circle in Kumase

TABLE 3.3

ESTIMATED ABSOLUTE POVERTY LEVEL
(US $ per capita)

Urban	307
Rural	150

Source: World Bank Data, 1983.

TABLE 3.4

ESTIMATED RELATIVE POVERTY INCOME LEVEL
(US $ per capita)

Urban	156
Rural	130

Source: World Bank Data, 1983.

cians, businesspeople, and the like, whose own surroundings present a stark contrast. Thus the colonial system is perpetuated.

On the other hand, the elite and its aspirants live in homes with carefully manicured gardens built for foreigners in the suburbs or government residential areas, in which they can shut themselves off in air-conditioned comfort (as long as the power stays on) and watch movies on their video cassette recorders. There is a hush in these residential areas, where the trappings of bourgeois life-style predominate. In Ghana, a person's position is validated by conspicuous consumption, and the big men bedazzle the masses with their fancy cars ("smiling Benz"), expensive clothing, affected speech patterns, and memberships in Western associations (Rotary, Masons). Their houses are generally inhabited by the nuclear family—the man, his wife, and their children. These men marry monogamously—their wives call themselves "Mrs."—but they actively and often openly engage in outside relationships.

Cross-Cutting Loyalties

In today's Ghana, as a result of Western impact and change, people face the dilemma of cross-cutting loyalties. Group loyalties are still promoted in the city, less to the kin group or tribe than to the state. The social system based on achievement rather than ascription has had a wrenching effect; role redefinition makes individuals responsible for themselves, potentially at the expense of the natal group. Accordingly, social status is now based less on ethnic group membership than on Western-oriented class. Colonial rule, the introduction of new religions, and the abundance and appeal of consumer goods have undercut traditional values and allegiances. Migration and mobility have carried people far—both socially and spatially—from their origins. They have gathered together people of diverse backgrounds, exposed individuals to new opportunities, and created fresh desires and aspirations. But hometown ties are not simply severed; they are maintained through formal and informal institutions, rural-urban continuity, and the constancy of basic loyalties.

SOCIAL POLICY

With the attainment of independence, and even during the period just preceding independence, Ghana's first government showed its intention of expanding the country's infrastructure to facilitate the most rapid modernization possible. In its various aspects—for example, education, transportation, and the press—the policy formation and implementation exhibited the state's desire to take over many of the roles and duties traditionally performed by members of the local group while introducing new services (see Table 3.5 for services budget). State involvement has varied in breadth and depth from regime to regime. Thus, state intrusiveness has not been steady; moreover, the ideological tone of each administration has colored the social programming emphasized, funding allocated, manner of implementation, and targeted and effective impact.

Educational Policy

Ghana's literacy is the highest and its educational facilities the best in West Africa.[4] During the Nkrumah years, educational policy was characterized by the provision for free elementary schooling (figures for school enrollment are given in Table 3.6). Some private-sector schools continued to operate, but they received no public funds except for an occasional small grant; most were absorbed into the public system. The Accelerated Development Plan for Education in 1951 and the consistently high monetary provision for education in Ghana's budgets and national development plans bear witness to the government's commitment to education.

The Ghanaian school system is modeled on the English one but is unique in its four-year middle school, interposed between the primary and secondary schools. In 1959, it was decided that middle-school pupils in their second or third year could sit for the Common Entrance Examination (for secondary-school admittance), enabling secondary-school entry from the lower levels of middle school.

The Education Act of 1961 legalized the government's decision to make education free. No tuition would be charged

TABLE 3.5

EXPENDITURE BY FUNCTION IN CENTRAL GOVERNMENT BUDGET (US $ millions)

	1973	1974	1975	1976	1977	1978	1979	1980	1981	1982
Total Expenditure	548.5	754.1	1146.2	1482.6	2136.6	3164.8	4295.7	4667.5	7719.3	9529.5
General Public Services	70.5	172.1	211.5	280.1	348.3	630.4	1114.2	843.1	-----	-----
Defense	37.2	58.4	89.0	92.2	112.3	167.5	189.8	174.8	-----	-----
Education	111.6	146.4	235.8	321.7	416.3	494.1	667.2	1025.6	-----	-----
Health	43.5	66.6	95.5	118.0	158.9	229.7	256.2	325.2	-----	-----
Social Security and Welfare	36.5	85.3	125.9	160.8	168.9	306.5	304.8	243.5	-----	-----
Social Security and Assistance	-----	52.8	79.3	100.2	88.1	-----	-----	-----	-----	-----
Welfare	-----	32.5	46.6	60.6	80.8	-----	-----	-----	-----	-----
Housing & Commun. Amenities	.1	-----	-----	-----	-----	-----	-----	74.9	-----	-----
Other Community & Soc. Serv	14.6	23.7	44.9	61.9	81.2	119.9	142.2	121.2	-----	-----
Economic Services	89.3	99.6	186.1	293.0	455.7	766.6	1078.8	967.4	-----	-----
Gen. Adm., Regulat. & Research	8.5	-----	-----	-----	-----	-----	-----	-----	-----	-----
Agriculture, Forestry, Fishing	39.2	41.6	76.2	106.9	192.2	385.7	445.7	571.0	-----	-----
Mining, Manufc. & Construction	2.3	17.5	28.4	32.5	51.0	76.8	99.3	103.5	-----	-----
Elect., Gas, Steam and Water	-----	2.0	2.9	2.7	2.7	11.3	8.1	4.5	-----	-----
Roads	24.7	29.1	65.4	111.3	149.6	162.8	352.5	185.8	-----	-----
Inland and Coastal Waterways	-----	-----	-----	-----	-----	-----	-----	-----	-----	-----
Other Transport. & Communic	3.7	9.0	13.0	11.6	34.4	62.0	98.9	93.1	-----	-----
Other Economic Services	10.9	.4	.2	28.0	25.8	68.0	74.3	9.5	-----	-----
Other Purposes	145.2	102.0	157.5	154.9	395.0	510.0	542.5	891.8	-----	-----
Adj. to Total Expenditure	-----	-----	-----	-----	-----	59.9	-----	-----	-----	-----

Source: Government Finance Statistics Yearbook. Volume VII, 1983. Washington, D.C.: IMF, p. 314.

TABLE 3.6

SCHOOL ENROLLMENT (adjusted enrollment ratios)

		1960	1970	Most recent estimate*
Primary:	Total	38.0	64.0	69.0
	Male	52.0	73.0	77.0
	Female	25.0	54.0	60.0
Secondary:	Total	5.0	14.0	36.0
	Male	9.0	21.0	44.0
	Female	3.0	8.0	27.0
Vocational (percentage of secondary)		12.6	23.3	3.5‡

*Most recent estimate is between 1979 and 1981.
‡1978.

Source: World Bank Data, 1983.

at the primary- or middle-school level. Responsibility for the preuniversity system was conferred on the central government ministry. By 1963, textbooks were provided free of charge; however, because of budgetary considerations book fees were reintroduced in 1966, after Nkrumah's overthrow.

Nkrumah was an outward-looking leader, and under his government, English language study was emphasized at the expense of Ghanaian languages. The 1951 plan made the vernacular the language of instruction, with the understanding that as soon as children were reasonably competent in English, the latter would become the language of instruction. English was a course of study from the first year and the sole language of instruction at the earliest possible stage.

Although primary education represented the major area of concern throughout the Nkrumah years, the entire educational structure was expanded. Under the Seven-Year Plan for National Reconstruction and Development, elementary education was regarded as a means of fitting youths "for all the jobs that need to be done," rather than only white-collar occupations. High priority was given to secondary schooling, and the technical education system was enlarged and reorganized to meet the country's economic needs; University College and the College of Technology and Science were both established. By 1965-1966, the student population in primary school was seven times larger than in 1951, in middle schools four times larger, in secondary schools fourteen times larger, and at the university level, twenty times greater. Tuition-free schooling resulted in a rapid increase in central government expenditures, so that between 1951 and 1966, operating costs had increased fourteenfold.

From the final year of the First Republic in 1965 until the terminal year of the Second Republic six years later, primary school enrollments fell whereas those of middle schools—the most rapidly expanding sector—increased by 70 percent. The post-Nkrumah period continued and completed the structural process begun in 1962: The six-year primary and four-year middle-school courses of instruction were reworked into eight years of primary and two-year courses for those not going on to secondary school. Curriculum reform at the elementary and secondary levels became a major objective of policy. The Second Republic broke with Nkrumah on language policy; the deemphasis of English as the language of instruction reflected Busia's cultural Ghanaian focus. During the first three and, if possible, the subsequent three years of primary schooling, the Ghanaian local language was to be the medium of instruction. The minimum goals were development of the basic reading, writing, speaking, and listening skills in English in the first year of school. Thus, the curriculum gave more time to Ghanaian languages and less to English than in 1964-1965.

Under the NLC, in mid-1969 local communities were granted more direct involvement in the management of their school systems, and the Ministry of Education, Culture and Sports was made responsible for establishing broad policies and general planning for education. The Second Republic placed actual administration into the hands of nine regional educational officers, and direct responsibility for local schools was borne by local district officers within each region. Such measures promoted broader participation by the citizenry at the local level.

The One-Year Development Plan of 1970-1971 enacted by Prime Minister Busia included measures to strengthen secondary education by increasing the number of places in form one (first of the four-year ordinary level course) and sixth form (the additional two-year advanced course for those wishing to proceed to university). The priority accorded to secondary schools, as well as teacher training, technical courses, and the university, represented a response to the real demands of the economy for human resources and for additional places in higher levels of schooling in accord with the expansion of lower levels.

At the same time, under the Student Loans Scheme Act of 1971 university students were required for the first time to contribute toward their own education. The government covered tuition charges, whereas the "maintenance charge" was to be paid by students. The scheme was abandoned one year later after Busia was overthrown.

Since 1972-1973, public education has been free in Ghana at all levels, except for textbook fees. During the first six years, 50 percent of class time is devoted to the study of language (English and vernacular) and mathematics. Teaching at this level is influenced by the CEE (Common Entrance Examination for secondary school), not the Middle Leaving Certification Exam. The official age of entry into primary school is six years, and the preuniversity program includes children between 13 to 17 years old, depending upon the year that a student entered secondary school. There are currently four programs of schooling; the two basic ones constitute six years of primary school. One is taught from the start in English and students successful on the CEE go right into secondary in their seventh year; the other initially employs the local language for teaching and students go through two years of middle school, sitting for the CEE in class 8. The other two programs of study follow primary education: a two-year terminal general education course or a two-year middle-school program, preparatory to secondary school or a vocational-technical course.

Under the SMC, the 1974 Education Act provided that in 1976 eighty additional primary schools would be built, 4,000 more teachers in training recruited, and a new medical school established in Kumase. In addition, recognizing the importance of the university as a socializing agent, the SMC proposed introducing compulsory basic military training in its curriculum.

Government interest in shaping educational programs to better ensure student participation in the goals of national government continues, changing with the ideology of the given government. Under the PNDC, there has been a move to restructure the entire educational system, reforming the content of curricula, adapting books assigned, and changing educational facility availability to rid students and society of negative attitudes and reflect reawakening of cultural pride. There had been a recent growth in the number and enrollment of private primary International Preparatory Schools, which charge high fees. Only children of the well-to-do can afford to attend these, and the children of lower economic groups are disproportionately enrolled in public institutions.

There has been a general burgeoning of the private sector of Ghana's educational sector—in part because there simply were not enough public schools, in part because parents felt that the existing schools were poor (with Ghana's economic decline, a massive exodus of professionals, including teachers, took place). And the expansion of the nongovernmental sector has affected the patterns of access to secondary schools: In 1972, more than 43 percent of form 1 students in the top five secondary schools came from the private primary sector, as compared with 6 percent in the remaining eighty secondary institutions. Schooling is clearly related to occupational eligibility in the urban sector, and elite schools have carried more clout; therefore, the children of less fortunate families have faced narrower job opportunities. Despite expansion, Ghana's educational system is still highly selective, with a broad elementary base, restricted secondary structure, and even narrower university level.

Population Planning

In March 1969, Ghana became the first West African country to adopt a national population policy. Heralded as a landmark in progressive planning, the government-approved position was published as an official policy paper, "Population Planning for National Progress and Prosperity."[5] The statement, which remains the basis of Ghana's policy, authorized the establishment of the National Family Planning Programme (NFPP) as an organic part of Ghana's social and economic planning and development activity.

Nine years earlier, state population planning had already begun with the formation of the Family Planning Committee in Accra. Then in 1961, the Christian Council established a family planning center at the YMCA in Accra, and in 1964, a second one in Kumase. In 1966, a group of Ghanaian doctors attended an International Planned Parenthood Federation (IPPF) conference in Denmark, and one year later, the Planned Parenthood Association of Ghana (PPAG) was founded and incorporated. Affiliated with the IPPF, PPAG receives most of its support from the federation and the balance from the U.S. Agency for International Development (U.S. AID) and the Ghana government. In June 1968, PPAG's Accra branch opened a clinic serviced by physicians and midwives. By late 1970, Accra boasted three such facilities.

The NFPP is located within the Ministry of Economic Planning. It uses facilities and personnel in both public and private sectors. The program's structure consists of a national planning council, with a secretariat that has two major divisions—information and education, and services. PPAG is situated within the service division's private-services unit. Primary responsibility for the provision of family planning services rests with the Ministry of Health, supplemented by PPAG and private medical personnel.

The program's principle objective[6] is to reduce Ghana's annual rate of growth and natural increase from 3.9 percent in 1970 to 1.75 percent in the year 2000. This objective reflects on understanding of the close relationship between population size and growth and the demand for social services, structure of the labor force, level of per capita income, and extent of agricultural self-sufficiency. In 1970, $1.31 million was allocated for family planning programs, increasing by 46 percent in 1976 but decreasing by 26 percent the following year; 89 percent of this allocation came from the Ghana government. Eighteen percent of the program funding in 1977 was allotted to the services branch, which operates three family planning delivery systems: (1) clinics, as part of maternal and child health services; (2) single-purpose clinics, such as PPAG; and (3) distribution of nonprescription contraceptives through commercial outlets. There were 156 government-established clinics throughout Ghana;

29 percent of the allotted funds went into information and education.

Information and services are available to all Ghanaians regardless of age, number of children, or ability to pay. Individual participation is entirely voluntary, and services are offered only to women. In 1978, only 4 percent of Ghana's married women of reproductive age used contraceptive devices: of these 55 percent used pills, 9 percent intrauterine devices, and 36 percent other methods. In 1977, 61 percent of the users were under 35 years of age; more than 50 percent had three children or fewer, and 17.4 percent had six children or more.

In Ghana, cultural factors present major obstacles to family planning. Children are a valued resource: They are often pivotal in reciprocal relationships and instrumental in reaffirming one's responsibility to others, in carrying out traditional obligations, in sustaining the balance of indebtedness, and in showing respect for custom and those who represent it. If motherhood is not the definitive attribute of being an adult woman, surely it is one of the more significant ones; many children attest to a father's virility. They are a source of labor and an insurance policy in their parents' old age. To choose to have few children in this society is a cultural unknown.

Even though the overall level of fertility remained virtually unchanged between 1960 and 1971, it fell among the younger females, particularly those between the ages of 15 and 24 and to a more marked extent among urban dwellers. These drops can be attributed to the decline in the number of marriages within this age group, which in turn is a consequence of the substantial increase in the number of girls attending school. This trend has meshed with further government measures to help reduce fertility, including not only increased female enrollment in school but also in the labor force and the limitation of paid maternity leave to the first three births.

Public Welfare Policy: Health and Nutrition

In traditional Ghanaian society, the family or kin group provided basic welfare for the individual. In the city especially, where this kind of mutual assistance is not assured and where

Housing in Obo, Kwahu, a town 100 miles north of Accra

the maximum opportunities and the dominant sociopolitical segments are to be found, the state has spent the most money on social amenities. By the same token, with rapid urbanization the primary infrastructural facilities in Ghana have been severely taxed and have disintegrated. Furthermore, within the cities, certain neighborhoods have been ignored; in Accra, these include Nima and Sabon Zongo, at least in part because they do not carry enough political clout. Such areas are characterized by abysmal sanitation, inadequate water supplies, limited electric power, and a high crime rate (theft).

The government has taken a strong position on the need for inexpensive and comprehensive health care, and budget allocations have been increased continually. In the mid-1970s, the country was spending twice as much on health services as in 1970; the ratio of physicians to population improved from 1:12,950 in 1960 to 1:9,930 in 1970—an improvement reversed by the phenomenal emigration rate of doctors fed up with Ghana's deteriorating quality of life. The Five-Year Development Plan for 1975–1980 stated the need for wide distribution of health services; yet the pattern's inequities have not been cured: As of 1980, 45 percent of Ghana's doctors and 23 percent of its hospital beds were still in the Greater Accra area, which contained only 10 percent of the country's population.

Life expectancy has increased from 44.8 years in 1960 to 54.5 years during the 1979–1981 period, and the infant mortality rate (per thousand) has gone down during those same years from 142.9 to 101. However, morbidity patterns have not changed since the 1960s, with malaria, bilharzia, typhoid, and onchocerciasis still threatening, and 30 percent of recorded deaths caused by parasitic and other communicable diseases. Accurate information on actual incidence of diseases, however, is lacking because only a small percentage of the ill request medical help and methods of keeping records are poorly developed.

Because tradition dies hard in Ghana, most people prefer the services of native healers and herbalists: Their diagnoses and remedies are more compatible with people's beliefs about causation—the supernatural and the powers of the elders—and with a philosophy of fatalism that obviate trust in Western curing. Indeed, according to estimates, in the 1970s only about one-fourth of the population accepted modern medicine, and this group was primarily composed of the urban educated.[7] Although native medicine enjoys no official support (the Ghana Medical Association does not recognize its achievements), the Ghana Psychic and Traditional Healers Association was founded in 1963. Moreover, traditional midwives (matrones), many of whom are herbalists, deliver more than 75 percent of the babies born and offer prenatal care and treat complications of pregnancy and delivery

State agencies in Ghana have focused attention not only on facilities and health knowledge, but also on housing, sanitation, water supplies, and malnutrition. The general health of the rural population and infant and maternal mortality have come under careful scrutiny. In 1970, the Danfa Project was inaugurated, under the aegis of the Ministry of Health and U.S. AID (through the University of California at Los Angeles medical school). In 1972, a decree prohibited traditional midwives from practicing, but the Danfa Project sought to train such practitioners in hygienic delivery and by 1979 ninety had been so trained. As a result, these matrones, who already have the confidence of the general population, help fill the country's need for medical personnel.

Modern medical services have been provided by the central and local governments, Christian missions, and private agencies, and they fall under the jurisdiction of the Ministry of Health. Government institutions have provided free medical care to civil servants and their families, paupers, war pensioners, and students at public schools. Certain tropical diseases, such as leprosy, are also treated without charge. Standard fees have been billed for all other medical care and unfortunately have discouraged those with little money.

The overall medical situation in Ghana has become critical. Korle Bu, the country's largest hospital, which is located in Accra, is described as a "morgue" because of the deteriorating and overcrowded facilities and a dire shortage of prescription drugs. Operations are performed even though antibiotics crucial to postoperative recovery may be unobtainable. A hospital in the Western Region has been functioning for years without a refrigerator; as a result the medical authorities there were powerless to control an epidemic outbreak of the measles in 1982. Regional disparities in medical services are persistent. Moreover, it is commonly understood that proper medical attention can be gained only through private services—a costly procedure. And, as already noted, the ranks of the doctors have been sorely depleted through emigration.

Nutritional balance has also been a problem throughout the country, causing poor health among Ghanaians. The change from 1960, when the population consumed an average of 43 grams of protein per day, until 1979–1981, when the figure was 44, is barely indicative of progress. During that same period, average caloric intake actually dropped from 92 percent to 88 percent of daily requirements. Severe protein energy-malnutrition is especially pronounced among immigrants in urban shanty-towns, who have no garden plots and whose incomes are used up by basic services like rent and electricity and by acquired habits, such as consuming nutritionless "status foods" like soft drinks. Food expenditures seem to vary little according to class; the urban wealthy tend to spend money on luxury items rather than on more and better food. Food shortages and inflation have been common since the early 1970s.

In 1976, prices of locally produced food (staple grains in the north, root crops in the south) went up 90 percent and imported food prices rose 70 percent. During the following year, the prices of basic foodstuffs such as rice and plantain and those prepared from cassava and maize soared beyond the buying power of the average worker. Concurrently, the Upper Region was experiencing near famine because of drought; international aid was diverted; and traditional crops (guinea corn and millet) had been abandoned in favor of the government-inspired and ineffective rice farming program. Children suffered from malnutrition. According to an Oxfam report, food needed by starving families, primarily outside the towns, was appropriated through irregularities by those who could turn a profit. Meat, fish, eggs, and poultry are the primary sources of protein for Ghanaians, and these products are more readily available in the south. Fishing is an important coastal industry, and even though fish farming was initiated in the north, it was abandoned in 1982 because of mismanagement and water problems.

Men traditionally have been given first priority on available food, so that children have frequently been malnourished and undernourished. Moreover, seasonal hunger occurs annually during the lean season of May through July or August, when the new harvest is reaped.

Changes in Ghana's government in the late 1970s and early 1980s exacerbated privation. The sale of essential commodities (canned milk, fish and meat, soap, and so on) was taken away from the marketwomen and the goods became scarce; supermarket shelves, once stocked with canned, bottled, and packaged provisions, as well as coolers containing refrigerated and frozen foods, became empty because of control pricing and the suspension of import licenses. Governmental programs, such as Operation Feed Yourself, were devised to create self-sufficiency in food and combat shortages. Their success was less than complete. Yet the commitment of recent governments, in combination with the difficulty of obtaining staple foods, has caused citizens to participate much more in food self-sufficiency. Even city dwellers are cultivating any available bit of land.

A predominant style of housing in Accra

Social Services: Water, Sanitation, Electricity

Social services are mainly available in urban areas. Running water is found primarily in higher-priced dwellings in urban and suburban areas. Most urban compounds have a communal pipe; consumers are charged for access to it at a rate to cover maintenance costs. Between 1970 and 1975, access to piped water was not increased in rural areas—where it remained low. As recently as 1981, water in Accra was in short supply and not always safe to drink.

Similarly, only in the newer or more expensive housing in major cities and suburbs are modern toilets common. Enclosed drainage or sewage systems are lacking, and sewage in the larger cities is generally carried in open ditches that line either side of the streets and that are fed by narrow drains from individual compounds. Standing pools of fetid water breed malaria-carrying mosquitos. In 1970, 92 percent of urban and 40 percent of rural dwellers had access to the disposal of excreta; these figures rose only for urban dwellers and by only 3 percent in 1975 (the most recent figure). Moreover, the disposal service was not through a sewage system: The majority of bulk waste is collected by the familiar man with a tall pail on his head, more often than not a migrant from the north. Collection is supposed to be a state service, but with the general decline, many compound owners or tenants are compelled to pay a "dash" out of their pocket to ensure service.

Throughout city areas, public latrines are situated to serve the many households that lack a privy. Public garbage dumps are often located in the same place. Since both garbage and night soil collection are irregular, the public toilets are malodorous eyesores. Under Rawlings's PNDC, clean-up exercises were initiated, and the local citizenry was encouraged or even coerced to participate in such ventures as hauling away roof-high piles of garbage.

Until 1966, electricity was produced by diesel-generating plants run by the State Electricity Corporation and the mines. Hydroelectricity, generated by the Volta Dam, replaced diesel power, and by 1972, the Volta River Authority (VRA) supplied 99 percent of the national electricity.[8] Nkrumah made the Volta Dam scheme the keystone of his economic plans. Valco, the U.S.-owned alumina smelter, purchases 60 percent of the generated energy. Since 1972, Ghana has been supplying electricity to Togo and Benin, even though only 20 to 22 percent of its own populace enjoy electric power and the electricity generated is available only to the prosperous south. Even in urban and wealthy suburban locales, electricity supply has become very undependable because of aging equipment and the lack of spare parts.

Public Services: Housing and Transportation

A good housing policy is important in basic human terms: Everyone should have a roof over his or her head. Beyond this, adequate housing correlates positively with a nation's economy; for example, it contributes to labor efficiency and political stability. In recognition of this fact, during the period of self-rule just prior to independence, the Gold Coast government set up the Ghana Housing Corporation, through which government projects were constructed and operated. Pledges to provide houses for the people in general or for workers have figured in the development plans, budgets, and political rhetoric of the various regimes.[9]

During the Second Republic, it was calculated that 16,000 new dwellings were needed, 7,000 in the urban area alone;

however, only 6,000 were built each year. During the second phase of Acheampong's rule—from mid-1974 until October 1975—measures were articulated to increase rural and urban housing. And when Flight Lieutenant Rawlings returned to power in December 1981, urban landlords were commanded to observe rent control, thereby making this basic need more affordable and accessible to the urban masses. In fact, neither the Ghana Housing Corporation nor any of the regimes has effectively dealt with Ghana's housing shortage—a failure apparently caused by intramanagement conflict, patronage and nepotism, financial mismanagement, political interference, and ultimately the inability to come up with either guidelines or a comprehensive housing policy.

The State Housing Corporation, the largest producer of housing, has little competition to stimulate supply, variation in quality, and differentiation of type. Moreover, those areas that really need housing construction are neglected, in part because of inefficiency. For example, by 1980 Accra, Kumase, and Sekondi-Takoradi needed over 100,000 new houses to replace their slum housing, occupied primarily by migrants. However, only 900 units were being produced annually, partly because of lack of patronage. Housing built for workers in Sekondi-Takoradi in the 1950s was allocated to local CPP officials or those proffering bribes. Accra, the political center of the country, has enjoyed the most State Corporation housing construction, and yet the housing shortage there is severe today.

Ghana's various modes of transportation are overseen by the Ministry of Transport and Communications.[10] Like all other components of the country's infrastructure, roads, railroads, and air transport had severely deteriorated by 1979. The 19,840 miles of paved roads in Ghana were in good condition by African standards in the early 1960s. Lack of maintenance, resulting from the need to import materials and the deficiency of foreign exchange to do so, has rendered some major routes—such as the road north from Kumase—barely passable. Road deterioration in turn has had disastrous effects on the economy by hindering the transport of foodstuffs from the north. Although roads have been falling into disrepair, a multilane highway was opened between Accra and Tema well before traffic warranted it. To rectify the road situation, the Rawlings government has successfully encouraged communities to pool their labor; for example, in a crash program in the Western Region, members of thirty villages repaired their 33-mile trunk road.

The State Transport bus line operates between cities, and Omnibus Services Authority and City Express carry local passengers. The private-sector transportation services supplement those of the state in the form of *tro-tros* (lorries), minibuses, and taxis, and are subject to political interference. New vehicle registrations averaged 10,000 from 1958 to 1963, dropped to 7,700 in 1964–1969 because of import restrictions and taxation, rose again in 1970-1971 to 12,800, but was again stymied by the reinstatement of import restrictions. The spare parts problem has been an enormous hindrance to owners of both private cars and public conveyances.

Like that of the rest of West Africa, Ghana's coast lacks indentations, so that no natural formations are available to act as shelter for shipping. Access to even the largest rivers, such as the Pra or the Volta, is restricted to canoes or to shallow draught launches. The first deep-water artificial harbor was constructed at Takoradi, the second in 1962 at Tema. The port system reflects a logical division of traffic between the two: Takoradi monopolizes the high-tonnage timber, manganese, and bauxite traffic; Tema has a larger share of trade because it handles the bulk of the cocoa exports, dry cargo imports, all crude oil imports, and the export of refined petroleum products. Ghana's shipping industry includes the government-owned Black Star Line, which has a fleet of sixteen freighters and provides passenger and cargo services, as well as acting as the agent for foreign lines. The two ports are connected by road, rail, and air transport, thus linking the three largest concentrations of population and economic activity—Sekondi-Takoradi, Accra-Tema, and Kumase.[11]

The 595 miles of railroad track in Ghana form a triangle between Accra, Sekondi-Takoradi, and Kumase. The heavy traffic moves between Takoradi and Kumase; the Accra/Tema–Kumase route is of secondary importance. The traffic pattern of the railroad system is unbalanced. Almost all inbound merchandise is moved by road; the trains carry outbound cargo, primarily manganese, bauxite, and timber. Outbound cocoa was initially carried by rail, but by 1966, 30 percent went by road, and by 1971, that percentage had risen to 50. A breakdown in facilities has resulted in decreasing traffic—a deterioration caused by extreme government neglect, foreign exchange problems preventing importation of needed parts for repair, and an increasing imbalance as road transport gains.

Both international and domestic travel is serviced by air. Airports for travel within Ghana are located in Kumase, Sunyani, Takoradi, and Tamale; Accra's Kotoka International Airport has both internal and external flights. Air service has become less regular than in earlier years. European airlines have cut back the number of flights considerably. In 1970, Pan American planes flew into Accra twice weekly; in 1982, the airline ceased operating in Ghana—a move already taken by Lufthansa. Ghana Airways, a state corporation, flies within the country, to selected coastal West African cities, and overseas to London. Its flights, however, are unreliable because of faulty maintenance resulting in breakdowns, overbooking of confirmed reservations, and mismanagement. As a consequence, many potential customers prefer to fly on other airlines or travel by a different mode.

In his 1983 plan, Rawlings set forth the need for an integrated transport policy, covering travel by all four modes. He proposed creating a Ghana Transport Board, and, congruent with his philosophy of decentralization, regional subsidiaries for passenger buses, freight buses, and shipping.

COMMUNICATIONS AND CULTURE

Mass Media

The Ghana government has been directly involved in the mass media through state-owned or -controlled publication of newspapers and periodicals, news agency enterprises, broadcasting, television, and film production. Urban Ghanaians are avid readers of newsprint, and many papers are available. In the early 1980s, four daily papers were published in English; the principal ones, the [People's] Daily Graphic and the Ghanaian Times, are both government owned and published in Accra; The

Pioneer, privately run and subject to government whim, comes out of Kumase. Of the fourteen newsweeklies, three are government owned. In addition, there are privately owned fortnightly publications and monthlies.

The Ghana Broadcasting Corporation (GBC) is the state-owned radio and television company. Ghana radio broadcasts in English but also has programming in six local languages. In 1979, there were 1,800,000 receivers and 65,000 loudspeaker boxes. Those who do not own a radio are not cut off because radios are played at such loud volume that programs are accessible to all. Fewer television sets are in use in Ghana—in 1979, an estimated 55,000—but here too the customary norm of sharing comes into play. GBC radio operates from 5:30 A.M. till evening, with periodic dead times; television programming begins in late afternoon and ends around 10:30 P.M.

"The strength of any government in Ghana can often be measured by its attitude to the press: the weaker its position, the less freedom it allows the newspapers."[12] Throughout Ghana's first twenty-five years of independence, the government has exercised greater and lesser amounts of control, although generally the media are used as a legitimacy engineering device. More often than not, the papers have been used by the state to publish governmental policy and programs. Even though the NLC lifted the censorship imposed by Nkrumah, criticism of the government was in fact not tolerated. During the Second Republic, Busia treated the press harshly; as a result it did not assert itself critically whereas the opposition press flourished.

Although the NRC commissioner for information admonished the press to be bold, objective, and courageous during Acheampong's entire rule, the press was nothing more than the administration's mouthpiece. The new constitution, anticipating the Third Republic, provided for the establishment of a press commission to protect the government-owned press from political pressure. In the interim between the sudden end of SMC II and the start of Limann's civilian rule, the AFRC appointed as editor to *The Daily Graphic* a newspaperwoman who exhibited mettle by criticizing the executions of former political figures.

Under the PNDC, the situation has been somewhat different. Although Rawlings is again at the helm, the PNDC has more

at stake than did the AFRC. The PNDC government has implied
that press neutrality is bogus and that it is the duty of the
media to provide the vehicle for the revolution. Newspapers
thus have extolled workers, decried neocolonialism and imperialism, and published articles excoriating the elite for their wicked
oppression of the masses. GBC radio and television, often
autonomous in name only, have been similarly expected to
broadcast programs documenting Ghana's cultural heritage and
to raise Ghanaian consciousness and self-pride. "Alien" music—
music primarily from the West—had in 1982 been declared
counterrevolutionary and for a time had been banned from the
air waves.

Informal Communication

Informal channels of communication follow kin and, in the
city especially, friendship networks. Churchgoers, Muslims attending mosque, neighborhood residents—all have access to
important pieces of information through their social and spatial
interconnectedness. The birth of a baby is significant news
because it enables a related person to attend to his/her obligations. But in addition to communicating information of this
traditional sort, informal channels keep people abreast of less
parochial goings-on; for those not literate and thus unable to
read the newspaper, or in times of scarcity when newsprint is
unavailable, the network substitutes.

Literature, Music, and the Arts

In Ghana, creative expression falls into two groups: that
rooted in the past and that of more recent origin. But there is
a strong carryover between the two.[13] Traditionally, the recital
of oral literature and the performance of music and dance are
all integrated and often incorporate works of traditional craftspeople and artists, for example, in clothing and paraphernalia.
Formal and informal occasions, such as festivals and rites of
passage, provide the setting for such cultural dissemination.

In many Ghanaian ethnic groups, public worship is neither
quiet nor solemn, but verbal, musical, and kinesthetically active.
The *durbar,* which marks the climax of annual festivals, is kept

exciting by drumming, singing, and dancing, and the participation of everyone present contributes to the solidarity of the group.

Music, like dance, not only finds its way into worship and festivals but also has a purely recreational function. Musicians have singular gifts; yet they express themselves through their membership in the group. Like the storyteller, the performing musician is guided by knowledge of tradition, of how to construct a phrase, and so on.

Artistic productivity is also disseminated in Ghana's cities through such means as television, radio, professional performance, and the printed word. The Arts Council of Ghana is the main organ through which the Ministry of Education and Culture has been fostering, developing, and dispersing cultural expression to the public. In addition, there are officially recognized national cultural associations like the National Music Association. Cultural promotion by the arts council is funded primarily by the state. Traditional music like the Akan *adowa* is recorded and sold on tapes and records. Groups like the African Brothers perform long narrative Twi-language songs in concert. The Ghana Dance Ensemble of the University of Ghana and the Arts Council Folkloric Troupe reflect the significance of the theatre in urban cultural life: These groups present choreographed arrangements of traditional Ghanaian dance both at home and abroad.

Ghanaian novelists,[14] poets, and playwrights are all well represented in modern African literary circles. They emerge from the traditions of oral literature; like old-time storytellers, they are members of the group yet stand apart in their vision, and like other artists, they must be comfortable with cultural images and be able to capture them, in their case through linguistic usage. All celebrate rituals of group life. Some use the rural setting, richly describing traditional custom and its accompanying values, such as fatalism and woman-as-mother. Most, however, depict city life, focusing on such themes as corruption, the appeal of materialism, and neocolonialism. A favorite theme is how traditional norms such as the centrality of the group have simultaneously been undercut and translated into modern terms.

Ghana Film Corporation, established in 1964, distributes films produced within and outside Ghana and produces news-reels, documentaries, and feature and commercial films. Like television programs, Ghana Film productions are notably tied up with governmental interests. Independent filmmaking, however, is gaining hold, and the movie "Love Brewed in an African Pot" has received international acclaim.

The arts, especially in their modern aspect, reflect the depressed situation of the country. Until the 1960s, Ghana was the leading West African country in contributing to contemporary African music, with such pioneers as E. T. Mensah, King of high-life, and E. K. Nyame (an inspiration for guitar bands), and bands like Ghanaba, which composed Afro-Jazz fusions. Poor facilities, nonenforcement of copyright laws, and depression of live music caused by inflation have led the young audience to turn to recorded Western sounds.

SPECIAL GROUPS

Women

In Ghanaian society, women have been traditionally loved and feared and have always represented a force to reckon with. The Akan, the country's largest ethnic group, is matrilineal, and it grants to its women a large measure of political power. Nkrumah realized "as go the women, so goes Ghana" and cultivated their love and goodwill. They became his chief field organizers and were responsible for party solidarity. He repaid their efforts by passing special legislation to admit women to the Ghanaian parliament. The complaints of the market women presaged his downfall.

Women have wielded much power in the economic sphere, most explicitly in their virtual monopoly of the marketplace. Their business sense has kept the market well supplied; however, they have also been closely identified with trade malpractice. In times of economic decline, they have become the government's scapegoat, a policy culminating in the AFRC razing of Accra's Makola Market to rid the country of the women's parallel distribution system.

Even though occupations in Ghana carry gender labels, the government has never discriminated against women in terms of salary. In line with past efforts, current governmental policy purports to raise the status of women by increasing the proportion of women in the labor force and educational institutions. After working for one year, female civil servants are eligible for paid maternity leave for up to three births.

In 1975, the government established the National Council on Women and Development (NCWD) to advise on issues affecting the full integration of women in national development. The NCWD has worked as a conduit for programs launched by the United Nations and other international bodies to reach women; for example, it expanded the coconut oil processing by women in the Western Region. Services for women are run by the Social Welfare and Community Development Departments, the Home Extension Unit of the Ministry of Agriculture, and the Public Health Unit of the Ministry of Health.

Aliens

Historically, long-distance migration has been typical of West African society. Hausas, Fulanis, Mossis, and Arab traders were certainly dealing with Ghana by the eighteenth century. In fact, until recent years Ghana was the major country of in-migration in West Africa, and the cosmopolitan acceptance of outsiders over a long time period had created favorable attitudes toward strangers. Most people migrated because of economics, and migrants experienced neither occupational nor residential segregation. After it gained independence, Ghana experienced a period of "accelerated immigration" resulting from CPP invitation to other West Africans, in line with Pan-Africanism and economic growth.

The development of hostility toward strangers and toward women in Ghana has been tied to the country's economic stagnation and decline, as well as the concern of indigenous people with competition from foreigners.[15] The Aliens Act of 1963 represented the country's first effort to establish immigration laws; new laws were not strictly enforced so that illegal entry continued. The Aliens (Amendment) Act 1965 decreed that noncitizens could enter only at named entry points. And then, in 1970, the Immigrant Quota Committee was set up to scrutinize immigrant applications. The number of foreign nationals decreased from 828,000 in 1960 to 562,000 in 1970, resulting in part from the better economic opportunities elsewhere and the enactment of the Aliens Compliance Order of 1969, which required all working aliens lacking a valid residence permit to leave Ghana within two weeks.

SOCIAL LIFE

The strong sense of interconnectedness instilled in Ghanaians, their appreciation for reciprocity, hospitality, and generosity, although at times onerous—a person cannot easily turn down a request for help from kin—has its celebratory side. Ghanaians are extremely sociable, and they can turn even the traditional obligations of tribe and family into social events. Festivals in Ghana are lavish affairs that aggrandize life-sustaining rituals into pageants; multitudes of people gather and march in procession, dance, pray, and enjoy themselves.

In countryside and city alike, these traditional occasions are feted. Urban dwellers may change the ceremonial aspects to accord with city values: promoting the material side and using the opportunity for display. However, village rites of passage and festivals provide an inducement for city people to visit homes, thereby affirming the town-country link.

Southern Ghanaian groups celebrate "First Fruits" festivals—the Ga *homowo* for corn, Krobo *nmayem* for millet, Akan *odwira* for yam—during which there is much eating, drinking, and socializing and the paramount chief occupies the center of activity. In the north, during Islamic ritual events such as the Salla marking the end of the Ramadan fast or the Damba spectacle commemorating the name of the prophet Mohammed, there are equestrian processions, chiefs and their retinues sit in state to receive homage, and music, dance, and feasting are often excessive. Rites of passage also provide ample opportunity for social intercourse. When a baby is a week old, an outdooring or naming ceremony is performed at dawn; at this time, the child is introduced to the group in which he or she was born

Procession during the annual nmayem (millet) festival in Odumase
(Krobo)

and the social fatherhood established. Among Ga, Akan, Ewe,
and northerners, this occasion provides a good excuse for the
members of the kin group and friends to celebrate. Puberty
celebrations (*dipo*) of Krobo girls involve village people: The
girls have their heads shaved and their naked bodies are layered
with many strands of beads, before they are led into the bush
for their initiation. A marriage or a death similarly calls for
group participation; the lavishness of the event depends on the
importance of the central figures and the wealth of the community. All these occasions include music. Among the Akan,
Ga-Adangme, and Ewe, voluntary musical associations are responsible for entertainment, which benefits not only the spec-
tators but the band members themselves.

     Less traditional events include the leisure-time and recrea-
tional activities engaged in by inhabitants of both the rural and
urban sectors. In this vein, the primacy of football (soccer) for
adults and boys as a spectator sport is incontestable. Ghana
has a national football league composed of regional teams. These

play weekly games, which are often as exciting in the stands as on the field—Ghanaians take the sport seriously! The teams compete for the Club Championship. On a wider scale is the African Cup of Nations, the competition for the African continent. For this event, Ghana's team is made up of players chosen from individual regional teams. In 1982, Ghana's Black Stars won the thirteenth cup, a victory that did a great deal for national solidarity, especially since they beat the team from Libya. When the players arrived home, a traditional libation was poured at the airport.

Both Kumase, the capital of Ashanti, and Accra have racecourses, which are well patronized by all sectors of Ghanaian society. Although many racehorse owners have been foreigners, there is also a sizeable contingent from the northern community, where riding is part of the traditional culture. In addition, there are sports clubs for participant sports, including football, tennis, and cricket. The relatively well-to-do can join Accra's polo club, once a haven for the British but now predominantly Ghanaian in membership.

High-life, the recreational West African urban dance form, is regularly found in Ghana's urban centers. Much like traditional dances, high-life encourages improvisation, and its lyrics speak of big city themes, such as good time girls and the reaffirmation of old norms simultaneous with the creations of new ones. And like the newspapers, the songs often praise or criticize governmental policy. Persons who are underage or cannot afford the admission price often dance outside clubs and hotels where bands are performing. Air-conditioned discotheques, with names like Black Caesar's Palace, have been taking over from the open-air dance clubs; the discotheques play recorded music, have higher entrance fees, and appeal to the well-to-do. Music is everywhere in Ghana's cities—blaring from house radios, record kiosks, and social clubs. Afro-American soul music and Caribbean reggae are overtaking high-life and traditional music in popularity, both for listening and dancing—so much so that their performers are regarded as cultural heroes by urban young people.

Drinking is a highly rated activity and can be enjoyed by all in a variety of locales. In addition to the dance spots, there are local bars, many of which sell *bubra* (beer on draught). In local areas, one can buy the traditional brews—*akpeteshie* from Ga women, palm wine in the Akan areas, *pito* (corn liquor) in the north—to drink on the spot or take home. A shortage of beer bottles led Prime Minister Busia to point to beer drinking in his corruptioin campaign—asking Ghanaians to "discipline their throats"—whereas the PNDC banned the selling of liquor during weekday afternoons ostensibly to cut down on work unproductivity.

More than 100 theaters show films in Ghana. Although some show British and U.S. movies, most cater to the tastes of the masses for Indian and Chinese films and spaghetti Westerns, all of which evoke hearty involvement from the audience, which roars along with the action.

Sunday in coastal areas brings friends and families to the beach, where they bathe, play football in the sand, eat, and drink a lot of beer. On a more informal note, in town and country during free hours people drop in on friends and family at home; hang out at the night markets where prepared-food sellers abound; or sit around the house playing the popular board game Ludu or watching television.

In all Ghanaian leisure-time activities, whether one is participating or watching, the social aspect is paramount. In social interactions, people generally behave according to certain normative patterns. Reciprocity and deference are two underlying principles that help forge social links, for example, between family member and family elder, or analogously between client and patron. According to custom, the successful person is expected to be generous, thereby promoting aid to group members. In African society, wealth is figured in terms of people: The wealthy man is one with many dependents. The "big men," who occupy positions of responsibility normally in the public realm, are thought to make decisions, give orders, look after the material well-being of their inferiors, the "small boys" in turn exhibit deference and reciprocate for favors by giving their support. Those who have achieved elite status in the city are expected, like village big men and chiefs, to help out as many of their close kin as possible; such aid for kin includes helping migrants find employment in the city.

Azu Mate Kole, chief of Krobo, sitting in state during the nmayem festival

IMPLICATIONS FOR SOCIAL CHANGE

Social change in Ghana was induced by the West and has taken a cyclical and uneven course. It has created regional disparities: Economic development has been uneven throughout Ghana. Although northerners are more progressive in their thinking than in the past, they continue to diminish the importance of schooling in general and schooling for girls in particular; despite the primacy of agriculture and a return to the soil, the emphasis on urbanization has undercut the status and esteem of the rural sector.

Second, regional social changes are coupled with those in the social structure of Ghanaian society. As the urban milieu has gained significance, traditional social roles and relationships have been redefined: Men and women, once partners, now compete in economic endeavors; obligations to kin have been more carefully delineated; new elites have supplanted the power of the chiefs. On one hand, the ethnic basis of society has given way to that of class; economic stagnation and decline have exacerbated the scarcity of resources and the rise in corruption. On the other hand, affirmation of traditional group loyalties has surfaced in ethnicity.

Although the process of social change has altered traditional attitudes, many—patience, reciprocity, fatalism, and the centrality of the descent group—have been reworked rather than discarded, thereby facilitating social continuity. Ascriptive identity (such as ethnicity) has been manipulated even as it has given way to achievement-based class. Services traditionally performed by the descent group have been taken over by the state, and neighborhoods and regions, like people, are treated according to the prestige that has accrued to them.

4

The Economy

Ghana's assets, both human and material, have been under-utilized, mismanaged, pulled in different directions, and caught in the stranglehold of hard times. They have been manipulated, unethically if not illicitly, by expatriates, bureaucrats, military men, government personnel, and individual citizens trying to survive.

Ghana's case has been of as much interest to economists as to observers of the political scene because the country held so much economic promise, in both theoretical and concrete terms, when it became independent. Nkrumah sought the advice of internationally known economists (most notably W. A. Lewis) in development planning. Moreover, Ghana's goals appeared attainable: Unlike most developing countries, it had a relatively high per capita income, a high real rate of growth in gross domestic product (GDP), and plentiful cash reserves available for investment.

Even before independence, however, Ghana's economy was described by the Sears Ross Report of 1952 as "fragile." The Ghanaian economy, set up by Britain to supply it with income in the most expedient manner, was overly dependent upon the earnings of cocoa. The First Republic expanded too quickly and in the wrong sectors and spent too much on imported goods, thereby depleting reserves to make up for the increasingly adverse balance of payments.

Thus, the promise gave way to crisis. The country's development planning has had a checkered history, and much of it has never been implemented; the GDP has steadily fallen;

cocoa's decline continues; and with oil bills consuming 40 percent of Ghana's foreign earnings, little is left for investment.

GHANA'S NATURAL RESOURCES

Ghana is well endowed with material resources,[1] in fact almost too much so—a situation that has led to an attitude of complacency. Starvation was traditionally unknown among the subsistence farmers, and if nature's bounty fell short, the folk attitude that "God will provide" was backed by the safety net of the extended family. Moreover, the country is endowed with certain resources that have proved attractive to European interests—to the extent that foreign traders and rulers moved in and encouraged the development of certain sectors. The foreign interest did not in the long run benefit Ghana; instead it created a classic relationship of dependency between Ghana and the European country—the legacy of which continues to threaten Ghana's stability today.

Agriculture

Agriculture is the basis of Ghana's economy, and its importance has been recognized, if not actively supported, by every regime since the First Republic (see Table 4.1). In 1970, the sector employed about 58 percent of the working population. Moreover, as hard times have worsened and the availability of foodstuffs has decreased, a significant proportion of the non-farming population has returned to the soil—commuting from town to hometown—to take up subsistence and cash-crop farming on family lands.

Ghana has three main farming regions: the coastal plain, the southern forest zone, and the northern interior savanna. The country's soils and climate are suitable for a range of field and tree crops. However, the soil is deficient in nutrients, which in combination with the fact that land is abundant and people have little capital, has made shifting agriculture the rational mode of farming. Agriculture is primarily the small-scale production of staples—maize, cassava, yam, cocoyam (taro), and plantain in the south, and maize, guinea corn, sorghum, millet,

TABLE 4.1

PRINCIPAL CROPS (thousand metric tons)

	1980	1981	1982
Maize	390‡	420‡	420*
Millet	66	73‡	90*
Sorghum	106	142‡	150*
Rice (paddy)	62	79‡	90*
Sugar cane	192‡	190*	220*
Cassava (Manioc)	1,800*	1,850*	1,900*
Other roots and tubers	1,420*	1,500*	1,540*
Onions	22*	22*	25*
Tomatoes	130*	140*	160*
Eggplants (Aubergines)	15*	15*	15*
Pulses	11*	11*	12*
Oranges	20*	30*	35*
Lemons and limes	30*	30*	30*
Bananas	7*	7*	7*
Pineapples	5*	5*	6*
Palm kernels	30‡	30*	30*
Groundnuts (in shell)	100*	90*	110*
Coconuts	160*	160*	160*
Copra	7*	7*	7*
Coffee (green)	2‡	2‡	3‡
Cocoa beans	250‡	230‡	190*
Tobacco (leaves)	n.a.	1*	1*

* FAO estimate.   ‡ Unofficial figure.

Source: "Ghana: Statistical Survey," Africa South of the Sahara,
1984-85. Fourteenth Edition (London: Europa Publications, Ltd.,
1985), p. 424.

and rice in the north. Subsistence farming is common in the north, cash cropping in the south.

Despite encouraging rhetoric, the various regimes have not produced any significant increase in agricultural productivity, and the country is still not self-sufficient in food production (Table 4.1). The growth of agriculture (as part of the GDP) from 1969–1971 to 1977–1979) was minus 0.1 percent, and in terms of per capita income, minus 3.1 percent. The production of staple foods like maize and yam, which are eaten everywhere in Ghana, had declined in 1975 by 8 percent from the average for 1961–1965. One-third to one-half of the GDP has been dependent upon the annual cocoa harvest.

Kaneshie Market, Accra

Indeed, in Ghana cocoa is king. In the forest zones of the south where it is grown, and in the country as a whole for which it has been the major export, its earning power, its impact on social relations, and its tie-in with the global economy have been fundamental to domestic social change. The cocoa industry was established by migrant farmers—"rural capitalists"—concerned primarily with expanding their business by acquiring more land, a process made possible by reconciling individual land use with corporate family ownership. The migratory farming process was successful because its traditional foundation recognized the importance of family obligations.

As in many developing countries, part of Ghana's colonial legacy is the persistence of a monocrop economy, even as its earning power has dramatically declined. Between 1958 and 1964, the world consumption of cocoa rose at an annual rate of 5.7 percent and production by 7.8 percent, resulting in a steady drop in price. At the same time, Ghana increased annual production of cocoa, raising its share in world production from 26 to 35 percent. Cocoa accounted for 64 percent of the country's

TABLE 4. 2

COCOA PRODUCTION (in thousand of metric tons)

Year	Production	Year	Production
1960-61	430	1970-71	413
1961-62	409	1971-72	454
1962-63	413	1972-73	407
1963-64	428	1973-74	340
1964-65	538	1974-75	376
1965-66	401	1975-76	396
1966-67	368	1976-77	320
1967-68	415	1977-78	271
1968-69	323	1978-79	265
1969-70	403	1982-83	180*
		1983-84	155*

* from International Cocoa Organization estimates, African Economic Digest IV, 50 (23 December 1983), p. 49.

Source: World Bank Data, 1983.

export earnings. In 1960, 20 percent of the labor force was employed in cocoa production.

Then in 1965, the world cocoa industry experienced its sharpest drop in price, undercutting Ghana's economic (and political) stability (see Table 4.2 and Figure 4.1). From a peak of 566,000 metric tons in 1965, the country's production dropped to 249,000 metric tons in 1979, exclusive of the cocoa smuggled across the borders. Ghana dropped from first to third place in world production, following the Ivory Coast and Brazil. The government, through the Cocoa Marketing Board, had imposed producer price controls; thus, even though food prices rose twenty-two times between 1963 and 1979 and cocoa prices in neighboring countries thirty-six times, Ghana's cocoa farmers' prices went up only six times. Given the soaring inflation rate, the hike was inadequate, and cocoa farmers neglected their trees, changed to farming foodstuffs, or smuggled their yield out of the country. Smuggling apparently accounted for approximately 15 percent of the harvest; in some regions, as much as 80 percent. In 1964-1965, Ghanaian cocoa output peaked at 557,000 metric tons and accounted for more than one-third of the world production; by 1984, that share dropped to less than 12 percent.

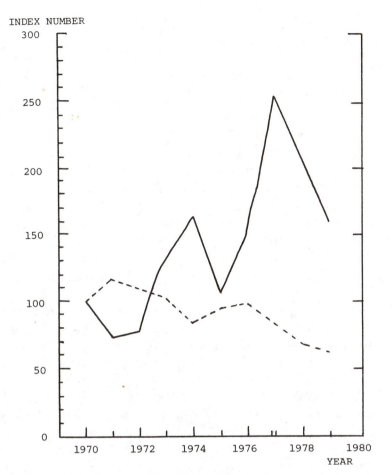

INDEX NUMBER

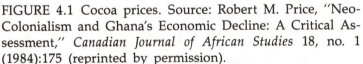

FIGURE 4.1 Cocoa prices. Source: Robert M. Price, "Neo-Colonialism and Ghana's Economic Decline: A Critical Assessment," *Canadian Journal of African Studies* 18, no. 1 (1984):175 (reprinted by permission).

Although other crops were exported—including coffee, palm kernels, and kola nuts—their impact on the Ghanaian economy was minor. Expansion of the cocoa industry took place at the expense of diversification. Cocoa earnings have enabled Ghanaians to broaden their tastes and increase their import of foreign consumer goods as well as industrial materials and spare parts: Economic dependency on the West has thus been assured (see

Table 4.3). Cocoa had at one time provided Ghanaians with a high per capita income relative to residents of other African countries; in 1950, it was highest in the region. But when the bottom fell out of the cocoa market, Ghana lost its primary source of revenue to pay its bills.

Minerals

The mining industry, which has been important throughout Ghana's history, continues to contribute to the country's foreign exchange earnings, even though its contribution to the gross domestic product (GDP) and as an employer of labor has declined in recent years. In 1960, gold, bauxite, and manganese constituted one-fourth of the country's total exports. By 1972, this contribution had decreased to 11.35 percent (industrial diamonds supplementing the percentage by 3.3) and remained at that level in 1975 (actually decreasing, as the contribution of diamonds dropped to 1.4 percent, a decline partly resulting from smuggling). Between 1972 and 1974, gold accounted for 72 percent of mineral exports, diamonds 1.6 percent, manganese 9 percent, and bauxite 3 percent. By 1980, diamond production was only 31 percent and gold only 43 percent of 1961 rates.

The output of the mining industry has been static in part because no new mines have been opened since the 1930s (see Table 4.4). In 1960, mining and quarrying employed 48,221 people; in 1968, 26,236 people; and in 1971, 24,144 people, or only 6 percent of the total work force. Despite this drop in production, there has been a rise in unit values of mineral exports on the world market and a consequent improvement in earnings.

In 1965, the State Gold Mining Company was established, and it controls 35 percent of the industry and supports five gold mines. The sixth mine at Obuasi in the Ashanti region, reputed to be the single largest cache of gold in the world, was leased to the London-based firm in Lonrho in 1968. Much of Asante material culture is based upon the gold trade—the various series of brass gold weights, gold dust boxes, decorative items for the chiefs' regalia, and of course the symbolic Golden Stool. Ghanaian women know and love gold jewelry, and the profession

TABLE 4.3

PRINCIPAL COMMODITIES ('000 cedis)

Imports	1977	1978	1979
Food and live animals	95,568	143,470	178,433
Beverages and tobacco	11,010	22,472	27,695
Crude materials (inedible) except fuels	45,800	42,551	48,344
Mineral fuels, lubricants, etc.	206,405	230,892	483,602
Animal and vegetable oils and fats	11,305	28,633	22,433
Chemicals	159,049	242,807	377,666
Basic manufactures	240,071	287,082	334,800
Machinery and transport equipment	343,232	547,562	768,775
Miscellaneous manufactured articles	40,929	50,368	62,079
Other commodities and transactions	39,943	85,939	42,172
Total	1,193,312	1,681,777	2,345,983

Total imports (million cedis): 2,906 in 1980; 3,041 in 1981; 1,939 in 1982.

Source: "Ghana: Statistical Survey," Africa South of the Sahara, 1984-85. Fourteenth Edition (London: Europa Publications, Ltd., 1985), p.428.

TABLE 4.4

MINING

	1980	1981	1982
Gold ore ('000 kg)	11.0	10.6	10.3
Diamonds ('000 carats)	1,149	836	684
Manganese ore ('000 tons)	250	223	160
Bauxite ('000 tons)	225	181	64

Petroleum (unofficial estimates, '000 metric tons): 300 in 1979; 400 in 1980.

Source: "Ghana: Statistical Survey," Africa South of the Sahara, 1984-85, Fourteenth Edition (London: Europa Publications, Ltd., 1985), p. 425.

of goldsmithing continues to be highly respected in rural and urban areas.

The decline in gold production—from 921,000 fine ounces in 1963 to 402,000 in 1978—is a function of a deteriorating economy beset by problems of transportation, antiquated machinery, and smuggling.

Bauxite, another important mineral, was already being mined during the first quarter of the twentieth century by the British Aluminum Company (BAC). It is ironic that bauxite constituted only 3 percent of Ghana's mineral exports in 1972–1974 because aluminum production was the economic justification for the massive Volta River Project undertaken by the First Republic. BAC, although initially interested, withdrew from the project and argued that the aluminum smelter for which the Akosombo Dam was to provide power was not warranted by global economic conditions. Nkrumah instead transacted a deal with the Kaiser Aluminum Company, which brought in Reynolds Aluminum at a 10 percent share, and created the consortium VALCO (Volta Aluminum Company). In fact, VALCO found it far more economical to import semiprocessed alumina from Korea. As a result, no new mines have been quarried in Ghana, no railroad (which would benefit the country in general) to transport the ore to the smelter built, and no alumina plant constructed.

Diamond mining, like gold mining in Ghana but unlike its sister industries elsewhere in Africa, has decreased in production. In 1956-1957, Ghana was second to Zaire in the value of production and export of diamonds, but by 1973-1974, although it maintained its place in the number of carats produced, it dropped to fifth place in the value of its exports—earning $12 million compared to Zaire's $60 million and Sierra Leone's $85 million. Ghana's diamonds are of industrial quality and are no longer mined by small-scale digging. The only operation has been run by Ghana Consolidated Diamonds, Ltd., which has maintained fairly constant levels of production. The industry's major problem, as it was with gold and cocoa, is not so much output as smuggling.

Timber

Ghana's forest zone supports its logging industry, and after cocoa, tropical hardwoods (obuke, wawa, utile, African mahogany, sapele, and makore are the most important) constitute the country's main export, generating about 10 percent of Ghana's export earnings. Log production developed rapidly during the early post–World War II years, expanded slightly in the 1950s, and has fallen since. Ghana's timber resources have been sorely depleted. As a consequence, the Timber Marketing Board, which governs marketing conditions for export, has very strictly controlled cutting and marketing—so much so that private foreign investors have been put off, exports have been curtailed, and output has stagnated.

More than one-half of Ghana's sawed timber is exported (see Table 4.5). The lumber industry was developed in the 1950s but has since stagnated; sawmills have been operating well below capacity. Besides restrictions on marketing and distributing, the timber industry, like so many other sectors in Ghana's economy, has been troubled by infrastructural woes. Long-distance hauling by train has been inefficient, and logs consequently lie rotting where they were felled.

Hydroelectric Power

In his conception of the Volta River Project (VRP), Nkrumah envisioned that the dam, built at Akosombo, would make power available for industry. However, for VRP to pay off, a major power-consuming industry had to be created; this led to the idea of aluminum production, which would annually consume half the power generated. Because Ghana lacked an indigenous monied class, Nkrumah had to seek foreign investment capital. And anxious to launch this highly ambitious project, he completed the financial arrangements for VALCO on disadvantageous terms: The Ghana government would provide power essentially at cost, grant special tax status for thirty years, and gain little employment relief as a mere 0.03 percent of its labor force (less than 1,000 persons) would be hired and these had to be housed by the government.

TABLE 4.5

EXPORT TRADE

Exports	1979*	1980	1981
Cocoa	1,846,269	1,942,176	1,091,258
Logs	54,192	n.a.	41,236
Sawn timber	60,235	n.a.	57,833
Bauxite	7,947	8,508	7,145
Manganese ore	29,243	n.a.	22,176
Diamonds	30,073	27,543	22,521
Gold	208,414	522,862	435,507
Total (incl. others)	2,863,000	3,458,000	2,924,000

*Provisional figures
1982 (million cedis): Cocoa 1,053.3; Total (incl. others) 2,402.0.

Source: "Ghana: Statistical Survey," Africa South of the Sahara,
1984-85. Fourteenth Edition (London: Europa Publications, Ltd.,
1985), p. 428.

Akosombo Dam

As mentioned earlier, the necessity of importing semiprocessed bauxite deprived Ghana of an integrated aluminum
industry.

Ghana's economic development has not been aided by VRP.
In fact, the project provides another unfortunate example of
"the development of underdevelopment" whereby more wealth

has been taken out of the country and nothing put back in. Ghana's electricity generation jumped from 527 million kilowatt hours in 1965, the year before the dam was completed, to 1560 million kilowatt hours in 1967, with little benefit to the country. The terrific depletion of Ghana's reserves and the stagnation and decline of the economy have meant that the industrial sector intended to be supported by the VRP has yet to be established.

Human Resources

When it attained independence, Ghana was well endowed with human resources. In the late 1950s, primary school enrollment was twice that of the next highest West African country. During those halcyon days, the public service was efficient, and the supply of skilled labor was adequate, with deficiencies occurring primarily within the professions. And yet for the Seven-Year Development Plan of 1964 to be fulfilled, the amount of skilled human resources had to triple because the stock of skills was small and the population growing fast.

The population has continued to grow whereas the reservoir of skilled labor, including professionals, has lost ground as the brain drain ravages the country in the face of economic travail. The state has not been successful in galvanizing its citizenry into increasing productivity. In 1970, 84 percent of the men and 64 percent of the women contributed to the country's work force. Yet, the work potential has not been utilized effectively, and unemployment and underemployment have become growing problems, especially in urban areas (see Table 4.6). Thus, even if terrific shortages of labor occur in select areas, there has also been terrible unemployment. The manufacturing sector, for example, has never been sufficiently developed to absorb labor. In 1960, 23 percent of the people were urban dwellers; yet 44 percent of the country's unemployed lived in the cities. Urbanization and migration to the urban areas accelerated unemployment—the larger the town, the greater the incidence of joblessness—particularly among those between the ages of 15 and 24.

Among persons with some schooling, employment levels are higher for the more educated; however, in the entire pop-

TABLE 4.6

ECONOMICALLY ACTIVE POPULATION (1970 Census)

	Males	Females	Total
Employees and workers on own account	918,736	1,046,109	1,964,845
Salaried employees and wage earners	662,715	94,648	757,363
Family workers	136,477	274,362	410,839
Total employed	1,717,928	1,415,119	3,133,047
Unemployed	141,467	57,104	198,571
Total labour force	1,859,395	1,472,223	3,331,618

In 1970 about 58% of the economically active population were in agriculture.

Source: "Ghana: Statistical Survey," Africa South of the Sahara, 1984-85. Fourteenth Edition (London: Europa Publications, Ltd., 1985), p. 424.

ulation, including those with no schooling, employment levels are higher for those with no education, because of the large number of primary- and middle-school dropouts within the educated force who cannot find jobs. One cannot help but wonder at the enormous expansion of the educational system undertaken without a parallel expansion in the appropriate job sectors. Middle-school dropouts, for example, seek clerical work, a sector that is saturated. They have a strong aversion to manual work—an attitude inculcated during the colonial era and reinforced in modern times—and often prefer no employment to a job they perceive as beneath them.

The higher the incidence of unemployment, the fewer female workers are likely to find work. Although they are noteworthy because of their influence in the marketplace, only about 3 percent of Ghana's economically active females work in the public or private sector; most pursue informal-sector work (such as small-scale trading) or a cottage industry (such as pottery made at home).

Migrants have been an important source of labor, but their contribution, in fact their labor-based migration, has been short-circuited by the processes of unemployment and underemployment. During Nkrumah's years as head of state, Ghana's economic expansion, coupled with Pan-Africanism and an open-door policy, attracted large numbers of international migrants, primarily from neighboring countries. Most were unskilled; a few were professionals. In terms of proportion, four times as many immigrants as indigenous people were employed in mining; many immigrants worked as craftspeople. And in 1971, aliens constituted 50 percent of the male merchant class. In southeast Ghana, more immigrant males were employed in the rural rather than the urban sector. Many of those who migrated to the city found daily life insuperable, because of high prices and low wages. They therefore moved into the informal sector and provided important services in petty enterprises. Some aliens have performed specialized roles: The Zabrama work as *kayakaya* (porters) and black marketeers in currency, the Hausa trade kola and art, and the Yoruba import textiles. Overall, they have made few inroads into the skilled sector, but they have contributed greatly to agriculture, mining, and service. As is the case with women who do not work in either the public or the private sector and whose work is not included in descriptive labor statistics, many of these informally employed aliens are not registered as workers.

International or interregional migrant workers have been supplemented by internal migrants, most notably rural dwellers moving to the city. In rural areas, underemployment constitutes a push factor in the decision to move, and immigrants unfortunately exchange it for urban unemployment. Those newly arrived in the city, like arrivals from other countries, lack skills and contacts and have difficulty locating employment in the formal sector. Those who find jobs are often hired for menial tasks that others cannot or will not do for reasons of custom, status, or taste. The night-soil collectors, for example, are generally northerners—Dagomba and Frafra—and night watchmen include northerners as well as Malians and Voltaics.

After independence, the percentage of expatriates who lived and worked in Ghana increased considerably, although their proportion still was not large—2.3 percent of the total population in 1960, decreasing to 1.5 percent in 1968. These non-Africans, who were predominantly Asians, Europeans, Lebanese, and Syrians, performed important economic functions. The Lebanese and Syrians, like the Yoruba and Hausa, operated tight trading networks. Large-scale wholesale and retail businesses were owned and operated by Europeans, Indians, and Syrians, whereas Syrians and Indians also ran smaller-scale merchandising establishments. Expatriate trading firms wielded considerable influence over their home governments and the Ghana government as well, and they were loath to encourage local manufacturing industries that would undercut their import/distribution activities. As a consequence, they hindered local industrial development, reinforced relations of dependency, and obstructed labor force expansion.

When in 1969 African and non-African aliens alike came under scrutiny and threat of deportation, all levels of economic activity suffered. The decree had been promulgated to keep the running of small businesses in the hands of Ghanaians, but it succeeded primarily in dissolving crucial trade networks, making certain commodities altogether unavailable, and depriving the country of the expertise necessary in running such businesses. Some Europeans remained as advisors, administrators, or managers ostensibly until the gaps in these upper echelons could be filled by trained Ghanaians. Some of the larger expatriate enterprises, such as department stores, were unaffected. However, as business ground to a halt in the mid-1970s, expatriate firms and businesspeople began to withdraw, and foreigners were no longer able to withstand the unmitigating and worsening shortages and left.

GHANA'S ECONOMIC STRUCTURE

Industry and Manufacturing

Nkrumah's dream was to develop Ghana into a modern state as rapidly as possible. Modernization implied industrialization. The CPP chose a socialist approach to ensure that economic progress would not occur at the expense of social justice, freedom, and equality. Since Ghana was in a transitional situation, its desire for economic independence from foreign competition could be achieved either by state control or by the establishment of an indigenous entrepreneurial class (which Nkrumah had no desire to create).[2]

Through industrialization, the Ghanaian government expected to reduce the country's reliance on manufactured imports and transform Ghana from an agricultural to a modern industrial state. The Industrial Development Corporation (IDC) was set up before independence to develop publicly owned commercial enterprises, and the First Republic channeled government participation in industry through the IDC until it was dismantled in 1961. According to the framework of the Second Development Plan, in 1959 there were three categories of industries: (1) state-owned and controlled, including railroad transport, electricity generation for public sale, radio broadcasting, waterworks, telecommunications, and cocoa export; (2) mixed state and private, with government participation mandatory; and (3) free enterprise. Subsequently, a fourth category, that of the cooperative, was appended to dissuade Ghanaians from initiating private business ventures. The development plan promoted the establishment of 600 factories, producing 100 products; however, by 1964 only thirty-seven government-owned industries were operating, including those built under the aegis of the IDC.

State farms, run by the State Farm Corporation (SFC), were set up in 1962 as part of the state corporation program to increase growth in the traditional agricultural sector, diversify exports, and reduce the need to import food. By 1964, these cooperative ventures were operating in only 1.2 percent of the cultivated farmland, and by 1965, the SFC was overseeing 105 farms. The ambitious goals of the Seven-Year Plan were not reached; productivity was low mainly because of labor redundancy, inadequate personnel, inefficiency, and corruption in management. After the 1966 coup, many farms were abandoned, some were sold to private foreign firms, and a handful continued as state businesses.

All in all, the state industries were eminently unsuccessful. Experimentation with state farms, industries, and controls went awry, apparently because the CPP used them as instruments of patronage and corruption. Joint state-private enterprises were more profitable than those run by the state alone—including a large textile plant and a soap factory set up with United Africa

Company and an oil refinery built by the Italian State Oil Firm.
After state control proved ineffective, the NLC offered foreign
business concerns the opportunity to take over state enterprises,
and in the years since, the government has floundered in
maintaining operation of such basic industries as telecommunications (which has retrogressed) and cocoa (which has declined).

Thus, Ghana's economy is predominately one of private
enterprise, with industry constituting a comparatively small
sector. Only a small group of large establishments use modern
forms of organization and capital-intensive technologies that
many regard as the manufacturing sector proper: the aluminum
smelter at VALCO (owned by two U.S. companies), the petroleum
refinery, sawmills and plants for processing timber, and factories
for cocoa processing. Other locally based industries produce
consumer goods, including crackers and cookies, cigarettes, and
cement.

Although the manufacturing sector has grown, factories
have been operating far below capacity. Ghana Industrial Holding
Company (GIHOC), for example, makes construction nails and
paper clips, and until 1980, it operated twenty-four hours a
day. However, because the country's economic crisis has worsened and terrific shortages of raw materials and spare parts
have developed, the company is now operating at less than 5
percent capacity.

Trade

Foreign trade has been crucial to Ghana. It has earned the
foreign exchange necessary for capital investment and enabled
the country to import essential consumer commodities and raw
materials.[3] Ghana's trading partners include the United Kingdom,
constituting 16.2 percent total trade in 1974; other European
Economic Community (EEC) countries, 25 percent; the United
States, 11.1 percent; USSR and Eastern European countries, 8.4
percent; and Japan, 6.1 percent. Patterns of foreign trade have
been significant insofar as they dovetail with and cement political
relations. During the early years of independence, the proportion
of Ghanaian trade with Britain—the former colonizer with whom

all sorts of ties remained—was larger than it is today. During that period, economic exchange with the Soviet-bloc countries was also strong; in 1966, it exceeded 20 percent of total trade. And in 1982, after his return to power, Rawlings signed major trade agreements with Libya, his major base of outside support.

Export earnings have been stable, fallen, risen, fallen—fluctuations resulting in large part from the size of the Ghanaian cocoa crop and the world cocoa price. As cocoa exports have increased, the country's dependence on imported foodstuffs and other consumer items has grown. Government controls have had little positive effect and have caused shortages. In 1968 for the first time in ten years, there was a trade surplus. Throughout the 1970s, the pattern was one of imbalance, with imports outdistancing exports. Attempts at industrialization have increased the dependence on imports since Ghana does not produce the necessary raw materials, such as the agricultural products needed for agrobased industry (sugar, cotton).

Between 1972 and 1974, external trade was based upon four exports: cocoa (60.8 percent), minerals (14.3), timber (14.1), and aluminum (6.6). After the 1973 oil crisis, oil imports rose two and one-half times in cost, and imported goods consisted of consumer items (23.8 percent), raw and semiproduced materials (40.1), capital (19.7), and fuels and lubricants (16.4 percent; up from 5 percent in the previous year). Low agricultural production has meant not only high prices for local foods but large expenditures for imported food.

Ghana's global dependence is a colonial legacy. Foreign trade has always been crucial to the export enclave set up during colonial Gold Coast days by foreign firms in conjunction with the British government. Through it, raw materials were exported and manufactured goods imported. Thus, like the geographic distribution of products, the ownership carried a colonial orientation. Trading, mining, and logging businesses and banks, shipping, and insurance companies were foreign owned when Ghana became independent. Infrastructural development coincided with foreign-oriented needs—an educational system to support the imposed civil service structure, the institutional setup of the export enclave—and profits were sent out of the country rather than being reinvested in Ghanaian enterprises.

Industrialization was accompanied by a reduction in foreign-owned enterprises, abetting Ghana's sense of independence. With stagnation and declines in economic fortunes, however, Ghana's trade has suffered.

Foreign-currency problems, taxation, and controls have all resulted in the curtailment of imports, including desirable consumer goods as well as spare parts essential to industry. Aggressive economic policies have included the limiting of private foreign investment, the abrogation of foreign debts, and Ghana's assumption of majority control in certain industries and banks. The dependence on cocoa has afforded Ghana little leeway around its dependence on the outside world and its income-earning capacity.

Domestic commerce centers on locally produced foodstuffs, and it is almost wholly controlled by Africans. Trading is the largest occupational category in Ghana: Very little of it can be classified as store trading; most is open market commerce. This informal-sector activity has been carried out by highly competitive entrepreneurs working on a small scale. It has been the potentially most rewarding economic activity for an untrained or illiterate woman, and in Accra the vast majority of gainfully employed women have been traders.

The significance of internal trade is reflected in amounts of monies spent on local foodstuffs—ten times as much as on imported foods. This trade includes raw foods—maize, yam, bananas, oranges, and other types of produce, and meat, fish, and poultry—as well as prepared foods. Throughout the country, in city and rural area alike women hawk everything from snack foods (fried plantain or yam, roasted peanuts or oranges) to a complete meal such as rice and stew. The marketplace belongs preeminently to the women's world. Male traders are few and specialize in such products as charcoal, meat, and Islamic paraphernalia. The latter two products are traded mainly by Hausa. Other types of exchange are similarly carried out as ethnic specialties: Yoruba women and men trade in textiles, Hausa in kola nuts, Ga women in fish.

Internal trade is highly flexible in Ghana; it easily accommodates other obligations, such as women's domestic responsibilities, sellers' varying levels of education, and entrepreneurs'

Salaga Market, Accra

different amounts of capital. At one end of the spectrum are the petty traders, who deal in the single cigarette, and at the other are the cloth traders who purchase multiple bolts of fabric. The clever and lucky salesperson has a chance for upward mobility.

Individual control of domestic distribution and sales has been cut down considerably by price controls and, under the PNDC, has been taken over first by the army and then by cooperative shops. Both represent an attempt to guarantee judicious distribution by depriving the market "queens" of their monopoly.

Finance

From the time of the First Republic until the present, Ghana's administrators have mismanaged the country's finances. In his visionary approach to development, Nkrumah sought revenue and loans to finance his ambitious plans rather than ensuring the country's year-to-year stability. Each of his successors, in attempting to neutralize and reverse the havoc, has set out a strategy in reaction to that of the preceding regime, either pursuing new policies that have been ineffective or returning to features of the course Nkrumah charted, which has also miscarried. In tandem with the state's changing tides, the economy has gone through phases of expansion and contraction, stabilization and liberalization, and stagnation and decline. And financial policy—what little there has been—has failed to rescue Ghana from the quagmire.

In Ghana, fiscal policy has called for price controls and trade restrictions to reduce demand for imports, or these restraints have been rescinded. Capital expenditure cuts have been instituted, freezing project development or halting unprofitable enterprises, and then a new capital improvement program has been launched. The cedi has been devalued in the wake of budgeting crises and then revalued. Different forms of taxation have been tried—direct deduction from wages and surcharges on merchandise, to name two.

The overall trend has been a rise in government expenditure as a result of expansion, ever-increasing demands for imported consumer goods and industrial materials, and political graft—but without parallel increases in revenue. Government receipts have either fluctuated or dropped, following the fortunes of cocoa. When controls have been imposed, they have not been properly supervised. As in other developing countries, low income levels and unsystematic collection procedures have produced little income from taxation.

The official positions of the Ghanaian government on the desirability of foreign investment, like policies of fiscal management, have fluctuated in line with ideology while also reflecting the scope of the economy at any given time. The combination of these two factors has created untenable inconsistencies. For example, Nkrumah launched a relatively large number of capital-intensive projects even though he lacked indigenous sources of capital. Thus although he inveighed against foreign investors and pursued policies unpopular with them, he needed and erratically sought such sources. Heavy expenditures, fluctuating revenues, and pervasive corruption resulted in budget deficits, which in turn necessitated heavy borrowing. In 1957, Ghana had external assets of $450 million; the country's enormous foreign-debt problem began within the next few years (see Table 4.7).

During the five years following the 1966 coup, the Ghanaian government gave more support to private entrepreneurial activities. Even though certain economic activities were reserved for Ghanaians, more open policies led the government to collaborate with foreign concerns and attempt to lure public and private capital from outside. Busia's government reoriented its political economic policy toward the West. After he was ousted from power during the January 1972 coup, governmental posturing and policy included little to attract foreign investment or deter it; international banks apparently refused Ghana credit in 1979 because it was far in arrears in short-term debt repayment.

The Limann administration offered concessions in hopes of attracting overseas money to complete the Bui Dam in Brong-Ahafo. Rawlings's reentry into power, initially characterized by such slogans as "down with Western imperialism" and by realignment with Libya, did little to ensure confidence in Ghana's stability for foreign investors. The terrific hardships imposed by

TABLE 4.7

SELECTED EXTERNAL DEBT-INDICATORS, 1970-1982 (US$ millions)

	1970	1975	1979	1980	1981	1982	1970-82
Total debt outstanding including undisbursed (DOU)	565.6	894.8	1,429.6	1,557.0	1,455.5	1,397.3	
External debt, disbursed and outstanding (DOD)	489.4	676.0	978.0	1,104.8	1,102.9	1,100.8	
Annual growth rate (%)	7.0	-3.8	14.6	13.0	-0.2	-0.2	7.0
As % of total GDP at m.p.	24.9	14.7	9.5	7.5	5.2	3.5	
As % of exports of goods & NFS	103.6	75.9	84.3	87.2	123.6	112.4	
External debt service	23.7	47.7	70.3	93.5	56.0	64.8	
Annual growth rate (%)	n.a.	76.7	7.5	33.0	-40.2	15.7	8.7
As % of total GDP at m.p.	1.2	1.0	0.7	0.6	0.3	0.3	
As % of exports of goods & NFS	5.0	5.4	6.1	7.4	6.3	6.6	
Interest Payments	11.7	19.3	30.2	28.4	25.3	27.7	
Annual growth rate (%)	n.a.	48.5	25.8	-6.0	-10.9	9.5	7.5
As % of total GDP at m.p.	0.6	0.4	0.3	0.2	0.1	0.1	
As % of total exports of goods & NFS	2.5	2.2	2.6	2.2	2.8	2.8	
Other Indicators							
Annual growth rate of imports of GNFS (%)	26.0	-3.7	9.0	17.3	-22.1	-13.9	5.2
Annual growth rate of exports of GNFS (%)	22.1	20.0	16.5	9.2	-29.5	9.8	6.3
Official reserves as months of imports of GNFS	1.2	1.9	3.0	1.7	1.7	1.8	

Source: World Bank Data, 1983.

TABLE 4.8

INTERNATIONAL RESERVES
(US $ million at 31 December)

	1981	1982	1983
Gold	48.2	68.8	72.5
IMF special drawing rights	0.7	0.2	2.2
Foreign exchange	147.3	142.2	142.6
Total	196.2	211.2	217.3

Source: "Ghana: Statistical Survey," Africa South of the Sahara, 1984-85. Fourteenth Edition (London: Europa Publications, Ltd., 1985), p. 426.

the 1983-1984 budget, however, succeeded in obtaining IMF and World Bank money.

The PNDC succeeded in attracting foreign aid: New commitments in 1983 amounted to $178 million, and total disbursements, $103 million. The IMF alone contributed another $239 million, and in 1984, $159 million. In 1984, apart from IMF money, new commitments and total disbursement rose to $460 million and $280 million, respectively. These figures include a 1983 World Bank Reconstruction Import Credit of $40 million and an 1984 Export Rehabilitation Project credit of $93 million.

Ghana's debt burden has been largely caused by foreign moneylenders, who have been overly eager to proffer loans, and by suppliers, who are keen on attracting new customers and quick to extend credit (see Table 4.8). The NRC's repudiation of some debts and rescheduling of others still left the country with a 1979 debt of $1,334.8 million; the debt servicing in 1979 amounted to $54.6 million.

GHANA'S ECONOMIC DECLINE

Economic Indicators

Some basic economic indicators clearly reveal the extent of Ghana's economic decline (see Table 4.9).[4] The 1979 per capita gross national product (GNP) of $400, although higher than figures for much of Africa, obscured the fact that between 1960 and 1979 the country's growth rate dropped an average of

TABLE 4.9

INDICES OF ECONOMIC PERFORMANCE 1961-1980

	Gold (1961=100)	Diamonds (1961=100)	Cocoa (1961=100)	Index of Manufacturing Production (1970=100)	Food per cap. (1965=100)	Consumer Price Index (1963=100)	Gross Domestic Investment[a] (1966=100)	GNP[a] per capita (1960=100)
1961	100	100	100			87	125	100.7
1962	106	99	95			95	--	102.8
1963	110	83	97			100	--	102.8
1964	103	83	101			102	--	102.8
1965	91	71	129			151	140	100.6
1966	82	88	95			171	100	97.9
1967	91	79	87			157	70	97.9
1968	89	76	96			169	75	99.1
1969	85	74	77			182	87	103.7
1970	84	79	85	100	99	189	110	111.6
1971	84	80	91	109	93	206	121	114.3
1972	87	73	107	85	81	227	60	108.2
1973	97	72	97	103	87	266	82	110.7
1974	74	80	81	101	88	315	115	113.9
1975	62	72	87	97	75	409	98	105.0
1976	64	72	92	74	74	639	67	96.1
1977	70	58	74	71	71	1383	44	94.4
1978	48		62		68	2401		94.4
1979	46		59		70	3695		94.4
1980	43	31				5547		
1961-70 (mean)	94.1	83.2	94.2			140.3	101.0	102.7
1970-79 (mean)	70.6	73.2[b]	83.5	92.5[b]	80.6	973.0	87.1	104.3

[a] At constant prices.

[b] 1970-1977.

Source: Robert M. Price. "Neo-Colonialism and Ghana's Economic Decline: A Critical Assessment." Canadian Journal of African Studies 18, 1 (1984), p. 166.

minus 0.8 percent a year. Despite tremendous efforts at productivity—in 1965, investment as a proportion of GNP was 22
percent—even ephemeral increases in output were tiny. Although
production showed an early flurry of growth, it stagnated and
declined. In 1969-1970, GDP rose 2.1 percent, but between 1970
and 1979, it dropped an average of 0.1 percent per year. During
the latter period, only services increased by 1 percent, with
agriculture and industry declining 0.2 and 1.5 percent, respectively. The structure of production shows the extent to which
growth has been idle—it registered $1,220 million in 1960 and
by 1979 had only increased to $10,160 million—and the extent
to which industry has not caught on. Agriculture constituted
41 percent of production in 1960 and *rose* to 66 percent in
1979; during the latter year, industry composed 21 percent of
the structure. In the 1974–1978 period, the GDP was estimated
at 5 percent; however, given a 2.8 percent annual population
increase and the upward spiraling of inflation, the decline in
per capita GDP and real income was 2.9 percent. The per capita
income that in the early postindependence days provided Ghanaians with a degree of comfort above that of other African
countries has been badly eroded.

Real income has dropped despite many wage and salary
increases since the first minimum wage legislation in 1960—
increases based more on politics than on productivity. With the
PNDC's 1983-1984 austerity budget, the minimum wage was
more than doubled to reduce glaring instances of inequity
between civil and public-service employees. Yet a worker earning
the minimum wage of ₵25 per day (equivalent to $9, up from
the 1960 rate of $.15) could barely afford to feed his or her
family once a day (see Table 4.10 for list of market prices).

Ghana's average annual rate of inflation of 7.6 in 1960–
1970 rose to 32.5 percent in 1970–1979; however, the latter
figure camouflages the triple digit rate of inflation that has
occurred almost every year after 1977. This inflation was caused
by wage increases not justified by productivity; by increases in
import prices (since 1973, the price of crude oil has gone up
925 percent); by bad harvests in 1976 and 1977 (local food
prices contributed considerably to total inflation; by an increase
in food prices of 150 percent in 1977 and 59 percent in 1978);

TABLE 4.10

MARKET PRICES OF SELECTED FOOD ITEMS IN ACCRA

Item	Unit	Average prices (¢)		
		January 1982	January 1983	April 1983
Maize	bag (50kg)	500	1,000	4,000
Maize	American tin (3kg)	30	80	200
Kenkey	ball	1	4	10
Cassava	tuber	10	15	25
Gari	American tin	15	65	190
Yam	tuber	45	80	160
Rice	bag (50kg)	600	900	1,200
Rice	American tin	80	200	200
Plantain	bunch (100)	160	250	1,000
Plantain	one	4	5	20
Tomatoes	3	4	10	40
Meat (beef)	lb	20	30	60
Bushmeat	(grasscutter)	250	450	600
Chicken	2lb	45	75	180
Eggs	crate (30)	80	90	180
Eggs	one	3	4	8
Sugar	American tin	70	150	300
Sugar	cigarette tin	5	15	25
Bread	loaf	4	disappeared	disappeared

Note: ¢2.75=$1.00

Source: J.A. Dadson, "Food and the Nation," West Africa, July 11, 1983, p.1597.

and by huge budget deficits. Since the early 1960s, the Ghanaian government has habitually resorted to financing, a policy resulting in mounting deficits from the banks and an excess demand in the economy. In this way the government has produced an inflationary trend. By 1978-1979, the country's overall budget deficit was $727.27 million.

The low degree of integration among various economic sectors in Ghana, by no means a recent phenomenon, has hindered efforts at diversifying production and increasing industrialization. Moreover, sectoral productivity has worsened. Between 1974 and 1978, the worst decline occurred in those sectors most closely allied to the state nexus. The resurgence of a subsistence economy and petty trading mark a reversion to economic activities outside state control.

The acute balance-of-payments problem may be the best known feature of Ghana's economy (see Table 4.11). The government has suffered continuous deficits in current accounts since 1959, except in 1972-1973 when it was able to enforce sharp cuts in imports and received favorable returns on exports. During the late 1950s, badly developed public services constituted a bottleneck to economic growth. Thus, the First Republic was involved in heavy public investment and infrastructural development—the expenditures for which were financed largely by the favorable cocoa revenues. Between 1961 and 1965, government expenditures grew faster than revenues, and when in 1960-1961 the deficit increased by 35.6 percent, it was financed with foreign reserves. The persistent problem of deficits is a legacy of the First Republic, exacerbated by waste and improper use of resources, as well as by a low tax ratio and difficulties in taxation. In 1971, the cumulative pressure of deficits of $206 million and depleted reserves (down from $39 million at end 1970 to $19 million one year later) and pressures to pay resulted in a balance-of-payments crisis and a 44 percent devaluation of the cedi. And like the payment crisis in 1966, it was "resolved" by a military takeover.

Themes that characterize social and political behavior are also evident in Ghana's economic rise and fall. The tolerance and patience of the citizenry, which allowed the situation to get out of hand, have also enabled the people to survive in the

TABLE 4.11

SUMMARY OF BALANCE OF PAYMENTS 1970-82 (million US$)

	1970	1975	1978	1979	1980	1981*	1982*
Exports of Goods	472.4	891.1	996.0	1177.4	1315.9	802.9	669.2
Imports of Goods	502.6	881.5	1072.8	1096.0	1313.0	985.8	707.8
Resource Balance	-30.2	9.6	-76.8	81.4	-2.9	-182.9	-38.6
Trade Balance	80.0	150.4	112.7	262.6	184.3	-22.3	98.2
Factor Services	-44.5	-36.3	-27.6	-39.0	-66.3	-62.7	-60.4
Net Transfers	7.0	44.6	58.3	79.4	79.7	82.9	82.4
Current Account Balance	-67.7	17.1	-46.1	121.8	16.3	-162.7	-16.6
Capital Account (net)		68.8	116.2	97.7	209.5	-85.1	179.7
Net Government Borrowing	67.8	23.7	114.4	100.7	189.7	58.8	148.0
Direct Private Investment		45.1	1.8	-3.0	19.8	26.3	31.7
Errors and Omissions	16.6	37.3	-145.6	-108.0	-158.6	-197.6	-106.7
SDR Allocation	--	--	--	14.2	14.3	12.7	--
Overall Balance	--	124.0	-75.5	125.7	-81.5	-262.5	56.4

* Provisional estimates

Source: IMF

face of fluctuations and continual decline in the Ghanaian economy. Individuals have been forced by scarcity to fight for themselves and have reactivated networks to redistribute goods and services as the state has increasingly lost control. Although Ghanaians are fatalistic about the state of the economy, their spirit of participation has been roused: People have gone from muted complaining to group demonstrations of anger and disapproval to creating productive strategies to cope with ambiguity and disarray. The old reciprocity has been resurrected in new ways as Ghanaians meet the challenge of their country's decline.

An Explanation of Ghana's Decline

The economic policymaking of each postindependence government depicts an encompassing picture of decline—fiscal crises, inequalities and scarcities, overextension and loss of state control, plummeting productivity, loss of morale, if not outright despair. Factors of internal and external origin[5] have been singled out to explain Ghana's underdevelopment.

Poor policy design—an inability or disinclination to plan rationally—has been pinpointed as a cause of Ghana's economic chaos. At an early stage, the state assumed too much responsibility for development at the same time as its external assets were dissipated, export earnings had stagnated, and foreign investment was falling. It placed too much emphasis on industrial development at the expense of agriculture, and within the agricultural sector, the small holder was disregarded if not victimized. Even though the early enthusiasm for state farm enterprises did not pay off, government policy continued to ignore peasant farmers; even cocoa farmers were undercompensated. Moreover, despite the centrality of cocoa to the economy, constraints on productivity (such as the age of the trees) were not carefully studied. The contraction of agricultural productivity furthered the country's dependency on food imports, eating up foreign exchange that could have been more profitably utilized elsewhere. Policy failures during the 1969–1979 period have been attributed to fiscal and monetary measures that produced extraordinary inflation, exchange rate policy, pricing, ceilings on interest rates, emphasis on distribution rather than production, and unplanned increases in expenditure.

Along with policy failure have been mismanagement, institutional weakness, and governmental malfunctioning. The government has often lacked the knowledge to act effectively, and its lack of direction has been exacerbated by vacillating ideologies among its administrations. Moreover, political instability has undermined opportunities for strategists to envision the results of their policies, as when Busia devalued the cedi. Because administrative agencies have proved incompetent to carry out their tasks, new ones have been added to the old. The proliferation of such offices has resulted in massive administration and little coordination. Mismanagement has meant that policies with potential have often gone untested. A corollary is the Ghanaian problematic work ethic. The wheels of government turn very slowly, partly because of the cumbersome bureaucratic machinery and partly because of the lassitude of government workers. The latter arrive late, take long breaks, barely apply themselves while behind their desks, and refuse to accept posts in rural areas.

The more the Ghanaian state has overseen economic regulation and management, the greater has been the scale of inefficiency, the overstaffing of parastatals, and the corruption. The state's economic policies have created a setting in which money is made through repugnant actions with unfortunate results: By undercompensating cocoa farmers, the government fostered a disincentive to produce high yields and a desire to smuggle the beans into countries where the growers' price was considerably higher.

Corruption is offered as another internal cause of Ghana's incapacitation. The country's economic structure and its exploitation may be regarded as a "kleptocracy" whereby bureaucratic/military functionaries have garnered extra income, often large amounts, through embezzling and other corrupt practices. Corruption has been observed in all the various regimes, although its prevalence varied. The CPP syphoned off monies for party purposes, and individual members enriched themselves. The National Housing Corporation handed over the allocation and administration of 800 houses built for workers in Sekondi-Takoradi to local CPP officials, to those offering bribes, and to Accra-based members of the Ghanaian parliament.

During the Second Republic, Busia launched a campaign against bribery and corruption; at that time policemen and customs officers extorted money at border crossings and government employees took bribes in exchange for favors. The economic policies of the Acheampong regime particularly abetted corruption and black-marketeering: Acheampong and his cronies openly pursued such immoral behaviors as ordering import licenses for themselves and their girlfriends. In the midst of Rawlings's revolution, robed judges were overheard wheedling bribes in exchange for favorable rulings.

The question has not been whether corruption exists in Ghana or even its extent, but whether it is rooted in Ghanaian historical, cultural, personal, or structural conditions, and thus whether it is a manifestation of underdevelopment or a cause. If corruption results from economic uncertainty, then it does not explain the etiology of the situation; however, if it was caused by other factors, then it may well be viewed as an agent of the country's deterioration. In any case, it is certainly bound up with the mismanagement and ineffectuality of the economic machinery.

Events beyond Ghana's control were a final internal cause of Ghana's decline. In 1976 and 1977, and again in 1982, 1983, and 1984, drought conditions prevailed in Ghana. Since farm water sources are predominantly rainfed and thus vulnerable, the development of adequate irrigation systems is crucial. In 1983, bush fires destroyed such field crops as plantain, yam, and cassava. The quadrupling of oil prices in 1973 helped drain the country's reserves. And the return of 1 million Ghanaians from Nigeria has strained Ghana's labor absorptiveness.

Domestic factors, such as state intervention, shortage of capital and technical know-how, neglect of infrastructural maintenance, decline in efficiency, fiscal mismanagement, and so on go far toward explaining the telescoping inequalities, regional imbalances, neglect of one sector in favor of another, and daily suffering endured by Ghana's citizens. These internal issues have fed into an already precarious economy—an economy, like many in the Third World, that is caught up in the vice of a colonial legacy, underdevelopment, and dependency. The British set up Ghana's economy in a manner inappropriate to Ghana's needs; they integrated it into the world capitalist system and undercut its potential for autonomy. They severely neglected the northern half of the country, even depleting its human resources by channeling labor southward into the cocoa farms and the mines. Focusing upon the export sector, they established a monocrop economy. Even though timber and minerals have brought in significant revenue, cocoa has overwhelmed them by its earning power. Moreover, all three products have been at the mercy of the world market. Although Ghana's leaders have attempted to break the country's dependence on cocoa, the extent of autonomy possible is limited. Thus Ghana has been a victim of cocoa fluctuations on the world market, which were particularly pronounced between 1960 and 1965. As a result of a drop in export earnings and of terms of trade, economic growth became more difficult. For example, attempts to correct regional imbalances in development required capital that the country simply lacked.

At the same time that cocoa revenues were dropping, the prices of imports were rising. Most prominent was the quadrupling of the price of crude oil. In addition, funds for spare parts and consumer items sapped the country's resources, and indebtedness to outside countries and to the banking system grew. Rather than employ the country's working capital for development, the government has used it to pay import bills, and outside wheeler-dealer suppliers have tightened their hold. Foreigners have encouraged patterns of consumption that are not in Ghana's interest and engaged in questionable if not illegal practices. Their enterprises have not been labor absorptive and have thus added to underemployment, and overall they have perpetuated colonial patterns.

These conditions working in concert help to explain Ghana's downward spiral and the loss of state control over the economy. No matter how competent its policymakers and implementers, as Ghana's export earnings depend upon an ever-changing world market, its fortunes could not be controlled from within. However, constraints imposed by structural dependence do not explain why the economy's descent was worse than ever when cocoa prices were booming in the late 1970s. Here issues of malfeasance and profiteering within Ghana cannot be disregarded.[6]

The state lost control over resources and hence lost its power as a redistributive center. Its attempts to enlarge the public sector and to ensure its productivity have not succeeded. Nkrumah's dream of raising the common person's standard of living has not been realized. Programs of economic growth have frequently given way to strategies for sheer survival. In its decline, Ghana has experienced a loss of income, of buying power, of commodities to buy, and of status among its own people and with the outside world.

STRATEGIES FOR ECONOMIC SURVIVAL

Suffer-Manage Strategy

Ghanaians have fashioned four strategies to respond to the worsening conditions in their country.[7] The first of these—the suffer-manage technique of survival—has enabled people to cope within conventionally approved codes of conduct. By this approach, as the cost of living has skyrocketed and basic necessities have either become terribly expensive or disappeared, people have tightened their belts and adjusted their tastes. The suffer-manage strategy is primarily an urban phenomenon. It is exhibited by people tied into the wage-earning sector, who are accustomed to the "perks" of modern living that they see dwindling and who are affected by a dropping real income coincident with the frightening hike in the cost of living.

The suffer-manage practitioners have learned how to deal with the shortages on all fronts. They have cut back on purchases, found substitutions, endured annoyances, returned to traditional usages, made purchases outside the country, or done without. Their eating behavior is characteristic: Their caloric intake has decreased and malnutrition has become a major problem. In Accra, following Rawlings's austerity program, many people ate a proper meal once a day and sometimes only once every two days. With the price of yams climbing as high as ₵400 per tuber off season and only decreasing to ₵100 in season, some people substituted cocoyam or cassava (popularly demeaned as "inferior" foods). The practice of buying prepared food from street vendors instead of cooking meals, common during Limann's time, was revived under the PNDC administration; the cost was lower because the food sellers could buy the ingredients at lower prices. Furthermore, they varied their fees according to how much protein matter was included in the portion. People also coped with Ghana's scarcities by driving to Lomé, Togo, where they commonly purchased soap, sugar, milk, rice, flour—whatever product was hard to find at home. Only those with foreign exchange, however, could exercise the option of leaving Ghana to make purchases.

The expense and shortage of gasoline and spare parts have affected private car ownership and travel in general. Those whose vehicles suffered cosmetic disrepair, like broken window handles, devised substitutes or left it unrepaired. More serious automobile problems, like a broken headlight, meant erratic usage or driving under perilous conditions. Many were forced to abandon their cars altogether. At the same time that more people clamored for public transportation, transport owners and drivers were afflicted by gas and spare parts shortages. Travelers were resigned to waiting for hours in long lines or walking long distances. Similar adversities struck health care, education, and other basic services.

This kind of coping necessitated a reallocation of time. Queuing in line for food, for example, or keeping one's personal network greased to increase access to goods in short supply required time and energy normally applied to work. Along with the rebudgeting of time, families had to rebudget the ways in which they spent their limited funds. More money went into basic necessities, as well as the transportation necessary to make purchases. More and more, housewives and even children sought ways to augment household income.

Beat-the-System Strategy

A second strategy—both cause and outcome of the chaos—is that of beat the system. Most Ghanaians have remained in the country to face deprivation, but unlike the suffer-manage types, the second group's survival has involved various forms of illicit dealings, known as kalabule and in its more recent form as warabeba. These schemes involve the activation of an

Queue for food, 1979

informal economy parallel to the country's formal one. Run outside of the bounds of the state, it sometimes competes with the formal sector, more often supplies what the formal sector cannot, and operates to the advantage of diverse groups of individuals—housewives, professionals, underworld people, the unemployed, government workers—but rarely to the advantage of the state.

Kalabule consists most notably of smuggling operations, especially for cocoa and to some extent for rice. In 1979, the former head of the Border Guards was executed for engaging in smuggling. An estimated four-fifths of the 1980 Volta Region crop of cocoa was either smuggled to Togo or left unharvested. Both gold and diamond smuggling have also taken their toll on the formal economy.

Hoarding when prices were low (on goods as diverse as toilet paper, soap, cloth, and tinned fish) and black-marketeering when goods were virtually unavailable were closely related to smuggling as kalabule methods of survival. The most visible people involved were the market women, and they were singled out for abuse and blamed for the sorry state of the economy. In fact, they were by no means the only ones involved in such activities: People of all walks of life hoarded goods and trade on the side—not out of wickedness but as a means of survival.

Corruption and embezzlement, two more components of the kalabule technique of maximizing gain, were mechanisms to divert monies and goods from the formal to the informal sector. This technique was evinced by the appearance of foods, such as grains and cooking oil donated by aid agencies, in their original containers in the markets. Less apparent and more heinous was the syphoning off of public funds into individuals' pockets and misuse of import licenses.

Outlawed by the PNDC, kalabule was succeeded by warabeba (derived from a Twi expression meaning "you will bring yourself"). The connotation was that the goods were available at high prices, but they were not out in the open as in kalabule times. The term implied that "you will suffer for it before you get it," and "you will only get it then by gaining access to the trader." The prices of warabeba goods surpassed those for Limann era kalabule goods. Soldiers took advantage of their role as distributors and confiscators: They were said to steal commodities or buy them at control price, then to give them to a middleman to sell at a higher price, and finally to pocket the profit. Creative strategies were mythicized. The very desirable Dutch wax cloth was seemingly nowhere to be found. But it was said that the cloth traders had retired to the broom section of the market, had tied the ends of the lengths of straw with a swatch of cloth, and the interested customer could choose a pattern of cloth from the brooms; the cloth was then brought out from hiding. Officials continued to be paid to be sure that they would carry out tasks that in fact were part of their jobs. Government workers sought out foreign exchange just as they had in the past, but they did so more discreetly.

The dual system created by the beat-the-system strategy furthered the deterioration of the already precarious economy. Those engaging in it sapped the formal sector and thus the state of the energies of its workers and the revenues they generated. It broke down social cohesion: The individuals involved put their own interests and those of their group above those of the state.

Escape-Migrate Strategy

The third coping mechanism is the escape-migrate strategy. Like the first alternative, its use is concentrated among the urban wage-earning people, who are most affected by fluctuations in the economy. Ghanaians traveled extensively in West Africa and to Europe in search of employment or commercial opportunities. Becoming significant in the mid-1970s, the escapist strategy took on drastic proportions by the end of the decade. It involved two groups of people: (1) the urban unemployed and unskilled, who sought positions elsewhere and were willing to perform even menial jobs, and (2) the skilled and highly educated. The brain drain resulting from the exodus of the latter group depleted the professions, the universities, and the secondary schools. The Nigerian and Liberian authorities became especially vigilant in regulating illegal entry, and a scandal erupted when forty-two Ghanaians suffocated in a prison in the Ivory Coast.

Return-to-the-Farm Strategy

The fourth strategy, like the first two, included people who had decided to stay in Ghana. Unlike these two strategies, however, it represented an innovative attempt at refining the traditional mode of survival—returning to the land. By withdrawing from the state-centered market economy, Ghanaians settled into subsistence and cash-crop agriculture—farming and raising cattle and poultry. Retired members of government, professionals, and entrepreneurs reactivated their rights to lineage land, relocated in the countryside, or spent increasingly larger blocks of time there. Given the proportional preponderance of agricultural-sector workers, this return to the land represents a reworking of customary economic behavior.

Ghanaians' Survival

The strategies and self-reliance of the Ghanaian people who chose to stay—manifested in their adaptability through innovation, on the one hand, and reactivation of traditional networks and behaviors, on the other—have kept them going and even enabled the state to continue, if not to flourish. Often strategies are mixed and matched, depending upon the individual's circumstances, needs, access to resources, and dependents or patrons. Emigration might prove necessary for a time in order to build up some capital; farming might be pursued when a family has small children to feed. The people of Ghana have coped and survived; they do not sit and introspect. Consumed by the exigencies of daily life, they deal in very concrete ways. Illegal activities multiply as people lose jobs or business dries up.

The paradox of Ghana's situation is that the very patience and fatalism of its people and the uncritical enthusiasm with which they embrace each new regime have allowed their situation to get so far out of hand, and yet these very attributes have kept Ghana afloat. The attitude of Ghanaians seems to be that once they were rich and today they are poor—that's how life is. But as they say, perhaps with patience, tomorrow they will be all right again.

5

Ghana and the International Order

Two prominent features have marked the development of Ghana's international relations since it gained independence. The first is diversity. Successive regimes have experimented with a variety of foreign-policy approaches that have run the gamut of nonalignment, open collaboration with the West, self-reliance, isolation, and supplication to foreign countries. The second characteristic is decline. When Ghana became independent in 1957 it assumed, by virtue of its birthright and the predisposition of its founding father, the mantle of leadership on the African continent. Since then Ghana's preeminence both internationally and regionally has persistently eroded, its influence has waned, and its original centrality has been replaced by a marginality reflective of severe, and perhaps inexorable, external deflation.[1]

In this chapter we are concerned with coming to terms with the manifold manifestations and underlying reasons for Ghana's changing international fortunes. We first examine fluctuations in foreign-policy approaches, then look at shifts in the structure of Ghana's external alliances. Next, we assess changes in Ghana's global standing and finally attempt to uncover the explanations and evaluate the implications of the paradoxical pattern of variety and weakness that has been the hallmark of Ghana's international contacts to date.

FLUCTUATIONS IN GHANA'S FOREIGN POLICY

Ghana's emergence as a sovereign entity on the world scene was not necessarily accompanied by a substantial increase in its freedom to maneuver. Like the citizens of other postcolonial states, Ghanaians had been exposed during the preceding centuries to a series of unequal contacts with the outside world. The inequality and marginality that marked the Gold Coast's uneven incorporation into the international system were glaringly apparent at the time of the country's independence. By 1957 the new state of Ghana was not only positioned on the periphery of the global nexus but was also subordinated, especially in economic terms, to external forces beyond its grasp.[2] All Ghana's leaders have been acutely aware of their country's dependence and of the limitations this condition imposed on the types of relations Ghana could conduct with other states.

Nkrumah's foreign policy can be described as activist, outward oriented, and multifaceted. For the first president, engaging in international politics was a vital extension of his efforts to reconstruct Ghana domestically. As an essential instrument of innovation, foreign policy was crucial to attract investment yet to challenge capital, to improve the quality of life, to enhance the meaning of change, and to alter the self-image of Ghana and Africa in the world arena.

The overall strategy developed by the leaders of the First Republic was aimed at breaking Ghana's inherited dependency through maximization of alternative sources of financing and realignment of levels of external interaction. The purpose of this counterintegration approach was not to withdraw from foreign contacts but rather to restructure Ghana's international ties by expanding their scope and increasing their range. Nkrumah's perspective was thus explicitly global: His sphere of operations was continental and international and his outlook at once historically conscious and forward looking.

Nkrumah was concerned with projecting a forceful, glorified African presence onto the world scene, thereby bringing about the rapid amelioration of the African condition.[3] The range of his foreign-policy interests was hence emphatically sweeping. The political focuses of Ghana's external relations revolved around three critical issues. The earliest and continually the most engaging issue was African liberation. A second, interrelated topic was Pan-Africanism. The CPP government underwrote preliminary conferences on African unity in the late 1950s, pioneered the creation of the first inter-African agglomeration (the Ghana-Guinea-Mali Union), helped to organize the Casablanca bloc of progressive African states, fostered personal ties among African leaders, and—despite initial hesitations—was instrumental in establishing the Organization of African Unity (OAU).[4] Pan-Africanism was inextricably linked by Nkrumah to the third political pillar of Ghanaian foreign policy at the time: socialism and nonalignment. Nkrumah forged the way for African participation in the Afro-Asian movement and, at the height of the cold war, purposefully diversified and balanced Ghana's ongoing links with the West with stronger and increasingly variegated ties to the Soviet bloc.

Nkrumah's conception of economic matters was broad as well, centering at the outset on elaborating trade links, encouraging foreign investments in capital-intensive projects, securing new sources of aid, and attracting labor from neighboring countries. Even later, when much energy was expended on renegotiating external debts and coming to terms with Ghana's creditors, Nkrumah persisted in promoting a variety of economic ties abroad.

In the military domain, the Nkrumah government constantly played an activist role. Foreign contacts were seen as ways to fortify Ghana's security by providing diverse sources of training and equipment. At the same time as Ghana's own military base was being solidified, the CPP regime engaged in armed ventures elsewhere, including the Congo intervention in 1960, the establishment of training camps for members of Southern African liberation movements, and the 1965 announcement of the intention to send forces to intervene in Rhodesia following Ian Smith's unilateral declaration of independence. These connections were rounded off by elaborate educational and cultural exchanges during the Nkrumah years.

To support the complex network of Ghana's external contacts in the early 1960s, Nkrumah augmented the machinery for the conduct of foreign affairs. The Ministry of External Affairs was expanded, over sixty ambassadors were dispatched to foreign capitals, and a special Bureau for African Affairs was created.[5] Thus, although the contradictions between political ends and economic needs, between the stress on investment and the challenge to foreign capital, between dreams of Pan-Africanism and overt subversion of African governments, and ultimately between continental concerns and Ghanaian interests became increasingly evident in the 1960s, these paradoxes need not overshadow the broad vision and heterogeneous nature of Ghana's foreign policy during the Nkrumah years.

The transitional government of the NLC consciously narrowed the terms of Ghana's international exchange. Ghana's foreign policy under the NLC was preoccupied with economic matters: The most important issues understandably were aid, investment, and debt rescheduling. Although the NLC verbally advocated Pan-Africanism, liberation, and nonalignment, it did not turn its attention to the political dimension of foreign affairs nor did it seek new avenues of cultural or military exchange.[6]

The scaling down of external interests and priorities was accompanied by a reduction in Ghana's foreign contacts. Twenty Ghanaian missions were closed, and the size of overseas delegations was pared down to conform to the new low-profile policy. The style of foreign relations also underwent a noticeable change: The leadership position endorsed by Nkrumah was relinquished without fanfare. Ghanaian concerns replaced African and global ones. Foreign policy shifted focus to more local concepts of development, and the previous emphasis on change was replaced by a more pragmatic concentration on the present. As a transitional government, therefore, the NLC sought to erase Nkrumah's excesses on the external front and to redirect the scope and content of Ghana's foreign policy.

Many of the substantive changes introduced by the NLC were pursued and further elaborated during the short years of the Second Republic. In Busia's capitalist political economy orientation, concerned as it was with augmenting productivity and rural growth under the guise of minimal state intervention, foreign policy was an indispensable tool for the effective execution of an investment-based free enterprise experiment. It was also another means of escaping from the continuing shadow of the Nkrumah period. If the state itself had to be temporarily mortgaged to further these development objectives, such an action was excusable, or so it was posited, if the necessary capital could be attracted to secure the ground for Ghana's economic future.

The foreign-policy strategy adopted by the Progress party government therefore involved collaboration with Western interests and financial concerns in the name of traditional partnerships, economic growth, and international responsibility. The scope of Ghana's foreign network was reduced accordingly; initiatives were carefully muted; a cooperative, low-keyed style was effected; and development issues were pushed to the forefront of external considerations. The collaborative stance of the Busia government was most evident in the constriction of Ghana's international contacts at this time. Such contacts came to focus almost entirely on economic matters: The subjects of foreign discourse included investment and aid, debt negotiations and development planning, economic policy and technical expertise. At the same time, Busia, in an attempt to counteract Nkrumah's stance on many issues, pulled back from nonalignment and Pan-Africanism. Rather surprisingly he called for a dialogue with South Africa, thereby discarding the clear internal consensus on the need to support African liberation movements.[7] This conscious curtailment of the topics in foreign policy was in keeping with the perception that it was inadvisable for Ghana to provoke Western concerns needlessly on matters without immediate import to the Ghanaian situation.

The conduct of Busia's foreign policy illustrates the changing substance of external relations. The reduced position of the foreign ministry imposed by the NLC continued throughout the Busia years. More to the point, trade and economic delegations, often headed by the prime minister himself, took on a critical role as funnels for foreign relations. This shift indicated the contraction of Ghana's international perspectives at this juncture: The critical lines of communication had become more a response to the need for negotiation between Ghana and its Western creditors than any concrete indication of policy initiatives.

The content of Ghana's international links during the brief years of the Second Republic helped to confirm the neocolonial image associated with the Progress party administration. Busia's conventional approach to global issues—a near obsession with reversing past patterns—precluded the adoption of an innovative, forward-looking conception of Ghana's position in the world arena. His policies fostered a prevailing sense of weakness in style, implementation, and results. If any pattern could be deduced from these links, it was one of an externally imposed logic that narrowed the terms of Ghana's international exchange.

The effects of foreign meddling in the Ghanaian political economy were high on the agenda of the military government of I. K. Acheampong when it came to power in 1972. Foreign policy was an inextricable part of the NRC's self-reliance program. The official stance became one of global disengagement and strident self-encapsulation. Although economic subjects were paramount in the NRC's external outlook, political topics were reinstated in Ghana's foreign policy during this regime. Indeed, the containment stance was accompanied by a new Ghanaian assertiveness, most readily apparent in the NRC's commitment to Nkrumah's notions of Pan-Africanism and African liberation. In 1973, Ghana took the chair of the OAU's liberation committee, renewed its pledge to assist freedom fighters, and engaged more actively in negotiations for the creation of an Economic Community of West African States (ECOWAS).[8]

Although these moves may have had little effect on Ghana's global position, they did alter the tenor of its external contacts. As cooperative efforts were amplified within Africa, Ghana's links with countries in the Northern Hemisphere assumed an explicitly confrontational tone. Disengagement was therefore coupled with a new militancy and self-reliance with a quest for cooperation among equals.

During the second half of Acheampong's tenure, when Ghana's economy was in almost complete disrepair, foreign-policy statements continued to articulate Ghana's goal of self-reliance at the same time as external actions belied their meaning. Foreign relations became the key vehicle for state survival and the primary hope for relief from economic chaos. Unable either to guide internal events or to stem a growing civilian revolt, Acheampong turned to foreign countries to prop up his floundering regime: His stance was one of overt supplication. Within the narrow range of economic concerns, the SMC dealt almost exclusively with the fulfillment of basic needs. By 1976 the substance of foreign relations revolved almost entirely around demands for food aid, working capital, supplier credits, and essential medical goods. All other considerations were thrust aside in this desperate effort to avert Ghana's total economic and political collapse.

The focuses of Ghana's external contacts at this juncture were no longer dictated by its ruler's preferences, but rather by inexorable needs. From Nkrumah's early stress on foreign policy as a means of attaining rapid qualitative improvements and Busia's emphasis on more limited maintenance and development concerns, Acheampong's objectives narrowed down to employing foreign contacts to ensure minimal survival. Past and future issues in foreign policy were noticeably absent: The present predicament became the sole concern. These circumstances make it hardly surprising that emphases shifted constantly, that policies were often haphazard, and that it was impossible to discern a logic behind maneuvers even in the limited economic sphere.

The regimes following that of Acheampong have had to operate within the substantive straitjacket inherited from their predecessor. SMC II under Akuffo institutionalized Ghana's dependence by acceding uncritically to IMF directives. And although Jerry Rawlings lashed out against imperialism and uncontrolled foreign influence, the Armed Forces Revolutionary Council was not in office long enough to formulate a cohesive foreign policy.

Hilla Limann, therefore, had little recourse but to court foreign concerns in an effort to attract sufficient capital to keep Ghana afloat. With an external debt of close to $4 billion, a worrisome backlog of over $1 billion in debt repayments, and few indigenous resources on which to draw, Ghana's leaders had few alternatives to increased dependence. During the brief civilian interregnum of the Third Republic, political economy and foreign policy became virtually synonymous. Not only did affairs with other countries hinge on economic subjects, but within this constricted spectrum survival issues replaced development concerns as the central topic of foreign policy.

The Provisional National Defence Council, unable to reverse past trends but also unwilling to bow to foreign interests, at first struck a strident antiimperialist posture. Fueled partly by economic considerations and partly by fears of externally backed conspiracies, Rawlings opted during 1982 to separate Ghana from its African neighbors and traditional Western partners in hopes of managing on the handouts of its most prominent ally, Libya. The PNDC made overtures to the Soviet bloc and Cuba as it tried to withdraw Ghana from the dependency web in which it was entangled.

But by 1983 Ghana was encumbered by a morass of unequal obligations that could not be dissolved by rhetoric alone. Although Rawlings continued to challenge the dependence on Western capitalism and to decry the neocolonialist ventures of his predecessors, he labored to acquire international approval and tangible Western support. IMF missions were entertained and foreign donors consciously placated in an effort to overcome external disinterest. Under the PNDC, Ghana's conformity to Western conventions differed more and more from the defiant parlance of many of Rawlings's original supporters.

Not only did the focus of Ghana's foreign policy fluctuate over the years; the actual nature of the country's external interests in the 1980s contrasted sharply with those in the 1960s. The range of topics embraced by the country's foreign policy lost the diversity of the early Nkrumah days: The focus shifted to securing foreign support to prop uneasy ruling coalitions. Passivity, always accompanied by Ghanaian dignity, replaced initiative as the trademark of exchanges with other countries. In the final analysis, the contents of Ghana's international links underwent severe substantive and qualitative constriction. Instead of a concern with change and amelioration, foreign policy came to be viewed as a means of persistence, then of preservation, and finally, of possible salvation. These strategies are a far cry from the vision of continental glory and international power entertained by Nkrumah at independence.

SHIFTS IN GHANA'S EXTERNAL ALLIANCES

Fluctuations in Ghana's foreign policy were accompanied by changes in the structure of its foreign partnerships. The tempo of these shifts, as well as their limitations on Ghana's international standing, can best be gleaned from a closer look at changing alliances on regional, continental, Third World, and global levels.

Ghana in West Africa

When Ghana became the first black African state to achieve independence from colonial rule, it seemed destined to be a leader in West Africa. But Nkrumah's preference for militant Pan-Africanism at the expense of closer links with his West African neighbors set the stage for over two decades of ambiguity in Ghana's ties with other countries on the West African littoral.

Indeed, Nkrumah disdainfully shunned notions of regionalism, viewed at that time as significant precursors to African unification. As he saw it, "even the idea of a regional federation in Africa is fraught with many dangers. There is the development of regional loyalties, fighting against each other. In effect, regional federations are a form of balkanization on a grand scale."[9] Although territorially based agglomerations were unacceptable to Nkrumah, he believed that ideological ones could play an important role. The CPP regime therefore forged a confederal alliance with Guinea and Mali in the hope of creating a progressive group of states committed to the ideas of radical Pan-Africanism. The Ghana-Guinea-Mali Union was designed to bring together the socialist regimes of West Africa in such a vanguard. Despite some ideological affinity, the countries' lack of territorial contiguity, differing precolonial and colonial experiences, and varying economic concerns virtually doomed this organization from the outset. And although the personal friendship between Nkrumah and Ahmed Sekou-Touré of Guinea survived Nkrumah's political demise, the union itself became one of the first failures in the attempt at transnational political unification in Africa.

Nkrumah's quest for an ideological network antagonized Ghana's most immediate neighbors [Togo, Upper Volta (now Burkina Faso), and the Ivory Coast] and created tensions with Nigeria and Senegal. As a result, Ghana's relations with bordering countries during the First Republic were both competitive and sporadic. Ghana's frontiers were more often closed than open, and other West African leaders were wary of what they considered Nkrumah's not very subtle efforts to subvert their power and undermine their regimes.[10]

The discord and suspicion fostered by Nkrumah lessened somewhat after his ouster. Both the NLC and the Progress party governments took pains to reestablish bilateral links with moderate West African states. They placed particular emphasis at the outset on establishing a modus vivendi with the surrounding francophone states—Ivory Coast, Togo, and Upper Volta. Kofi Busia's first journey outside Ghana after his election was to the Ivory Coast. Other officials visited Togo, Upper Volta, and Dahomey (now Benin). Even relations with Nigeria, which had been marked by intense hostility, were repaired somewhat immediately after the change in government in both countries. Although a short period of quiescence ensued in Ghana's West African ties, the Ghanaian-Nigerian connection was strained during the Nigerian civil war. Busia further aggravated ties with Nigeria and other West African states when he expelled tens of thousands of nationals from these countries.

At the time of Busia's political demise in 1972, Ghana's relations with nearby states were again at a low ebb, and Acheampong tried to alter this picture. The West African connection was, in fact, a critical facet of the SMC's quest for self-reliance. Acheampong therefore made a concerted effort to improve ties with Ghana's neighbors. Ghana and the Ivory Coast signed a friendship and cooperation treaty in 1973, and Ghana hosted the heads of state of Dahomey and Togo. President William Tolbert of Liberia paid a visit to Acheampong and ratified an agreement to create a joint cooperation commission; trade treaties were negotiated with Niger and Nigeria. Diplomatic links were renewed with Gabon, and declarations of friendship were promulgated with other states. The intricate variations of specific relationships with other West African states gave substance to Acheampong's search for meaningful regional links. These efforts culminated in 1975 when Ghana actively endorsed the creation of the Economic Community of West African States (ECOWAS),[11] a regional economic association aimed at achieving the gradual integration of West African economies. The ECOWAS framework enabled Ghana to concentrate horizontal ties in a multilateral framework and to use the West African forum as a stepping stone for concrete exchanges with other countries.

Acheampong's West African alliance did not survive the upheavals of the late 1970s. Nigerian-Ghanaian relations were strained once again following the Nigerian decision to cut oil exports to Ghana in the wake of the June Fourth (1979) Revolution. The porous Togolese and Ivorian borders became the center of contention in Ghana's relations with these countries as smuggling activities increased in the kalabule economy. By 1979 when the Third Republic was inaugurated, Ghana had developed an unequal bilateral relationship with Nigeria and the Ivory Coast, the magnet countries for Ghanaian migration. Tensions with these states persisted throughout Limann's term of office. Stories of mistreatment of Ghanaian migrants in the Ivory Coast and Nigeria led to official Ghanaian protests. An atmosphere of recrimination clouded Ghana's relations with the stronger West African states.

These tensions did not abate after Jerry Rawlings's return to office. Nigeria complained about the harassment of Nigerian nationals by the PNDC. Rawlings, in turn, suggested that other countries harbored armed dissidents of the new regime. In early 1982, Ghana finally sealed its land borders in an attempt not only to avert subversive activities against the government but also to contain smuggling operations. This closure generated undue suffering in January 1983, when over 1 million Ghanaians expelled from Nigeria tried to make their way home to their beleaguered country. Only in the midst of the repatriation effort was the frontier with Togo reopened. Since then, Ghana has tried to repair relations with the Ivory Coast, Nigeria, and Burkina Faso (Upper Volta).

Ghana, Pan-Africanism, and Continental Unity

If ambiguity characterizes Ghana's regional connections, the country's continental links have been marked by an admixture of fierce theoretical commitment and of fragile real ties. Kwame Nkrumah was perhaps the most forceful postcolonial propagator and elaborator of the Pan-African dream. "The emancipation of the African continent is the emancipation of man. This requires two aims: first, the restitution of the egalitarianism of human society, and, second, the logistic mobilization of all our resources towards the attainment of that restitution."[12] Nkrumah defined the goals of Pan-Africanism in political terms: the creation of a continental power united in its commitment to liberation, development, and global reciprocity. "A union of African states will raise the dignity of Africa and strengthen its impact on world affairs. It will make possible the full expression of the African personality."[13]

Nkrumah devoted considerable energy to promoting his notion of African unity. In the late 1950s he hosted a series of conferences for independent African states with a view to preparing the groundwork for the creation of a United States of Africa. He allied himself with like-minded leaders (Abdel Nasser, Patrice Lumumba, Ahmed Sekou-Touré, Modibo Keita) who were also committed to the idea of political unification. In 1960, with the Congo crisis in full swing he despatched Ghanaian troops to aid Lumumba's precarious regime and to serve notice that Ghana would stand by its African brothers against any external attempts to meddle in its affairs.

In 1961 in anticipation of a major Pan-African drive, Nkrumah spearheaded the creation of the Casablanca bloc. This association of progressive African states championed maximum African unity and global nonalignment. The verve with which Nkrumah pursued his Pan-African dream alienated as much as it enthralled his African cohorts. During the years preceding the establishment of the OAU in 1963, the continent was divided between moderate and radical states, between Pan-Africanists and advocates of regionalism, between proponents of functional cooperation and adherents of political union; in short, between pro- and anti-Nkrumah forces.

The organization finally created at the Addis Ababa summit was a far cry from the political superpower that Nkrumah had conceived. But the OAU nevertheless was the first concrete embodiment of continental unity. Nkrumah's role in its symbolic and actual gestation cannot be underestimated. Indeed, after 1963 the OAU provided the main multilateral setting for Ghana's African policy and the key channel for Ghana's inter-African contacts. Within the OAU, special attention was given to the issue of liberation in southern Africa. When the 1965 summit was held in Accra, Ghana was once again at the forefront of the African call for the complete and total decolonization of the continent. To accentuate this commitment, just prior to his ouster Nkrumah called for the creation of a Pan-African command and promised to send a Ghanaian detail to fight against the rebel white regime of Ian Smith.

Nkrumah emerges, in retrospect, as the embodiment of African nationalism and the personification of the quest for continental unity. Even though his relations with other African states were often intermittent and problematic, his contribution to the establishment of an African community has survived after his domestic political power ended.

During the years after Nkrumah's withdrawal from the political scene, Ghana's continental activism lapsed. Although both the NLC and PP governments proclaimed their continuing support for the OAU, in reality neither administration encouraged Ghanaian militancy in the African arena. Formal contacts with other African states continued within the OAU framework until Busia broke the continental consensus on the South African question: In 1969 he challenged the organization's unwillingness to communicate with the white rulers of South Africa and called for a constructive dialogue with the racist state. This move effectively detached Busia's Ghana from African currents and exposed his regime to severe criticism at home.

Acheampong sought to bring Ghana back into the continental fold after the uncomfortable Busia hiatus. He reaffirmed Ghana's commitment to Nkrumah's vision, encouraged active participation of Ghanaians in OAU activities, pledged funds to the organization, assumed the leadership of the OAU liberation committee, and put out a call for volunteers for African freedom.[14] This Ghanaian involvement in the OAU and its allied organs continued unabated throughout the 1970s, despite the SMC's capriciousness on other issues. Although Hilla Limann, in the Nkrumaist vein, reavowed the importance of inter-African cooperation, in November 1980 he closed down the Libyan embassy in Accra, and at the OAU summit in Nairobi he led the opposition to the decision to hold the 1982 meetings in Tripoli.

When the PNDC came into office, one of its first actions was to restore diplomatic relations with Libya, which gave Ghana oil on concessionary terms. In fact, Muammar Qaddafi was rumored to have backed Rawlings's return to power. The close alliance between Rawlings and Qaddafi at the outset of PNDC rule cast a shadow on Ghana's continental activities. When the OAU summit to be held in Tripoli was twice postponed in 1982, Ghana was accused of siding with Libya and of creating discord within the continent.[15] During 1983 and the early part of 1984, however, Ghana made an effort to reconsolidate continental relations. Close ties with Libya nevertheless continue.

Ghana's advocacy of the Pan-African cause and its preference for regularizing contacts with other African states through the OAU machinery have survived internal domestic upheavals and external criticisms. The symbolic value that Nkrumah attached to the notion of continental unity has been adopted and refined by the next generation of Ghanaians. But Ghana's own standing in Africa has not kept pace with the commitment of its citizens, nor have Ghanaian activities on the continental level always been consistent with the appeal for inter-African harmony: All too frequently a gap has developed between Ghana's assertion of Pan-Africanism and the fragmented status of its African alliances.

Ghana and the Third World

Ghana's relations with Third World countries began with Nkrumah's quest for new partners. The first president of Ghana fostered links with countries in North Africa, the Middle East, Asia, and Latin America. In the Middle East, he nurtured contacts not only with Egypt and other progressive Arab states, but also with Israel. In Asia, he established close personal relationships with Jawaharlal Nehru and Mao Tse-tung, and sought to augment direct contacts with other leaders as well. He was one of the first African statesmen to recognize the revolutionary regime of Fidel Castro and to establish an African connection with South America. Kwame Nkrumah placed Ghana at the forefront of the nonaligned movement, and what is more significant, he helped to mold Third World states into a strong coalition at the United Nations. Indeed, Nkrumah was one of the first African leaders to recognize the importance to the continent of this international body. He was instrumental in forming the nonaligned Group of 77, and in creating an active and cohesive African bloc at the United Nations.

Nkrumah's sensitivity to Third World issues was not shared by the leaders of the Second Republic. But as global ties shifted in the early 1970s, Ghanaian interest in Third World matters was revived. The country's previously subdued relations with the Arab world assumed a new urgency in the wake of the 1973 oil crisis and the rupture of diplomatic relations with Israel. Ghana strengthened its ties with Egypt and established new links with Saudi Arabia and the Gulf states. The country's connection with India, initiated by Nkrumah, was renewed by Acheampong and pursued by Limann and Rawlings. Contacts of some significance were maintained with China, and Latin American relations, previously very sparse, were amplified into an important horizontal network during the Acheampong years.

Ghana made initial contacts with Third World countries at the United Nations, which remained the major forum for Ghanaian interactions with other states in the Southern Hemisphere. By the close of the 1970s, Ghana appeared at least superficially to be creating a web of horizontal ties independent of the North-South underpinnings of traditional foreign alliances. This image was buttressed by the activities of SMC emissaries in the African, Caribbean, and Pacific (ACP) group negotiations with the European Economic Community. Under Acheampong, Ghana's lateral connections along the Third World axis were solidified.

Acheampong's successors have continued in this direction. Hilla Limann paid special attention to nurturing ties with moderate Arab states and even increased trade and aid relations with Israel. The Far East link was developed as special projects were established with Brazil. Jerry Rawlings has maintained many of these contacts and paid particular attention to those with Cuba and India. But even though the pace of South-South exchanges has not abated, their importance has been reduced. Fragmentation within the Afro-Asian bloc and Ghana's growing dependence on industrialized states have made the connection with the nonaligned world simply less useful in recent years. The pattern of diversification and restriction so noticeable in Ghana's inter-African relations has therefore repeated itself in the broader Third World context.

Ghana and the Industrialized World

Inevitably, the most complex and variable aspect of Ghana's foreign alliances has been relations with the industrialized countries of the Northern Hemisphere. Reluctance and necessity have intertwined to make Ghana's contacts with these states fraught with vacillations and inconsistencies. This checkered history commenced with Nkrumah's conscious effort to expand Ghana's contacts beyond the country's traditional ties with Britain and Western Europe. The CPP's campaign to sever the colonial umbilical cord took two main forms. First, the party appealed for closer relations with the noncolonial or smaller industrialized states of the Western world, such as Italy, Holland, and Germany. Second and better known, it intentionally created close connections with Eastern bloc countries, especially with the Soviet Union. By 1964, Ghana had established a complex set of relations with the USSR in areas ranging from cultural and educational exchanges to military aid and barter commodity agreements.[16] However problematic this effort later proved, the counterintegration strategy of Nkrumah, based on the careful balancing of Eastern and Western ties, distinguished Ghana's foreign links immediately after independence from those of most newly independent African states.

The Progress party did not pursue many of the contacts initiated by Nkrumah, much as it neglected the diverse links he had forged within Africa and the Third World. Determined to reverse the Nkrumaist inheritance on this critical front, the PP made moot its connections with the Soviet Union and allowed arrangements with Eastern European countries to lapse. At the same time, Ghana actively courted closer relations with the West. The British tie was nurtured with an almost vindictive intensity; Kofi Busia became the first Ghanaian anglophone head of state to visit Paris. German and U.S. ties were developed. Under Busia, Ghana's external alliances had narrowed to the familiar neocolonial constellation central to the foreign relations of most African states in the immediate postindependence period.

As Ghana's reliance on the Western world grew, its channels of communication multiplied. Besides conventional diplomatic interaction, Busia displayed a marked preference for personal diplomacy: He consequently encouraged negotiations with the West on a collective basis. Discussions with Western countries were frequently held in concert (through the IMF or the group of creditors that ironed out the first debt-rescheduling program). During the short years of the Second Republic, the countries and agencies involved in the conduct of Ghana's foreign relations became more heterogeneous than ever before.

Acheampong, at least during the first part of his tenure, tried to break away from the exclusively Western network created by the PP regime. He confined contacts with the West to unavoidable transactions, and even these were carefully balanced by a renewed effort to rekindle Eastern European connections. But Acheampong's notion of nonalignment was accompanied by a strong preference for disengagement from the industrialized world in general. He was unable to sustain this defiant stance throughout his years in office. Economic and historical factors dictated that Ghana's involvement with Western agglomerations continue and indeed grow. More to the point, these persistent attachments lost some of their initial complexity. Vital discussions with industrialized countries (including the Soviet Union) were conducted in a consolidated manner. The Lomé accords with the EEC further confined Ghana's direct access to the West. Vertical ties were therefore not discarded at this juncture, but they were aggregated in a more collective mold.

This mediated pattern of contact with Northern Hemisphere countries became even more institutionalized under Akuffo, Rawlings, and Limann. The IMF, Ghana's creditors, and multinational conglomerates joined forces to deal with the succession of short-term Ghanaian regimes in the 1978–1982 period. Distinct, separate, bilateral connections with either Western or Eastern countries were kept at a minimum as Ghana began to experience the effects of the neglect and disinterest of the industrialized world. And when a creditors' conference was convened in November 1983 to deal with Rawlings's economic recovery program, representatives of Western governments, large firms, banks, and the IMF cooperated to formulate policy together. Ghana's capacity to deal separately with these various concerns and regimes was severely curtailed.

The precariousness of Ghana's global standing reflects the deflation in its alliances with the First and Second Worlds. Despite fluctuations in partners, emphases, and channels of interaction, Ghana has been unable to withstand the international marginality that has become part and parcel of the process of its economic and political decline.

The Pattern of Ghana's External Alliances

The nature of Ghana's foreign associations has altered dramatically in the quarter of a century since independence. From an involvement with global and Third World matters under Nkrumah, the arena of Ghana's critical alliances has moved to the African and the West African level. Although Ghana is still tenaciously present in global forums, its most consistent bilateral interactions are being conducted with its neighbors.

Reduction in the scale of the country's activities has accompanied the development of a greater distance between Ghana and the industrialized world. This shift has also resulted in a decrease in the number of Ghana's foreign partners. Although Ghana interacts today with more states than it did at the end of its first decade of independence, these connections are mostly indirect and lack the individualized tone of former engagements.

The shrinking of the Ghanaian framework of external interchange becomes even more visible when the channels and modes of exchange are analyzed. At first, vertical links were established on a conventional bilateral foundation; today the most important contacts are made either on a nongovernmental basis or between Ghana as a member of certain multilateral associations and multinational groupings in the industrialized world. Mediated structures of international communication, both formal and nonformal, have replaced more direct bilateral channels. The once significant horizontal agglomerations that Ghana could use to cushion its dependence on the industrialized world have been transmuted into a new source of unequal ties much closer to home.

CHANGES IN GHANA'S PLACE IN THE INTERNATIONAL ORDER

Shifts in the substance and structure of Ghana's external exchanges have directly affected the nature of the country's global standing. Within the framework of inherited dependency on other countries, Ghana's international position has undergone subtle variations, fluctuations, and even significant mutations since independence. These changes illuminate the process of global decline and detachment—the cardinal feature of the history of Ghana's foreign contacts.

Ghana as a Leader of Africa and the Nonaligned World

At independence, Ghana's standing in the international arena was determined to no mean degree by the institutionalized dependence created during the period of British rule. But within this confining setting, Kwame Nkrumah and the CPP developed nuances, appended subtleties, and created new reciprocities and exchanges. Nkrumah's efforts concentrated on removing the ideological and normative aspects of Ghana's global subordination as a precondition for eventually disentangling the country from more material forms of inequality. By carving a niche for Ghanaian action, Nkrumah, at least during the first five years of his tenure, was able to pit the various realms of dependency—the political and the economic, the military and the cultural—against each other. Thus Ghana under the First Republic attained a certain autonomy in the international arena unrivaled in the African continent at the time.

The confrontational style adopted by Nkrumah inevitably evoked sharp reactions, especially in the West. Two main tools were employed to suppress Nkrumah's quest for independence. First, foreign countries tightened the credit terms on loans extended to Ghana; the most glaring example of the use of such methods was the VALCO contract signed in the early 1960s. Second, and more drastic, latent sanctions were imposed on the CPP government by forcing it to borrow large sums of money at high interest supplier credit rates. Nkrumah inevitably became trapped in the contradiction between the need for foreign investment and the desire to defy the organization of the world system. Foreign debts accumulated, and Ghana became entangled in a dependency far greater than that inherited at independence. The risks of effecting a precipitous challenge to the existing order were harshly driven home in the final years of Nkrumah's tenure.[17]

The accumulation of a massive commitment to outside financial concerns had a disastrous impact on Ghana's state socialist political economy, which was already suffering from internal dissent, worker unrest, rampant bureaucratic corruption, and reduced economic productivity. The combination of these forces isolated the CPP and its leader and eventually brought about the demise of the First Republic.

Nevertheless, under Nkrumah Ghana exerted a tangible influence on continental and global matters. Ghanaian policies radiated and impinged on affairs of other countries, and even though Nkrumah was not tolerated everywhere, he could hardly be ignored. Thus, although tensions between the government of Ghana and other African states mounted during this phase and acrimony with the West grew as well, Nkrumah did succeed not only in easing some of the psychological and political restraints of reliance and in uncovering certain spheres for independent action, but also in projecting an influence beyond Ghana's frontiers that had to be noticed.

Ghana as a Neocolony

Ghana's global stance during the NLC and Busia years was more acquiescently dependent than at any time since the country attained independence. The government championed collaboration with the West as a means of obtaining economic benefits and as a vehicle for inducing economic growth. The virtues of an unequal relationship were defended as a sign of mutuality and joint concern. The responses of Western countries to this shift in Ghana's demeanor were understandably supportive: Ghana was granted generous terms by its creditors; new capital disbursements were offered, and a perceptible rise in foreign investment took place. The line dividing external support and foreign interference was, however, exceedingly thin. The IMF, the World Bank, and privately contracted academic advisors attempted to introduce an economic package that would revive the economy and minimize the repercussions of the PP's spending spree during its first year in office.

Within Ghana, workers and younger intellectuals resisted these foreign incursions, ethnic cohorts were no longer willing to support the Asante-Brong power structure, and Busia was increasingly subjected to criticism from his own ruling coalition. When the prime minister succumbed to foreign pressures to devaluate the cedi, he sealed the fate of his regime. The National Redemption Council's coup of January 13, 1982, brought this Ghanaian experiment with state capitalism to a close.

During the 1966–1972 period, any measurable impact that Ghana might have made outside its borders may be attributed to the residue of respect and experience it accumulated during the Nkrumah years. But even this backlog of possible influence was dissipated under Busia's guidance: In effect, from a position of some import at the forefront of African interests and global leverage, Ghana became one of many weak countries seeking to attract a modicum of foreign consideration.

Ghana as a Self-Reliant State

Although by 1972 the extent and intensity of Ghana's dependence were not at issue, the premises upon which this external reliance hinged could be redefined. Ghana's new military leaders opted for a policy of conscious, voluntary, and vocal disengagement. These early NRC moves did not evoke the hostile response that could have been anticipated in light of the Nkrumah experience. The World Bank granted Ghana a loan despite Acheampong's repudiation of medium-term debts. Foreign business concerns continued to express an interest in investments in Ghana. Most significant, at a Rome meeting in March 1974 major creditors acceded to Ghana's demand for a moratorium on debts and reopened the government's credit line.[18] This willingness to come to terms with Ghanaian requests may be viewed as a sign of the change in attitudes that accompanied the energy recession crisis of 1973 and the growing awareness of the problems related to the contraction of global resources. On another level, this tendency to support rather than suppress disengagement measures of the type employed by Acheampong can be seen as an indication of the trend toward redefining the terms of North-South exchanges.

By 1975 Ghana's unequal posture vis-à-vis the industrialized world had not been alleviated, nor had its global position been altered in any significant way. But at least the notion of self-reliance did suggest a way of meeting Ghanaian needs and of reasserting a constructive Ghanaian presence in the African arena: An external role in keeping with Ghana's size, location, and resources seemed to be in the making.

Ghana as a Global Supplicant

The self-confidence resulting from Acheampong's early international successes and from the concomitant restoration of Ghanaian national pride induced Ghana's military leaders to take advantage of the seemingly opportune international climate to extract more visible material concessions from abroad. Beginning from a perceived position of relative strength in terms of raw materials, Ghana, in conjunction with other West African states, sought to reap political and economic benefits from an agreement to reenter the global arena following its self-imposed encapsulation. Some of the assumptions underlying this new militancy were, however, exceedingly problematic. First, Ghana's material well-being came to depend on the degree of economic interest it could elicit from abroad. Because Ghana's resource base was limited, possibilities for it to play one foreign country against another were sparse. Second, and much more pernicious, African and Third World solidarity, which had wrung admissions of moral responsibility for underdevelopment from the industrialized world, could not endure once these superficial rhetorical points had been scored. At this juncture, new sources of inequality among African states emerged, based strictly on material criteria.

But at first it seemed as if Ghanaian demands would be fulfilled. Western countries issued important statements on decolonization, racism, and self-determination. In the economic sphere gains were made in commodity negotiations as stabilization provisions were inserted in trade agreements between the industrialized world and a Ghana operating within the West African community. But external reactions to the idiosyncratic moves of the Acheampong regime quickly began to take on a different complexion. Hesitant to invest in a collapsing economy, uneasy about Acheampong's internal policy, and unwilling to offend a sovereign state, most foreign governments, multinational corporations, and international financial organizations simply extricated themselves from Ghanaian ventures. Their response was one of uncompromising avoidance. Without a fortuitous boom in cocoa prices (the proceeds of which Acheampong rarely funneled into state coffers), it is unlikely that SMC I could have withstood the demands by Ghanaian citizens for its resignation. As it was, by mid-1977 Acheampong's days were numbered.

At the end of the 1970s, Ghana was more dependent on external aid and more detached from the center of foreign concerns than at any previous point in its history. The areas that had allowed Ghana some degree of maneuverability during the Nkrumah era had been systematically closed off by his successors. Ghana faced the unsavory prospect of coping with the complex problems of survival in an atmosphere of international indifference.

Ghana as an African Dependency

As Ghana's extra-African options receded, the possibilities of relieving the internal economic chaos by appealing to foreign concerns diminished accordingly. Efforts to obtain such support nevertheless persisted. Ghana's leaders after Acheampong struck out in three major directions. First, they attempted to enhance Ghana's international acceptability. Akuffo and Rawlings bowed to IMF directives, and both Limann and Rawlings actively courted foreign capital. Second, both Akuffo and Limann tried to nurture relations with the Eastern bloc in hopes of once again diversifying the sources of external support. And, third, both governments came to rely more extensively on sustenance from countries closer to home. The ECOWAS connection was highlighted as an avenue to Western funding and as a direct source of some relief. In all these cases, the working presumption was that Ghana could not subsist without massive injections of foreign assistance.

Responses to these appeals were initially scanty and hesitant. In most instances, investors were reluctant to commit funds to a country teetering on the verge of collapse. When some foreign interest was evinced, it was accompanied by tough demands for special concessions. Ghana did receive some relief from its neighbors, and especially from Nigeria, which extended petroleum credits and undertook to champion the Ghanaian cause abroad. The ineffectiveness of these external gestures during the PNP years, much like the ineptitude of internal measures, aroused domestic criticism and exacerbated social cleavages.

During the early 1980s, Ghana became even more exposed to external influences. At the same time, the country's regional subordination became more pronounced. Its growing dependence on Nigeria made its contacts closer to home progressively uneven and unequal. An internal African dependency was added to the external one. Ghana's global remoteness was aggravated.

Ghana at Bay

When Rawlings returned to power, he brought with him anti-imperialist slogans and a determination to combat retrogressive forces on the domestic front. This stance dictated that Ghana detach itself from outside global and regional infringements: Ghana's borders were sealed and its traditional allies spurned. Such moves evoked external exasperation and made other countries unwilling to cooperate with the populist regime; in West Africa, Ghana's withdrawal triggered hostility and growing impatience. For a while it appeared that Ghana would be abandoned to fend alone in a fragmented continent and within an unsympathetic global environment.

By 1983, however, Ghana's leaders were compelled to repair their fences within Africa and abroad. Their new appeals for foreign aid were coupled with conciliatory gestures toward Ghana's neighbors. Although Rawlings did not attenuate his anti-interventionist position at this juncture, he was left with little choice but to look outward for assistance. Thus the PNDC has reaffirmed at least in its actions the ambiguities inherent in Ghana's position of external supplication and continental dependence.

The Spiral of External Deflation

Ghana's global leverage, regardless of shifts in foreign policies and external allies, has decreased since independence. If in the halcyon days of early independence Ghana's leaders sought to extend Ghanaian interests through foreign interchanges, by the 1980s initiative had given way to passivity and Ghana was left to cope with the little it was allotted by the increasingly remote international community. Ghana's initial unique dynamic had dissolved into an undistinguished posture on both internal and international fronts.

6

Ghana's Future

GHANA'S PAST: CONTINUITY AND INSTABILITY

Contemporary Ghana projects a paradoxical image of permanence and flux. Public life has been rife with uncertainty and decay; yet old patterns have persisted, fundamental norms have been retained, and existing relationships have become more elaborate. New social forms and innovative ideas thrive even while political arrangements consistently falter. The dynamics of the interplay between the state and the social order—the two autonomous components whose interaction has varied so significantly over the years—illuminate the situation of flux that is the hallmark of the Ghanaian experience today.

On the political front, Ghanaians have witnessed more fluctuations in national affairs than the citizens of perhaps any other country on the continent. Rapid and frequently contradictory changes in administrations have weakened central institutions, undermined their legitimacy, hampered their ability to act, and rendered them less and less relevant to the majority of the population. The Ghanaian state is in a process of decline, but it has not yet collapsed. Ghanaians continue to search for appropriate means to rehabilitate the infrastructure of political life and for alternatives to the formal administrative and judicial systems. In many cases they have revived traditional institutions or constructed other frameworks for meaningful participation. Political activities are everywhere apparent even though political structures have been incapacitated.

Ghanaians' attitudes toward their society have gradually become more ambivalent in the years since independence. Some

198

have suggested that these feelings border on the fatalistic, and to be sure the common belief in a bright future that bound Ghanaians together only two decades ago is not always apparent today. But some essential values do persist: The commitment to a democratic ethos has not wavered; deeply embedded notions of participation and just distribution have continually guided the evaluation of political behavior and still stand as the primary goals of social action. Many Ghanaians concur on the diagnosis of the sorry state of their society, and at present the consensus is so negative that it lacks a constructive dimension.

On the economic front, a struggle for survival has replaced the promise of development. The country's leaders have systematically assaulted the economic foundations of Ghana by their poor policies, inept use of resources, widespread mismanagement, and condoning of unbridled foreign intrusions. As the potential of the country's economy has been dissipated, Ghanaians have devised mechanisms to cope with economic uncertainty and food insecurity: They have returned to farming the land, refined barter arrangements, restructured agricultural production, and revitalized the parallel economy. In the early 1980s economic conditions in Ghana reached a nadir. Ghanaians, however, have built buffers against the sharp vacillations of the economy and managed somehow to maintain themselves in face of growing adversity. These economic activities point out both the patience of Ghanaian society and the opportunism of its members. Fluctuations and scarcity require endurance and ingenuity; Ghanaians in the 1980s have exhibited these two characteristics with great regularity.

Ghanaian society has undergone many mutations in the course of the past few decades. The quality of services has eroded relentlessly. Ghanaians could once boast that their education, health, and welfare systems were unmatched in the sub-Saharan region. Today the entire educational network is in disarray; medical facilities are hopelessly inadequate; the transportation system is grinding to a halt because of poor road maintenance and the absence of spare parts. Still, this pervasive regression has not affected the people's unflinching belief in knowledge and the remedial powers of technology. Cultural activity, far from slowing down, has expanded as creativity in music and the arts has been unequivocally pursued. Individual mobility is everywhere in evidence; so too is the continuing importance of communal life. Traditional values, such as patience and reciprocity, have helped keep social life on a relatively even keel. Nevertheless, ethnicity and class consciousness are much more prominent than in the early postcolonial period. The contradictory themes of antagonism and tolerance permeate the contemporary social scene in the country.

The fluidity of domestic affairs has been reflected in Ghana's relations with the outside world. Ghana's preeminence in Africa—the password of the Nkrumah years—has yielded to greater dependence and reliance on other nations. Although Ghana's foreign partners have varied over the years, the country's international standing has unmistakenly deteriorated. Ghanaians, nevertheless, remain prominent in the multilateral and continental civil service corps, and personal and institutional contacts with international bodies flourish despite the country's reduced status. The cosmopolitan nature of Ghanaian life has been retained. Ghana maintains a position of deference and subordination within the global order, but Ghanaian pride endures and is recognized on both foreign and domestic fronts.

Ghana, therefore, has undergone a complex process of expansion and fragmentation since independence. As the state framework has inexorably disintegrated, other mechanisms have been revived, redefined, and developed. These dual cycles accentuate not only the ambiguity present in Ghanaian society but also its essential strength. The state and the local community, once more closely interrelated, are growing apart; simultaneously, however, new relationships are evolving and innovative alternatives are being explored.

Ghana of the 1980s displays an admixture of rationality and magic. Social, economic, political, external, and geographic themes intertwine to create a context both confusing and familiar. Unpredictability characterizes all segments of the Ghanaian arena at the same time that identifiable long-established patterns flourish. Throughout, the vibrancy of Ghanaian life provides an excitement that pervades both continuity and movement, perseverance and change.

The manifold ways of coping with uncertainty, intriguing in themselves, cannot obscure the fact that state-society relations in Ghana have not yet yielded a formula for constructive interchange between state and society. It is not easy to explain the causes for the combination of collapse and vitality that characterizes contemporary Ghana nor to isolate the factors that have sustained this pattern. Historical variables undoubtedly play a part; so, too, do the scarcity of resources, the contingency of attachments to state institutions, the personal frailties of political leaders, the inability to inject national structures with Africanized contents, institutional weaknesses, social strife, and the dependency of Ghana on the world economy.[1] The precise amount of each of these ingredients remains unclear. What is evident is that the role of the state in Ghana requires a basic reformulation if a viable partnership between its institutions and the people, resources, and values within its boundaries is to be sustained in the future.

GHANA'S CHOICES

The future of Ghanaian society is as nebulous as its recent past. Few Ghanaians envisaged twenty-five years ago that the harvest of independence would be so meager; still fewer Ghanaians today can look ahead with confidence. Ghana is at a crossroads: The way Ghanaians deal with the complex realities of the present will have a direct bearing on the directions their society will take on the eve of the twenty-first century.

The all-embracing process of impoverishment in Ghana during the past few decades first created problems of accountability and then accentuated the difficulties of governing in conditions of absolute scarcity. Insufficient attention has been paid by policymakers to meeting the challenge of state enfeeblement and its deleterious byproduct of societal dispersion. Ghanaians now must come to terms seriously and courageously with these problems.

Causes of Ghana's Dilemma

The fundamental issue currently confronting Ghana's government and people is to find ways to make Ghana flourish again. The process of reconstruction requires attention to four root causes of the present Ghanaian dilemma. The first relates to the nature of Ghana's government. Some Ghanaians support authoritarianism in the hope of reinstating order in their country. The concept of a benevolent dictatorship is gaining currency; however, given the administrations' past record, the mechanisms needed to ensure the honesty and skill of future leaders remain unclear. Other Ghanaians advocate reducing the size of the state apparatus, not only to align government activities more closely with institutional capacities and to lower the cost of the bureaucracy, but also to increase the margin for individual creativity. The form of the state structure and its functions require further exploration.

The second aspect of the reordering process must focus on social relationships. Ghana today is deeply divided along class and ethnic lines. Many Ghanaians would like to create a state that would reflect the pluralism in Ghanaian society while allowing each divergent strand to retain its own identity. The vision of a multiplicity of existing groups acting in concert is considered too idyllic by others; they maintain that without altering the social order and the distribution of wealth within the country, Ghanaian society is doomed to years of strife. In this view, structural reorganization is a prerequisite for reviving the society. In either case, some adjustments clearly must be made to avert further social dissolution.

The third area of Ghana's rehabilitation is the economy. Some people stress the need to augment the quantity of existing resources through the expansion of production; others are more concerned with better resource coordination and utilization. These all concur, however, on the absolute importance of alleviating poverty if Ghana is to overcome its present predicament and begin to fulfill its economic potential. Some important steps in this direction have been taken during 1984 and 1985.

The fourth requirement for Ghana's reconstruction is a reassessment of the normative underpinnings of society. The traditional personal values of Ghanaian citizens must be reordered for the country's reconstruction to have substance and conviction. Tolerance is a crucial value in a heterogeneous setting, but when it permits uncontrolled opportunism among those in power it becomes pernicious. Deference is at odds with the quest for self-realization, and status consciousness does not sit well with an egalitarian ethos. Similarly, fatalism and participation do not comfortably intermix. A reassertion of deeply ingrained notions of justice can help establish practicable norms for common behavior, as can the redefinition of guiding values.

A workable formula to reunify Ghana must include special emphasis on linking political changes to economic shifts and normative alterations to social adjustments. The rehabilitation process therefore possesses dimensions both within and outside Ghana. This duality does not mean that foreign models should be blindly transposed on the Ghanaian context; efforts of this sort have proved unsuccessful. It also does not imply that reconstruction can be achieved by completely excluding foreign elements: Such a notion is a prescription for the total atomization of the Ghanaian state. Approaches to rebuilding Ghanaian society therefore center on various ways of redesigning the basic components of the Ghanaian environment and their mode of interaction domestically and internationally to give coherence and purpose to the future of Ghana.

Options for Ghana's Reconstruction

Several possible scenarios for restructuring come to mind. The first is a benevolent reconciliation between the social and the political orders.[2] In this option, the state will adapt itself to its reduced position; existing local self-reliance mechanisms will be fortified; the techniques devised to cope with impoverishment will be refined and elaborated. Inevitably, central institutions will be pared down to meet these new realities. National structures will provide an arena for exchange and a funnel for communication with the outside world, and perhaps they will be empowered to use enforcement devices. The connection between the state and society will, however, depend mostly on the existence of common practical concerns. The Ghanaian state will not be endowed with greater authority or legitimacy than it can muster at the moment. It may, however, maintain a measure of organizational significance.

The benevolent reconciliation option can be implemented if a new formula for social and political exchange is designed.

National policymakers would have to surrender some of their control over central institutions, and political leaders would have to forego attempts to penetrate into the countryside. Such restraint has not been an outstanding characteristic of Ghana's leadership since independence. In the same vein, individuals and groups would have to reduce the scope and the intensity of their demands on government. Here too, historical precedents are hardly encouraging, especially as economic conditions have continued to deteriorate. Foreign creditors would have to evince some forebearance—a trait they have not exhibited with great regularity.

Reconciliation, although it requires few policy changes, necessitates the conscious limitation of expectations. The scenario does not hold much promise for the revitalization of Ghanaian society; it does, however, suggest ways of arriving at a modus vivendi that will ensure a modicum of social, political, economic, and normative reciprocity.

A second scenario focuses on reform and includes greater state intrusion into the social and economic affairs of the Ghanaian population. In this plan, state managers might attempt to assume greater control over local affairs by impinging more directly on citizens' daily lives. For Ghana to move in such a direction therefore involves authoritarian or populist policy changes so that the state would infiltrate into the rural areas and demand more obedience to government directives.

This option can be set in motion only if the state center is enormously strengthened. Massive injections of resources and arms are required to implement such a policy,[3] which also demands forceful leadership and an institutional efficiency heretofore lacking in Ghana. The realization of the choice depends, too, on the acquiescence of the Ghanaian population—people who have repeatedly demonstrated their low tolerance for autocratic rule. Therefore, by following the intrusive scenario the state might augment centrifugal tendencies and unleash widespread conflict while attempting to gain control over the divisive strands of Ghanaian society.

The third alternative takes a quite different direction: It hypothesizes that given Ghana's present situation, the country may be ripe for recolonization. In this rather dreary scenario, local institutions can no longer contend with the myriad of conflicting forces at work on the Ghanaian scene; Ghana's salvation must come from the outside. Recolonization may take on several distinct forms: It may allow the return of the former metropole (a possibility surely farfetched today); it might involve the subordination of the country to a consortium of industrialized states or to certain multilateral agencies (such as the International Monetary Fund and the World Bank). A less radical type of external takeover may come in the form of Ghana's subjugation to newly influential African states or to a regional entity into which Ghana would be incorporated on an unequal basis.

For these foreign intrusions to preempt Ghanaian sovereignty, certain international conventions would have to be drastically altered. Indeed, this option presupposes foreign interest in Ghana and woefully underestimates the force of Ghanaian national pride. Nevertheless, some recent events have underlined the vulnerability of Ghana to greater foreign incursions. For Ghana to be recolonized, the state itself would have to forfeit all ties to society, and local level self-reliance techniques practiced by the rural population would have to prove unable to ensure sheer survival. Should the specter of recolonization materialize in the future, this approach would probably be more an outcome of the dispersion of Ghanaian society than a mechanism for its reconsolidation. Such a scenario would effectively erase any earlier gains without pointing to viable methods for societal rehabilitation.

Many observers have suggested that recent events have set Ghanaian society on a revolutionary course. The internal contradictions within the social and political orders have, in this view, reached such unmanageable proportions that they can only be resolved by a total rearrangement of power relations in the country. This fourth option has held a particular allure for those who are convinced that nothing short of a basic structural upheaval can save Ghana from total breakdown.[4] The revolutionary choice stresses first the elimination of inequities, social privilege, and unharnessed opportunism. It highlights the need for a thorough revamping of the normative system to fundamentally alter social relations. In this perspective, the reaffirmation of the centrality of the state can be achieved only

after a lengthy, and perhaps violent, process of societal transformation. The political metamorphosis that will take place at
this juncture will put the state under the direct supervision of
newly liberated social forces.

The preconditions for revolution in Ghana, regardless of
the consistency with which this possibility has been raised, are
simply not abundantly in evidence at the moment. Poverty alone
does not cause revolutionary upheavals; if it did, the entire
African continent would be in continuous turmoil. Revolutions
require powerful groups that not only possess a strong consciousness but also are capable of attracting support for their
cause. In Ghana, those groups, which in the past could hope
to amass wealth and status from proximity to the state, are
now powerless. To be sure, class divisions have become more
pronounced, and class awareness has increased as scarcity has
set in. But Ghanaians do possess alternatives to state institutions;
their protest does not have to focus on the center. The widespread
detachment and indifference prevalent in many sectors of Ghanaian society further weaken the prospects for an imminent
revolutionary campaign. A revolution is especially improbable
today because of the failure of past attempts. The revolutionary
option will undoubtedly be debated at length in the future, but
as long as the structural situation in Ghana remains essentially
the same, these discussions will continue to be removed from
the concrete realities of the Ghanaian situation.

The prospects for democracy in Ghana have been raised
and rejected consistently. The democratic precepts at the root
of the Ghanaian social order, the well-honed skills of political
observation and debate, and the strong tradition of participation
in public life all lend support to a democratic resolution to the
current crisis in Ghana. In this fifth model, the constitution
could be altered to grant Ghanaian citizens adequate representation and access to decisionmaking processes. The concept of
a developmental democracy, currently in vogue in some academic
circles, proffers an image of a future state government based
on a peculiarly indigenous brand of democracy suited to conditions of scarcity.[5] The introduction of democratic institutions
in Ghana has been tried several times and has failed. Perhaps
the lack of success was due to complicated constitutional pro-

visions, to inadequate preparation, or to the social background of those supporting the democratic precepts. More probably these experiments have floundered because interest in the state core has diminished, because political struggles have followed the lines of social cleavages, because democratic rhetoric has outstripped a true commitment to the participatory ethos, and because duly elected leaders have been unwilling to entertain sustained criticism. The prevalence of a democratic ethos in society cannot easily be translated into the construction of a democratic political order when the state itself is either weak or irrelevant. In Ghana, democratic options, like their revolutionary counterparts, are both enticing and elusive.

The five alternative scenarios for the future of Ghana are diverse and complex. Each option suggests a formula for reorganization of the socioeconomic and political foundations of Ghanaian life, each relies on either policy or structural adjustments, each relates to both domestic and foreign factors, and each contains a myriad of obstacles for its eventual fulfillment. These models show some ways that social relations may be redesigned so that new kinds of linkages around the existing Ghanaian entity may be realized. They are not, however, entirely reflective of current trends.

A sixth scenario, which claims to be both the most realistic and the most sobering, suggests that Ghana will continue in the immediate future to stagnate along lines familiar from the recent past. Processes of fragmentation in the economic, social, and political spheres will persist. Already identifiable cleavages may grow, and strife may, in this perspective, expand into open conflict. The economy, however chaotic, will deteriorate even further and political life will be characterized by more plots, putsches, and coups. As the socioeconomic and political implosion involved in such a dynamic takes root, social groups may become even more hesitant about their involvement with the state. In these circumstances, state institutions will be less capable of meeting public demands, and the state framework will become even less relevant than it is today. The vision of prolonged stagnation essentially means that Ghana will continue to decline without irretrievably falling apart. In this option, conditions will worsen beyond what has been conceived as possible; yet

Ghanaian society will somehow survive. The probability of this eventuality rests on the supposition that piecemeal interventions by leaders or foreign elements cannot make a dent in the inexorable process of decline. Those who unhappily uphold this view foresee the decay of the country and hold little hope for its improvement.

The gloominess inherent in the prospect of ongoing deterioration has led some people to conclude that not only is it impossible to resuscitate Ghana but that such a task is not desirable. To their minds, the only viable option left open to Ghanaians is to oversee the dismantling of their state. This position rests on the fact that association with national institutions, far from promoting and encouraging progress, has only increased the vulnerability of many Ghanaians and limited their prospects for advancement. State structures, at best, have functioned inefficiently; more frequently they have disrupted productive activities, intruded needlessly into the lives of citizens, and orchestrated discord. With the national economy at a standstill, survival for the average Ghanaian depends little, if at all, on the efforts of politicians, policymakers, or international civil servants. Interaction within the national community has exacerbated social tensions. In short, the benefits of disengagement from the existing order far outweigh the questionable returns from participating in national affairs.

The process of taking apart a state is no mean feat. Despite the fragility of so many societies in the contemporary world, few precedents exist for such an undertaking. In Ghana, social groups constantly overlap and intermingle; their formal separation would not be neatly accomplished. Individuals associate with a variety of organizations in their daily lives; depriving them of such access may create new impediments to survival. Although the de facto existence of the state in Ghana has been in doubt for some years, the international system still provides it with a de jure status that it is unlikely to withdraw.[6]

Not only are the technical aspects of state dismemberment problematic, but the alternatives are unclear. The intentional breakdown of Ghana could lead to local communal autonomy, to complete atomization, to the construction of symbolic or ethnic communities, and, on another level, to the redefinition of regional politics. The present international system conceives of the state as the basic political unit; the outcome of state demise remains poorly defined. In the early 1980s, Ghana appeared to be on the verge of collapse. However, this danger may be lessening in view of the improvement in the country's economy during 1984 and 1985. Nevertheless, the ramifications of state dissolution—a possibility heretofore considered beyond the purview of conventional social science research—must be studied with greater urgency. Regardless of the desirability or practicality of state decline, this prospect can no longer be summarily discounted.

Summary

Barring any major shifts in Ghanaian fortunes, Ghanaian society will probably experience variations of reconciliation, reform, recolonization, and stagnation during the next few years, facilitated by repeated and contradictory military interventions. At the same time, the search for more far-reaching revolutionary or democratic solutions will intensify as the fabric of the Ghanaian state continues to be fragile.

Whether Ghanaians will be able to apply their ingenuity and resourcefulness in the quest for a more suitable and locally appropriate model of interaction or whether they will surrender to decay will have a direct bearing on the shape of Ghanaian society and its well-being in the future. Ghanaians therefore have an important role to play in molding their own destiny in the last decades of this century.

IMPLICATIONS FOR AFRICA

In the twentieth century, Ghana has emerged as a microcosm of social, political, and economic processes in Africa. Ghana's recent history exemplifies the intricacies of the contemporary African experience: It details the problems of development and underdevelopment; it exposes directions of growth and lays bare the profound roots of recession and poverty; it embodies the essence of suffering and promise at the heart of present-day Africa.

The Ghanaian proclivity for experimentation has made Ghana into a veritable laboratory for the investigation of different approaches to endemic African problems. The strengths and weaknesses of various strategies for survival and growth can be isolated by focusing on trends in Ghana; so, too, can the planned and unplanned outcomes of policy initiatives. Despite their country's poor performance record, Ghanaians may yet hold the key to the resolution of some of the most intractable problems confronting Africans today.

Ghana, therefore, is a continuing object of fascination and a seemingly endless source of creativity. To uncover the various layers of recent Ghanaian history is to begin to comprehend the subtlety of analysis in the continent as a whole. Ghana has provided and will continue to offer an original challenge to those truly trying to understand the complex processes in Africa and perhaps elsewhere in the world.

Notes

CHAPTER 1. HISTORICAL BACKGROUND

1. F. M. Bourret, *The Gold Coast: A Survey of the Gold Coast and British Togoland, 1919–1946* (Stanford, CA: Stanford University Press, 1949); J. D. Fage, *Ghana: A Historical Interpretation* (Madison: University of Wisconsin Press, 1959); J. D. Fage, *A History of West Africa* (Cambridge: Cambridge University Press, 1969); W.E.F. Ward, *A History of the Gold Coast* (London: Allen & Unwin, 1948).

2. Ward, *A History of the Gold Coast*, p. 104.

3. Ivor Wilks, *Asante in the Nineteenth Century: The Structure and Evolution of a Political Order* (London: Cambridge University Press, 1975); Robert Rattray, *Ashanti* (London: Oxford University Press, 1923) and *Religion and Art in Ashanti* (London: Oxford University Press, 1927); Fage, *Ghana: A Historical Interpretation* and *A History of West Africa*; Francis Agbodeka, *African Politics and British Policy in the Gold Coast 1868–1900: A Study in the Forms and Force of Protest* (Evanston, IL: Northwestern University Press, 1971); David Kimble, *A Political History of Ghana, 1850–1928* (Oxford: Oxford University Press, 1963).

4. Basil Davidson, *Africa in History* (New York: Collier Books, 1974).

5. John K. Fynn, *Asante and Its Neighbors, 1700–1807* (Evanston, IL: Northwestern University Press, 1971).

6. Fage, *Ghana: A Historical Interpretation*; Fynn, *Asante and Its Neighbors*; Rhoda Howard, *Colonialism and Underdevelopment in Ghana* (New York: Africana Publishing Co., 1978).

7. Agbodeka, *African Politics and British Policy*; Kimble, *A Political History of Ghana*.

211

8. Kimble, *A Political History of Ghana*, p. 268; see also Agbodeka, *African Politics and British Policy.*

9. Agbodeka, *African Politics and British Policy*, pp. 55f; see also Michael Crowder, *West Africa Under Colonial Rule* (Evanston, IL: Northwestern University Press, 1968); Adu Boahen, "Politics in Ghana, 1800–1874," in A.J.A. Ajayi and Michael Crowder, eds., *History of West Africa*, vol. 2 (New York: Columbia University Press, 1973).

10. Crowder, *West Africa Under Colonial Rule*, p. 211; David Apter, *Ghana in Transition* (New York: Atheneum, 1966), pp. 120–122.

11. Apter, *Ghana in Transition*, pp. 124–130; Crowder, *West Africa Under Colonial Rule*, pp. 221–223.

12. Howard, *Colonialism and Underdevelopment in Ghana*, p. 60.

13. The best analysis of nationalism in this early period may be found in Kimble, *A Political History of Ghana.*

14. The role of voluntary associations is discussed in Yaw Twumasi, "Prelude to the Rise of Mass Nationalism in Ghana, 1920–49: Nationalists and Voluntary Associations," *Ghana Social Science Journal* 3, no. 1 (1976):35–46. Also see Thomas Hodgkin, *Nationalism in Colonial Africa* (New York: New York University Press, 1958); and Immanuel M. Wallerstein, *The Road to Independence: Ghana and the Ivory Coast* (The Hague: Mouton, 1964).

15. Some facets of the cocoa industry are discussed in Howard, *Colonialism and Underdevelopment in Ghana;* and Beverly Grier, "Underdevelopment, Modes of Production and the State in Colonial Ghana," *African Studies Review* 24, no. 1 (1981):438–494.

16. Quoted in Dennis Austin, *Politics in Ghana, 1946–1960* (London: Oxford University Press, 1964), p. 55.

17. The topic of the youngmen is covered well in Roger Genoud, *Nationalism and Economic Development in Ghana* (New York: Praeger, 1969).

18. For more details on Nkrumah's confrontation with the British see Kwame Nkrumah, *Ghana: The Autobiography of Kwame Nkrumah* (Edinburgh: Thomas Nelson and Sons, 1959).

19. Editors of *Spark*, *Some Essential Features of Nkrumaism* (Accra: Spark Publications, 1964).

20. Some of these findings have been analyzed by Bob Fitch and Mary Oppenheimer, *Ghana: End of an Illusion* (New York: Monthly Review Press, 1960).

21. Austin, *Politics in Ghana*, pp. 209–247.

22. Ibid., p. 250. For more details also see Bankole Timothy, *Kwame Nkrumah: His Rise to Power* (Evanston, IL: Northwestern

University Press, 1963); and F. M. Bourret, *Ghana: The Road to Independence* (London: Oxford University Press, 1960).

23. The CPP's maneuvering power is demonstrated on the local level by Maxwell Owusu, *Uses and Abuses of Political Power: A Case Study of Continuity and Change in the Politics of Ghana* (Chicago: University of Chicago Press, 1970).

CHAPTER 2. THE PENDULUM OF GHANAIAN POLITICS

1. Editors of *Spark, Some Essential Features of Nkrumaism* (Accra: Spark Publications, 1964), p. 27.

2. For different views on the consolidation of the party, see Henry L. Bretton, *The Rise and Fall of Kwame Nkrumah: A Study of Personal Rule in Africa* (London: Pall Mall Press, 1966); Trevor Jones, *Ghana's First Republic: The Pursuit of the Political Kingdom* (London: Methuen, 1976), pp. 92–140; Ben Amonoo, *Ghana 1957–1966: The Politics of Institutional Dualism* (London: Allen & Unwin, 1981); and Jon Kraus, "On the Politics of Nationalism and Social Change in Ghana," *Journal of Modern African Studies* 7, no. 1 (1969):107–130.

3. For different views see Tawia Adamafio, *A Portrait of Osagyefo Dr. Kwame Nkrumah* (Accra: Ministry of Information, n.d.); Basil Davidson, *Black Star: A View of the Life and Times of Kwame Nkrumah* (London: Allen Lane, 1973); T. Peter Omari, *Kwame Nkrumah: The Anatomy of an African Dictatorship* (Accra: Moxon Publications, 1970); David E. Apter, *Ghana in Transition*, rev. ed. (New York: Atheneum, 1966); Bankole Timothy, *Kwame Nkrumah: His Rise to Power* (Evanston, IL: Northwestern University Press, 1963); Ali A. Mazrui, "Nkrumah: The Leninist Czar," *Transition* 26 (1966); and Robert H. Jackson and Carl G. Rosberg, *Personal Rule in Black Africa: Prince, Autocrat, Prophet, Tyrant* (Berkeley: University of California Press, 1982).

4. Kwame Nkrumah, *Consciencism: Philosophy and Ideology for Decolonization and Development with Particular Reference to the African Revolution* (New York: Monthly Review Press, 1964), p. 73. Also see Colin Legum, "Socialism in Ghana: A Political Interpretation," in William H. Friedland and Carl G. Rosberg, eds., *African Socialism* (Stanford, CA: Stanford University Press, 1964), pp. 131–159; Kenneth Grundy, "Nkrumah's Theory of Underdevelopment: An Analysis of Recurrent Themes," *World Politics* 15, no. 3 (1963):438–454; and Ayi Kwei Armah, "African Socialism: Utopian or Scientific?" *Presence Africaine* 64 (1967):6–30. For a good critique see Kwame Ninsin, "Nkrumah's Socialism: A Reappraisal" (Department of Political Science, University of Ghana, Legon, October 1978).

5. On Nkrumah's policies, see A. W. Seidman, *Ghana's Development Experience*; E. N. Omaboe, "The Process of Planning," in Birmingham et al., eds., *A Study of Contemporary Ghana. Volume One—The Economy of Ghana*, pp. 439–468; Emily Card, "The Political Economy of Ghana," in R. Harris, ed., *The Political Economy of Africa* (Cambridge, MA: Schenkman Publishing Co., 1975), pp. 49–92; Tony Killick, *Development Economics in Action: A Study of Economic Policies in Ghana* (London: Heinemann, 1978).

6. Convention People's Party, *Programme of the Convention People's Party for Work and Happiness* (Accra: n.d.); and Douglas Rimmer, "The Crisis in the Ghana Economy," *Journal of Modern African Studies* 4, no. 1 (1966):17–32.

7. Tony Killick, *Development Economics in Action: A Study of Economic Policies in Ghana*. For NLC policies, see also E. O. Boateng, *Inflation in Ghana: Problems and Prospects*; Reginald N. Green, "Reflections on Economic Strategy, Structure, Implementation, and Necessity: Ghana and the Ivory Coast," in Philip Foster and Aristide Zolberg, eds., *Ghana and the Ivory Coast: Perspectives on Modernization* (Chicago: University of Chicago Press, 1971), pp. 231–264.

8. Richard Jeffries, *Class, Power and Ideology in Ghana: The Railwaymen of Sekondi* (London: Cambridge University Press, 1978), p. 74. Also see Jon Kraus, "Strikes and Labour Power in Ghana," *Development and Change* 10, no. 2 (1979):252–286.

9. Bob Fitch and Mary Oppenheimer, *Ghana: End of an Illusion* (New York: Monthly Review Press, 1966), p. 129.

10. Details on the coup may be found in A. A. Afrifa, *The Ghana Coup: 24th February 1966* (London: Frank Cass, 1967); A. K. Ocran, *The Myth is Broken: An Account of the Ghana Coup d'Etat of 24 February 1966* (London: Longman, Green, 1968); and Anton Bebler, *Military Rule in Africa: Dahomey, Ghana, Sierra Leone and Mali* (New York: Praeger, 1973).

11. For a description of the internal structure of the NLC, see Robert Dowse, "Military and Police Rule," in Dennis Austin and Robin Luckman, eds., *Politicians and Soldiers in Ghana* (London: Frank Cass, 1976), esp. p. 18; and Robert Pinkney, *Ghana Under Military Rule* (London: Methuen, 1972).

12. K. A. Busia, *Africa in Search of Democracy* (London: Routledge and Kegan Paul, 1967), and *Idem, The Position of the Chief in the Modern Political System of Ashanti*, 2d ed. (London: Frank Cass, 1968).

13. Republic of Ghana, *Outline of Government Economic Policy* (Accra: Government Printer, 1967), esp. pp. 5–7.

14. Paraphrase from Victor T. Le Vine, "Autopsy of a Regime: Ghana's Civilian Interregnum, 1969–1972" (Unpublished Paper, Mimeo., n.d.), p. 6. Also see Dennis Austin, "Return to Ghana," *African Affairs* 69, no. 274 (1970):71.

15. On the programs of the Busia years, see Tony Killick, *Development Economics in Action: A Study of Economic Policies in Ghana*; James Pickett, "Development Planning in Ghana," *Economic Bulletin of Africa* 12, no. 1 (1976):9–18; Cameron Duodu, "Will Devaluation Rescue the Ghanaian Worker?" *African Development* 6, no. 2 (1972):7–8.

16. These problems are highlighted in David Goldsworthy, "Ghana's Second Republic: A Post Mortem," *African Affairs* 72, no. 286 (1973):8–25.

17. The cedi (¢) is the Ghanaian unit of currency introduced by Nkrumah. ¢1 = 100 pesewas.

18. Republic of Ghana, *The Charter of the National Redemption Council* (Accra, n.d.).

19. A good overview may be found in Donald Rothchild, "Military Regime Performance: An Appraisal of the Ghana Experience, 1972–1978," *Comparative Politics* 12, no. 4 (1980):459–479; and Michel Prouzet, "Vie Politique et Institutions Publiques Ghaneénes," *Revue Française d'Etudes Politiques Africaine* 145 (1978):51–85.

20. Jon Kraus, "The Political Economy of Conflict in Ghana," *Africa Report* 25, no. 2 (1980):9–16; Colin Legum, "Ghana," in *Africa Contemporary Record* (1978–79); *Africa Report* 24 (1979).

21. See Richard Jeffries, "Rawlings and the Political Economy of Underdevelopment in Ghana," *African Affairs* 81, no. 324 (1982):307–317.

22. Donald Rothchild, "Ghana's Economy—An African Test Case for Political Democracy: President Limann's Economic Alternatives," in Colin Legum, ed., *Africa Contemporary Record 1979–1980* (London: Holmes and Meier Publishers, 1981), pp. A137–145.

23. For election background, see Austin and Luckham, *Politicians and Soldiers in Ghana*, and Moses Danquah, ed., *The Birth of the Second Republic* (Accra: Editorial and Publishing Services, 1969).

24. Jeffries, *Class, Power and Ideology in Ghana*, p. 139. Also see David Smock and Audrey Smock, *The Politics of Pluralism: A Comparative Study of Ghana and Lebanon* (New York: Elsevier, 1975).

25. Duodu, "Will Devaluation Rescue the Ghanaian Worker?"

26. David Brown, "Borderline Politics in Ghana: The National Liberation Movement of Western Togoland," *Journal of Modern African*

Studies 18, no. 4 (1980):575–609, and "Who Are the Tribalists? Social Pluralism and Political Ideology in Ghana," *African Affairs* 81, no. 322 (1982):37–69.

27. Naomi Chazan and Victor T. Le Vine, "Politics in a 'Non-Political' System: The March 30, 1978 Referendum in Ghana," *African Studies Review* 22, no. 1 (1979):177–208. The article gives full details about the referendum.

28. Jon Kraus, "Ghana: The Crisis Continues," *Africa Report* 23, no. 4 (1978):14–21. Also see Jim Silver, "Class Struggles in Ghana's Mining Industry," *Review of African Political Economy* 12 (1978):67–86.

29. The analysis of SMC II is based on Naomi Chazan, *An Anatomy of Ghanaian Politics: Managing Political Recession, 1969–1982* (Boulder: Westview, 1983), pp. 215–279.

30. See Emmanuel Hansen and Paul Collins, "The Army, the State, and the 'Rawlings' Revolution,'" *African Affairs* 79, no. 314 (1980):3–12; Kraus, "The Political Economy of Conflict in Ghana," pp. 9–16; and Jeffries, "Rawlings and the Political Economy of Underdevelopment in Ghana," pp. 307–317.

31. Naomi Chazan, "Ethnicity and Politics in Ghana," *Political Science Quarterly* 98, no. 3 (1982):461–485. The most detailed description of the 1979 elections is that in Robert Vineberg, "The 1979 Elections in Ghana: A Vote for Political Stability and a Return to Civilian Control" (Jerusalem: Harry S Truman Research Institute, mimeo, 1979). Also see Donald Rothchild and E. Gyimah-Boadi, "Ghana's Return to Civilian Rule," *Africa Today* 28, no. 1 (1981):3–16. Many of these points are emphasized in Richard Jeffries, "The Ghanaian Elections of 1979," *African Affairs* 79, no. 316 (1980):397–414. Also see Chazan, "Ethnicity and Politics in Ghana," pp. 475–484.

32. E. Gyimah-Boadi and Donald Rothchild, "Rawlings, Populism, and the Civil Liberties Tradition in Ghana," *Issue* 12, no. 3/4 (1982):64–69; and Donald Rothchild and E. Gyimah-Boadi, "Ghana's Demodernization and Development Strategies," in John Ravenhill, ed., *Africa in Economic Crisis* (London: Macmillan, 1984), forthcoming.

33. *Policy Guidelines of the Provisional National Defence Council* (Accra: May 1982), p. 8.

34. Jerry Rawlings, as quoted in *West Africa* (24/31 December 1984), p. 2637.

CHAPTER 3. SOCIETY AND CULTURE

1. The stool symbolizes group solidarity; it embodies the spirit of ancestors and signifies their presence; indeed, it represents the continuity between the living and dead.

2. Much has been written on the concept of destiny in Africa. As it applies to Ghana in particular, see M. J. Field, *Religion and Medicine of the Ga People* (London: Oxford University Press, 1937), pp. 192–99; Meyer Fortes, *The Web of Kinship Among the Tallensi*, published for the International African Institute (London: Oxford University Press, 1949), pp. 227–229; Helaine Minkus, "The Philosophy of the Akwapim-Akan of Southern Ghana," Ph.D. dissertation (Northwestern University, 1975).

3. Richard Jeffries, *Class, Power and Ideology in Ghana: The Railwaymen of Sekondi* (London: Cambridge University Press, 1978).

4. The discussion of Ghana's education system draws on C. K. Graham, *History of Education in Ghana: From the Earliest Times to the Declaration of Independence* (London: Frank Cass, 1971); Betty George, *Education in Ghana*, U.S. Department of Health, Education, and Welfare (DHEW), pub. no. (OE) 75-19119 (Washington, DC: Government Printing Office, 1976); R. B. Bening, "Colonial Policy on Education in Northern Ghana, 1908–1951," *Universitas* 5, no. 2 (1976):58–99; John Bibby and Margaret Peil, "Secondary Education in Ghana: Private Enterprise and Social Selection," *Sociology of Education* 47, no. 3 (1974):399–418; Lois Weis, "The Reproduction of Social Inequality: Closure in the Ghanaian University," *Journal of Developing Areas* 16, no. 1 (1981):17–30, and "Schooling and Patterns of Access in Ghana," *Canadian Journal of African Studies* 15, no. 2 (1981):311–322.

5. A. A. Armar and A. S. David, *Country Profiles: Ghana* (New York: The Population Council, 1977); S. K. Gaisie, N. O. Addo, and S. B. Jones, "Population Policy and Its Implementation," in J. C. Caldwell, ed., *Population Growth and Socioeconomic Change in West Africa* (New York: Columbia University Press, 1975), pp. 408–424; Dorothy L. Nortman, *Population and Family Planning Programs*, 11th ed. (New York: Population Council, 1982); *Population Policy Compendium: Ghana* (New York: UN Fund for Population Activities, 1981).

6. See Gaisie et al., "Population Policy and Its Implementation," p. 414, for NFPP's operating principles.

7. For traditional attitudes and recourse to traditional modes of practicing medicine, see Robin Horton, "African Traditional Thought

and Western Science," *Africa* 27, nos. 1 and 2 (1967):50–71 and 155–187; *Africa-Link* (International Population Planning Foundation—Africa Region, 1980); "Power in Local Herbs," *The Mirror*, February 13, 1971.

8. Douglas Rimmer, "Ghana: Economy," in *Africa South of the Sahara 1980–81*, 10th ed. (London: Europa Publications, 1980), pp. 438–445.

9. Dennis Austin, "Ghana: Recent History," in *Africa South of the Sahara 1980–81*, pp. 428–438; Ken Kwaku, "Ghana Housing Corporation and the Politics of Housing 1956–1972," *Ghana Social Science Journal* 4, no. 1 (1977):1–18.

10. A. M. O'Connor, *The Geography of Tropical African Development* (Oxford: Pergamon Press, 1978); Douglas Rimmer, "Ghana: Economy"; D. Hilling, "The Evolution of a Port System—The Case of Ghana," *Geography* 62, pt. 2 (1977):97–105; John F. Due, "The Problems of Rail Transport in Tropical Africa," *Journal of Developing Areas* 13, no. 4 (1979):375–393.

11. E. A. Boateng, "Ghana: Physical and Social Geography," in *Africa South of The Sahara*, pp. 427–428.

12. Colin Legum, ed., "Ghana," in *Africa Contemporary Record: Annual Survey and Documents* (New York: Africana Publishing Co., 1978–79), p. B-628.

13. Herbert M. Cole and Doran H. Ross, *The Arts of Ghana* (Los Angeles: Museum of Cultural History, UCLA, 1977); J. H. Kwabena Nketia, "The Musician in Akan Society," in W. d'Azevedo, ed., *The Traditional Artist in African Society* (Bloomington: Indiana University Press, 1973), pp. 79–100.

14. Well-known novels include Asare Konadu, *A Woman in Her Prime* (London: Heinemann, 1967); Kofi Awoonor, *This Earth, My Brother* (London: Heinemann, 1971); Ayi Kwei Armah, *The Beautyful Ones Are Not Yet Born* (New York: Collier, 1969).

15. For attitudes toward strangers, see Nelson Addo, "Immigration into Ghana: Some Social and Economic Implications of the Aliens Compliance Order of 18 November 1969," *Ghana Journal of Sociology* 6, no. 1 (1970):20–42; Gaisie et al., "Population Policy and Its Implementation"; Margaret Peil, "The Expulsion of West African Aliens," *The Journal of Modern African Studies* 9, no. 2 (1971):205–229; K. C. Zachariah and Julien Conde, *Migration in West Africa: Demographic Aspects* (New York: Oxford University Press, 1981).

CHAPTER 4. THE ECONOMY

1. General works relating to sectors of Ghana's economy—resources, finance, patterns of distribution, economic indicators—include Birmingham et al., *A Study of Contemporary Ghana. Volume One.* For a description of the country's basic resources, see also A. W. Seidman, *Ghana's Development Experience* (Nairobi: East African Publishing House, 1978); Polly Hill, *The Migrant Cocoa-Farmers of Southern Ghana: A Study in Rural Capitalism* (Cambridge: Cambridge University Press, 1963).

2. Tony Killick, *Development Economics in Action: A Study of Economic Policies in Ghana* (New York: St. Martin's Press, 1978). For description of industry and manufacturing, also see Tony Killick, "The State Promotion of Industry: The Case of Ghana Industrial Development Corporation. Part I," *Ghana Social Science Journal* 2, no. 1 (1972):27–50, and "The State Promotion of Industry: The Case of Ghana Industrial Development Corporation. Part II," *Ghana Social Science Journal* 3, no. 1 (1976):18–34; Seidman, *Ghana's Development Experience*; C. Dorm-Adzobu, "The State and Industrial Development in Ghana," *Ghana Social Science Journal* 1, no. 1 (1971);108–115; E. N. Omaboe, "The Process of Planning," in Birmingham et al., *A Study of Contemporary Ghana. Volume One.*

3. For discussion of trade see E. O. Boateng, *Inflation in Ghana*; Seidman, *Ghana's Development Experience.*

4. Statistics are drawn from various issues of *Africa Report* and *West Africa*, as well as Walter Birmingham, I. Neustadt, and E. N. Omaboe, eds., *A Study of Contemporary Ghana. Volume One—The Economy of Ghana* (London: Allen & Unwin, 1966); "Ghana: Statistical Survey," in *Africa South of the Sahara, 1980-81.* 10th ed. (London: Europa Publications, 1980), pp. 445–553; "Ghana's Statistical Survey," in *Africa South of the Sahara, 1984-85.* 14th ed. (London: Europa Publications, 1984), pp. 424–429; Donald Rothchild, "Ghana's Economy: An African Test Case for Political Democracy: President Limann's Economic Alternatives," in Colin Legum, ed., *Africa Contemporary Record*, vol. 12 (New York: Holmes and Meier, 1979–80), pp. A137–145; E. O. Boateng, *Inflation in Ghana: Problems and Prospects*, Institute for Social, Statistical and Economic Research (ISSER) (Legon: University of Ghana, 1978); World Bank, *Accelerated Development in Sub-Saharan Africa: An Agenda for Action* (Washington, DC: World Bank, 1983).

5. For internal causes, see Richard Jeffries, "Rawlings and the Political Economy of Underdevelopment, *African Affairs* 81, no. 324 (1982):307–317; Steve Mufson, "End of a Dream," *Wall Street Journal*, March 28, 1983; Victor Le Vine, *Political Corruption: The Ghana Case* (Stanford, CA: Hoover Institution Press, 1975); Kofi Tetteh, "The Roots of Corruption," *West Africa*, March 29, 1976; Herbert Werlin, "The Roots of Corruption—The Ghanaian Enquiry," *Journal of Modern African Studies* 10, no. 2 (1972):247–266; Naomi Chazan, "Development, Underdevelopment and the State in Ghana," *African Studies Center Working Papers No. 58* (Boston: African Studies Center, Boston University, 1982). For external causes, see J. A. Dadson, "Ghana: Food and the Nation—1 and 2," *West Africa*, July 11, 1983 and July 18, 1983; Elliot J. Berg, "Structural Transformation Versus Gradualism: Recent Economic Development in Ghana and the Ivory Coast," in P. Foster and A. Zolberg, eds., *Ghana and the Ivory Coast: Perspectives on Modernization* (Chicago: University of Chicago Press, 1971), pp. 187–230; Alan Urbach, "Ghana's 20 Years," *New African Development* 11, no. 3 (1977):184–190; Rhoda Howard, *Colonialism and Underdevelopment in Ghana* (New York: Africana Publishing Co., 1978).

6. Robert M. Price, "Neo-Colonialism and Ghana's Economic Decline: A Critical Assessment," *Canadian Journal of African Studies* 18, no. 1 (1984):163–193.

7. Chazan, "Development, Underdevelopment and the State in Ghana"; Deborah Pellow, "Coping Responses to Revolution in Ghana," *Cultures et Developpement* 15, no. 1 (1983):11–36.

CHAPTER 5. GHANA AND THE INTERNATIONAL ORDER

1. The discussion in this chapter is based on Naomi Chazan, "Political Economy and Foreign Policy in Ghana" (Paper presented at the Twenty-Fourth Annual Meeting of the African Studies Association, Bloomington, IN, October 1983).

2. The theme has been taken up by numerous scholars. See, for example, Ann W. Seidman, *Ghana's Development Experience* (Nairobi: East African Publishing House, 1978); Rhoda Howard, *Colonialism and Underdevelopment in Ghana* (London: Croom Helm, 1978); and Robert Szereszewski, *Structural Changes in the Economy of Ghana, 1891–1911* (London: Oxford University Press, 1965).

3. For an overview of Ghana's foreign policy, see W. Scott Thompson, *Ghana's Foreign Policy, 1957–1966* (Princeton, NJ: Princeton University Press, 1969). Nkrumah's foreign policies are summarized

in editors of the *Spark, Some Essential Features of Nkrumaism* (Accra: Spark Publications, 1964). For an excellent analysis of the political economy of foreign policy at this time, see Rolf Hanisch, *Ghana and the Cocoa World Market: The Scope of Action of a Raw Material Exporting Country of the Periphery in the World Market* (Hamburg: SSIP, 1976).

4. Kwame Nkrumah, *Africa Must Unite* (London: Heinemann, 1963).

5. Details may be found in Michael Dei-Anang, *Administration of Ghana's Foreign Policy* (London: Institute of Commonwealth Studies, 1976).

6. For an overview, see Olajide Aluko, "Ghana's Foreign Policy Under the National Liberation Council," *Africa Quarterly* 10, no. 4 (1971):312–329; and W. Scott Thompson, "Foreign Policy Under the National Liberation Council," *Africa Report*, May-June 1969.

7. On the dialogue with South Africa, as well as other aspects of Busia's foreign policy, see David Goldsworthy, "Ghana's Second Republic: A Post Mortem," *African Affairs* 73, no. 286 (1973):8–25.

8. For the main principles of foreign policy at this time, see "Acheampong's Africa Policy," *Afriscope* 7, no. 9 (1973):32–33; and Olajide Aluko, "After Nkrumah: Continuity and Change in Ghana's Foreign Policy," *Issue* 5, no. 1 (1975):55–62.

9. Nkrumah, *Africa Must Unite*, p. 214.

10. One aspect of the West African relationship is covered in Olajide Aluko, *Ghana and Nigeria, 1957–1970: A Study in Inter-African Discord* (London: Rex Collings, 1976).

11. Interview with the late Colonel R.J.A. Felli, then commissioner for foreign affairs, Accra, July 1977.

12. Kwame Nkrumah, *Consciencism: Philosophy and Ideology for Decolonization and Development with Particular Reference to the African Revolution* (New York: Monthly Review Press, 1964), p. 78.

13. Nkrumah, *Africa Must Unite*, p. 193.

14. "Acheampong's Africa Policy."

15. See Leon Dash, "Ghana's Rawlings, 34, is Admirer of Gaddafi," *Washington Post*, February 17, 1982, in which Rawlings's early connections with Libya are discussed.

16. Chris Stevens, "In Search of the Economic Kingdom," *Journal of Developing Areas* 9, no. 1 (1974):3–26.

17. Hanisch, *Ghana and the Cocoa World Market*.

18. "Ghana's Debt: Ambiguity Sanctified," *West Africa* 2967 (April 29, 1974), pp. 485–489.

CHAPTER 6. GHANA'S FUTURE

1. These explanations are elaborated in Dennis Austen, "Things Fall Apart?" *Orbis* 25, no. 4 (1982):925–949.

2. For an expansion on this option, see Donald Rothchild and Michael Foley, "The Implications of a Scarcity for Governance in Africa," *International Political Science Review* 4, no. 4 (1983):311–326.

3. I. William Zartman, "Issues of African Diplomacy in the 1980s," *Orbis* 25, no. 4 (1982):1025–1043.

4. For one example, see the excellent analysis by Kwame Akon Ninsin, "Ghana: the Failure of a Petty Bourgeois Experiment," *Africa Development* 7, no. 3 (1982):37–67.

5. This idea is suggested in Richard L. Sklar, "Democracy in Africa" (University of California, Los Angeles: African Studies Department, 1983).

6. Robert H. Jackson and Carl C. Rosberg, "Why Africa's Weak States Persist: The Empirical and the Juridicial in Statehood," *World Politics* 35, no. 1 (1982):1–24.

Acronyms

ACP	African, Caribbean, and Pacific group
AFRC	Armed Forces Revolutionary Council
ARPB	Association of Recognized Professional Bodies
ARPS	Aborigines' Rights Protection Society
BAC	British Aluminum Company
CDR	Committee for Defence of the Revolution
CPP	Convention People's party
CVC	Citizens' Vetting Committee
CYO	Committee on Youth Organization
ECOWAS	Economic Community of West African States
EEC	European Economic Community
GBC	Ghana Broadcasting Corporation
GDP	gross domestic product
GIHOC	Ghana Industrial Holding Company
GNP	gross national product
IDC	Industrial Development Corporation
IMF	International Monetary Fund
IPPF	International Planned Parenthood Federation
NAL	National Alliance of Liberals
NCBWA	National Congress of British West Africa
NCD	National Commission for Democracy
NCWD	National Council on Women and Development
NDC	National Defence Committee
NFPP	National Family Planning Programme
NLC	National Liberation Council

NLM	National Liberation movement
NRC	National Redemption Council
NUGS	National Union of Ghanaian Students
OAU	Organization of African Unity
OFY	Operation Feed Yourself
PDC	People's Defence Committee
PFP	Popular Front party
PNDC	Provisional National Defence Council
PNP	People's National party
PP	Progress party
PPAG	Planned Parenthood Association of Ghana
RDC	Regional Development Corporation
SFC	State Farm Corporation
SIB	special investigation board
SMC II	Supreme Military Council II
TUC	Trade Union Congress
UGCC	United Gold Coast Convention
UGFC	United Ghana Farmers Council
UNC	United National Convention
VALCO	Volta Aluminum Company
VRP	Volta River Project
WDC	Worker's Defence Committee

Selected Bibliography

The scholarly literature on Ghana is vast. The following introductory list represents only a small portion of a large body of works on virtually every aspect of Ghanaian life.

HISTORICAL BACKGROUND

Agbodeka, Francis. *African Politics and British Policy in the Gold Coast 1868–1900: A Study in the Forms and Force of Protest.* Evanston, IL: Northwestern University Press, 1971.

Apter, David. *Ghana in Transition.* rev. ed. New York: Atheneum, 1966.

Austin, Dennis. *Politics in Ghana, 1946–1960.* London: Oxford University Press, 1964.

Boahen, Adu. *Ghana: Evolution and Change in the Nineteenth and Twentieth Centuries.* London: Longman, 1975.

Bourret, F. M. *The Gold Coast: A Survey of the Gold Coast and British Togoland, 1919–1946.* Stanford, CA: Stanford University Press, 1949.

Busia, Kofi A. *The Position of the Chief in the Modern Political System of Ashanti.* 2d ed. London: Frank Cass, 1968.

Claridge, W. W. *A History of the Gold Coast and Ashanti.* London: John Murray, 1915.

Ellis, A. B. *A History of the Gold Coast of West Africa.* New York: Negro Universities Press, 1969 (orig. published: London: Chapman and Hall, 1915).

Fage, John D. *Ghana: A Historical Interpretation.* Madison: University of Wisconsin Press, 1959.

Fynn, John K. *Asante and its Neighbors, 1700–1807.* Evanston, IL: Northwestern University Press, 1971.

Howard, Rhoda. *Colonialism and Underdevelopment in Ghana*. London: Croom Helm, 1978.

Kay, G. B., ed. *The Political Economy of Colonialism in Ghana: A Collection of Documents and Statistics, 1900–1960*. Cambridge: Cambridge University Press, 1972.

Kimble, David. *A Political History of Ghana, 1850–1928*. Oxford: Clarendon Press, 1963.

Nkrumah, Kwame. *Ghana: The Autobiography of Kwame Nkrumah*. Edinburgh: Thomas Nelson and Sons, 1959.

Rattray, Robert. *Ashanti*. London: Oxford University Press, 1923.

————. *Religion and Art in Ashanti*. London: Oxford University Press, 1927.

Reindorf, Carl C. *The History of the Gold Coast and Asante*. Accra: Ghana Universities Press, 1966.

Timothy, Bankole. *Kwame Nkrumah: His Rise to Power*. Evanston, IL: Northwestern University Press, 1963.

Wallerstein, Immanuel M. *The Road to Independence: Ghana and the Ivory Coast*. The Hague: Mouton, 1964.

Ward, W.E.F. *A History of the Gold Coast*. London: Allen & Unwin, 1948.

Wilks, Ivor. *Asante in the Nineteenth Century: The Structure and Evolution of a Political Order*. London: Cambridge University Press, 1975.

POLITICS AND GOVERNMENT

Afrifa, A. A. *The Ghana Coup: 24th February 1966*. London: Frank Cass, 1967.

Amonoo, Ben. *Ghana 1957–1966: The Poliitics of Institutional Dualism*. London: Allen & Unwin, 1981.

Austin, Dennis. *Ghana Observed: Essays on the Politics of a West African Republic*. Manchester: Manchester University Press, 1976.

Austin, Dennis, and Luckham, Robin, eds. *Politicians and Soldiers in Ghana, 1966–1972*. London: Frank Cass, 1975.

Beckman, Bjorn, *Organizing the Farmers: Cocoa Politics and National Development in Ghana*. Uppsala: Scandinavian Institute of African Studies, 1976.

Bing, Geoffrey. *Reap the Whirlwind: An Account of Kwame Nkrumah's Ghana from 1950–1966*. London: McGibbon and Kee, 1968.

Bretton, Henry L. *The Rise and Fall of Kwame Nkrumah: A Study of Personal Rule in Africa*. London: Pall Mall Press, 1966.

Chazan, Naomi. *An Anatomy of Ghanaian Politics: Managing Political Recession, 1969–1982.* Boulder, CO: Westview Press, 1983.

Davidson, Basil. *Black Star: A View of the Life and Times of Kwame Nkrumah.* London: Allen Lane, 1973.

Dunn, John F., and Robertson, A. F. *Dependence and Opportunity: Political Change in Ahafo.* London: Cambridge University Press, 1973.

Fitch, Bob, and Oppenheimer, Mary. *Ghana: End of an Illusion.* New York: Monthly Review Press, 1966.

Genoud, Roger. *Nationalism and Economic Development in Ghana.* New York: Praeger, 1969.

Jeffries, Richard. *Class, Power and Ideology in Ghana: The Railwaymen of Sekondi.* London: Cambridge University Press, 1978.

———. "Rawlings and the Political Economy of Underdevelopment in Ghana." *African Affairs* 81, no. 324 (1982):307–317.

Jones, Trevor. *Ghana's First Republic 1960–1966: The Pursuit of the Political Kingdom.* London: Methuen, 1976.

Kraus, Jon. "The Political Economy of Conflict in Ghana." *Africa Report* 25, no. 2 (1980):9–16.

———. "Rawlings Second Coming." *Africa Report* 27, no. 3 (1982):59–66.

Ladouceur, Paul André. *Chiefs and Politicians: The Politics of Regionalism in Northern Ghana.* London: Longman, 1979.

Le Vine, Victor T. *Political Corruption: The Ghana Case.* Stanford, CA: Hoover Institution Press, 1975.

Nkrumah, Kwame. *Consciencism: Philosophy and Ideology for Decolonization and Development with Particular Reference to the African Revolution.* New York: Monthly Review Press, 1964.

Okeke, Barbara E. *4 June: A Revolution Betrayed.* Enugu: Ikenga Publishers, 1982.

Olorunsola, Victor. *Societal Reconstruction in Two African States.* Washington, DC: University Press of America, 1977.

Omari, T. Peter. *Kwame Nkrumah: The Anatomy of an African Dictatorship.* Accra: Moxon Paperbooks, 1970.

Owusu, Maxwell. *Uses and Abuses of Political Power: A Case Study of Continuity and Change in the Politics of Ghana.* Chicago: University of Chicago Press, 1970.

Pinkney, Robert. *Ghana Under Military Rule.* London: Methuen, 1972.

Price, Robert M. *Society and Bureaucracy in Contemporary Ghana.* Berkeley, CA: University of California Press, 1975.

Rothchild, Donald. "Military Regime Performance: An Appraisal of the Ghana Experience, 1972–1978." *Comparative Politics* 7, no. 4 (1980):459–479.

Saaka, Yakubu. *Local Government and Political Change in Northern Ghana.* Washington: University Press of America, 1978.

Staniland, Martin. *The Lions of Dagbon: Political Change in Northern Ghana.* London: Cambridge University Press, 1975.

Zolberg, Aristide. *Creating Political Order: The Party States of West Africa.* New York: Rand McNally, 1966.

SOCIETY AND CULTURE

Amedekey, E. Y. *The Culture of Ghana: A Bibliography.* Accra: Ghana Universities Press, 1970.

Assimeng, Max. *Social Structure in Ghana.* Accra: Ghana Publishing Corporation, 1981.

Birmingham, Walter, Neustadt, J., and Omaboe, E. N., eds. *A Study of Contemporary Ghana, Volume II: Some Aspects of Social Structure.* Evanston, IL: Northwestern University Press, 1967.

Caldwell, John C. *African Rural-Urban Migration: The Movement to Ghana's Towns.* Canberra: Australian National University Press, 1969.

Cole, Herbert M., and Ross, Doran H. *The Arts of Ghana.* Los Angeles: Museum of Cultural History, UCLA, 1977.

Field, Margaret J. *Religion and Medicine of the Ga People.* London: Oxford University Press, 1937.

Fortes, Meyer. *The Web of Kinship Among the Tallensi.* London: Oxford University Press, 1949.

Foster, Philip. *Education and Social Change in Ghana.* Chicago: University of Chicago Press, 1965.

Goody, Jack, ed. *Changing Social Structure in Ghana: Essays in the Comparative Sociology of a New State and an Old Tradition.* London: International African Institute, 1975.

Graham, C. K. *History of Education in Ghana: From the Earliest Times to the Declaration of Independence.* London: Frank Cass, 1971.

Kilson, Marion. *African Urban Kinsmen: The Ga of Central Accra.* London: Hurst and Longman, 1974.

Opoku, Kofi Asare. *West African Traditional Religion.* Accra: FEP International, 1978.

Pellow, Deborah. *Women in Accra: Options for Autonomy.* Algonac, MI: Reference Publications, Inc. 1977.

Zachariah, K. C., and Conde, Julien. *Migration in West Africa: Demographic Aspects*. New York: Oxford University Press, 1981.

THE ECONOMY

Anyane, S. La. *Ghana Agriculture: Its Economic Development from Early Times to the Middle of the Twentieth Century*. London: Oxford University Press, 1963.

Birmingham, Walter, Neustadt, J., and Omaboe, E. N., eds. *A Study of Contemporary Ghana, Volume One: The Economy of Ghana*. London: Allen & Unwin, 1966.

Boateng, E. O. *Inflation in Ghana: Problems and Prospects*. Legon: ISSER, 1978.

Chambers, Robert, ed. *The Volta Resettlement Experience*. London: Pall Mall Press, 1970.

Chazan, Naomi. "Development, Underdevelopment and the State in Ghana." *African Studies Center Working Paper No. 58*. Boston: African Studies Center, Boston University, 1982.

Foster, Philip, and Zolberg, Aristide, eds. *Ghana and the Ivory Coast: Perspectives on Modernization*. Chicago: University of Chicago Press, 1971.

Hanisch, Rolf. *Ghana and the Cocoa World Market: The Scope of Action of a Raw Material Exporting Country of the Periphery in the World Market*. Hamburg: SSIP, 1976.

Hill, Polly. *The Migrant Cocoa-Farmers of Southern Ghana: A Study in Rural Capitalism*. Cambridge: Cambridge University Press, 1963.

Killick, Tony. *Development Economics in Action: A Study of Economic Policies in Ghana*. London: Heinemann, 1978.

Leith, J. Clark. *Foreign Trade Regimes and Economic Development: Ghana*. New York: Columbia University Press, 1974.

Peil, Margeret. *The Ghanaian Factory Worker: Industrial Man in Africa*. London: Cambridge University Press, 1972.

Pellow, Deborah. "Coping Responses to Revolution in Ghana." *Cultures et Developpement* 15, no. 1 (1983):11–36.

Pickett, James. "Development Planning in Ghana." *Economic Bulletin of Africa* 12, no. 1 (1976):9–18.

Price, Robert M. "Neo-Colonialism and Ghana's Decline: A Critical Assessment." *Canadian Journal of African Studies* 18, no. 1 (1984):163–193.

Rimmer, Douglas. "The Crisis in the Ghana Economy," *Journal of Modern African Studies* 4, no. 1 (1966):17–32.

Rothchild, Donald. "Ghana's Economy: An African Test Case for Political Democracy: President Limann's Economic Alternatives," in Colin Legum, ed., *Africa Contemporary Record*, vol. 12. New York: Holmes and Meier, 1979–80.

Seidman, Ann W. *Ghana's Development Experience*. Nairobi: East African Publishing House, 1978.

Szereszewski, Robert. *Structural Changes in the Economy of Ghana, 1891–1911*. London: Oxford University Press, 1965.

FOREIGN RELATIONS

Aluko, Olajide. "After Nkrumah: Continuity and Change in Ghana's Foreign Policy." *Issue* 1 (1975):55–62.

―――. *Ghana and Nigeria, 1957–1970: A Study in Inter-African Discord*. London: Rex Collings, 1976.

Dei-Anang, Michael. *Administration of Ghana's Foreign Policy*. London: Institute of Commonwealth Studies, 1976.

Felli, R.J.A. "Principles and Current Aspects of Ghana's Foreign Policy." *Vierjahrber* 69 (1976):161–166.

Nkrumah, Kwame. *Africa Must Unite*. London: Heinemann, 1963.

Owusu, Maxwell. "Economic Nationalism, Pan-Africanism and the Military: Ghana's National Redemption Council." *Africa Today* 22, no. 1 (1975):31–52.

Thompson, W. Scott. "Foreign Policy Under the National Liberation Council." *Africa Report* 14 (1969).

―――. *Ghana's Foreign Policy, 1957–1966*. Princeton, NJ: Princeton University Press, 1969.

Index

231